Frane Adam (Ed.)

Social Capital and Governance

Gesellschaftliche Transformationen
Societal Transformations

herausgegeben von/edited by

Eckhard Dittrich, Nikolai Genov, Raj Kollmorgen, Ingrid Oswald, Heiko Schrader, Melanie Tatur

Band/Volume 11

LIT

Frane Adam (Ed.)

Social Capital and Governance

Old and New Members of the EU in Comparison

With a Preface by Thomas Luckmann

LIT

Bibliographic information published by the Deutsche Nationalbibliothek
The Deutsche Nationalbibliothek lists this publication in the Deutsche Nationalbibliografie; detailed bibliographic data are available in the Internet at http://dnb.d-nb.de.

ISBN-10: 3-8258-9658-7
ISBN-13: 978-3-8258-9658-4

A catalogue record for this book is available from the British Library

Ziegelstr. 30
D-10177 Berlin

Auslieferung:
LIT Verlag Fresnostr. 2, D-48159 Münster
Tel. +49 (0) 2 51/620 32 - 22, Fax +49 (0) 2 51/922 60 99, e-Mail: lit@lit-verlag.de

Distributed in the UK by: Global Book Marketing, 99B Wallis Rd, London, E9 5LN
Phone: +44 (0) 20 8533 5800 – Fax: +44 (0) 1600 775 663
http://www.centralbooks.co.uk/acatalog/search.html

Distributed in North America by:

Transaction Publishers
New Brunswick (U.S.A.) and London (U.K.)

Transaction Publishers
Rutgers University
35 Berrue Circle
Piscataway, NJ 08854

Phone: +1 (732) 445 - 2280
Fax: + 1 (732) 445 - 3138
for orders (U. S. only):
toll free (888) 999 - 6778
e-mail:
orders@transactionspub.com

Contents

Part II.
National Case Studies

Graphs

Tables

Preface

Thomas Luckmann

In countries where modernisation has progressed the furthest, as in most EU member states, members of society no longer share the same value system. Although older certainties were already shaken in the early phase of modernisation, only a few generations ago certain traditional orientation patterns were taken for granted in Europe as part of a common notion of reality in a group of societies. Despite national differences, internal class cleavages and conflicts of interest, one may assume that at the bottom of the whole civilisation there remained a reasonably coherent core of values.

Those times have passed. In addition to generations of conservative philosophers in Great Britain, Germany and, prominently, in post-revolutionary France many keen observers of another ideological bent recognised the risks which, along with the gains in liberty and material benefits of technological modernity, the loss of coherence in modern societies brought to collective and individual life. Among sociologists of the former generation it was Emile Durkheim in particular who trenchantly diagnosed the ills of a society that had lost its traditional coherence without developing what he called organic solidarity to match the requirements of a complex division of labour. Others including Marx, Spencer and Max Weber analysed the nature and problems of modern society and some proposed their own remedies. But it can be said that it was Durkheim who started the search for ways and means to oppose the anomie that threatened the cohesion of modern societies. 'Intermediary' institutions – the concept has been known in sociology since Durkheim – were to be the countervailing force. By mediating between the individual and the primary, 'big' institutions in society which had emerged in consequence of the progressive institutional specialisation of functions, they would nourish the growth of organic solidarity. The anonymous 'big' institutions such as the invisible hand of the market and the all-too-seeing eye of the bureaucratic state perform the role of ancient fate in inexorably governing life in modernity, the 'intermediary' institutions allow individual human beings to actively contribute to the production and transmission of the repertoire of values and orientations in their society, thus influencing the operation of the powerful primary, functionally differentiated institutions and thus, even if continuing to be locked in the iron cage of modernity, to borrow Weber's term, becoming, at least to a limited degree, masters of their own fate.

A local parish community, a chapter of the parent-teachers association, an ecological group, a soccer fan club, a rehabilitation support group, a local section of the 'Volunteers for X' may all be true mediating structures that can suitably soften the negative aspects of modernisation: 'anomie', a lack of cohesion and solidarity, disorientation and 'alienation'.

Among the terms found in the conceptual field to which 'intermediary institutions' belong and which prominently include 'civil society', 'social capital' has become particularly popular in contemporary social research. In spite of its theoretical weaknesses, it has outlasted its competitors partly because no other can match the catchiness of the word and partly because it seemed to promise the possibility of quantification in an analogy with its economic inspiration. However, this promise did not materialise. The methods used in studying those aspects of social reality that are covered by this term have proved less than adequate and the attempts at quantification illusory.

For various reasons, and despite a critical discussion of the concept, at least during the meetings I had the pleasure to attend, the European group of social scientists whose findings are presented in this volume have continued to use 'social capital' as a heuristic device. The results show that for comparative purposes, here especially between the 'old' and 'new' European Union members and with a glance at the United States, the concept does have its uses if, namely a big 'if', the pitfalls of overgeneralising from weak data are avoided. Like with most social research, investigations of 'social capital' sometimes tend to jump from one or two halfway plausible indicators, usually 'measured' by responses to (pseudo)standardised questions, to assertions about the strength or weakness of 'social capital' in a given society. Fortunately, the research group was (mostly) aware of the dangers of such procedures and the results of their investigations can be read with some confidence. A preface is not the place to expound at length on one's own methodological caveats and preferences. Fortunately, the first chapter by Frane Adam offers a sound overview of these matters and provides a proper perspective on the collective product.

Introduction
The Structure and Intention of the Volume

In the last decade, social science research has been strongly influenced by discussions regarding social capital. Especially following the publication of Putnam's study of civicness and institutional performance in Italian regions we have witnessed perhaps the unprecedented acceptance, study and application of this concept. It is one of those sociological concepts that has not merely remained confined to the social sciences but has also entered broader public debates. The range of issues to which this concept is applied is indeed wide, probably more than with other comparable concepts. In fact, one may approach practically any social entity or situation through the conceptual framework of social capital. This can be interpreted either as evidence of the heuristic potential of this conceptual framework or, as the manifestation of its inflation, of it having turned into a cure-all and becoming robbed of any distinct meaning.

On the other side, the 'added value' of this concept is potentially high. However, if social scientists are to realise its potential and meaningfully employ it in social research it must be applied within a coherent methodological framework. This does not imply a unified research programme, as some authors suggest. Instead, the problems of its definition, operationalisation and measurement, along with the difficulty of the ontological status of social capital – its sources, forms and consequences – must be resolved coherently within a particular approach or research programme.

* * *

For epistemological reasons, it is impossible to devise a single concept and a single valid measure of social capital. First, we do not have a strong consensus on what social capital is: it seems that the more popular the concept becomes, the further we get from such a consensus. True, it is possible to discern a 'genotype' of social capital since, regardless of their disciplinary or theoretical background, most authors agree with Coleman's formulation that we are dealing with certain aspects of the social structure which enable social action. However, this formulation is too broad for a more unified research programme. Alternatively, there is already an impressive (and growing) body of 'phenotype' definitions and applications in concrete social scientific research.

On the other side, social capital has many meanings and refers to different phenomena. In this sense, we are dealing with a number of phenotype applications of a concept, which are only loosely related to its genotype definition. Due to this and the fact that social capital is a strongly context-specific phenomenon it is unrealistic to expect or demand a unified operational definition. The most we can do in methodology is to achieve greater transparency and verifiability by precisely defining the level and context of research and using appropriate research tools.

Proceeding from a more in-depth analysis we can discern a number of ambiguities and inconsistencies which further contribute to quandaries as to definitions and measurement. For example, decreasing trust in political institutions is not always a sign of decreasing social capital. It might also be an appropriate and intelligent reaction to incompetent political decisions or corruption. A well-organised civil society can also be a manifestation of a rent-seeking system. Rich interpersonal contacts can be an expression of negative social capital whereby an individual can realise their goals by utilising their contacts and acquaintances even though they do not have suitable competencies or do not meet meritocratic criteria. Some settings involve substantial amounts of *bonding* social capital, but lack b*ridging* social capital.

* * *

Here, our discussion is based on a thesis that would be accepted by many, possibly even most, researchers of social capital. Namely, that co-operation is an essential determinant of social capital. Put differently, it is a genotype definition with a whole range of phenotypical applications. Conceiving social capital as a genotype with many applications means that we have to do with different research programs. Four of them are the most relevant. The first is connected with civic participation, civil society and governance and this is the context in which our analysis is embedded. Expressing this another way, we are interested in how social capital in the form of co-operative norms and behaviour is transformed into participation, associational involvement and institutional co-ordination. The second actually represents a continuation and extension of the human capital concept whereby social capital is seen as an additional resource which accelerates the circulation and transfer of knowledge and information. The third approach – based on network analysis – focuses on informal interactions while the fourth joins collective action theory with social capital.

The texts in this volume fall within the first research programme and aim to demonstrate how social capital in the form of co-operative norms and actions facilitates the self-organisation of civil society, its internal ability to articulate policy relevant alternative proposals and how this influences the efficiency and responsiveness of governance at different (local, national, trans-national) levels.

The contributions in the volume Social Capital and Governance are the results of research, discussions and peer-reviewing within Research Group 5 of the CONNEX Network of Excellence within the 6th Framework Programme (Democratic and Efficient Governance in a Multi-level Europe, whose main co-ordinator is Prof. Beate Kohler-Koch from Mannheim University) undertaken since the end of 2004.

The intention of the contributions is to focus on the less known and so far less investigated aspects of social capital in the context of civic participation, governance and civil society at both national and EU levels. The role of new EU members is particularly stressed.

There are nine contributions (along with a preface and introduction) that are mostly co-authored and written by 17 researchers from various universities and countries (10 from Slovenia, two from the Netherlands, two from Poland, two from Croatia and one from Sweden). The volume is divided into two parts: comparative studies and national case studies.

While the authors deal with different aspects and use specific approaches there is a common denominator that is quite easy to detect. Not only do they all concentrate on civic participation and its interrelation with social capital, but they also try to practice methodological reflexivity and a triangulation strategy meaning that they use various data sources and, in some cases, a combination of quantitative and qualitative data.

In the first text (*Frane Adam, The Distribution of Social Capital and the Quality of Data from Cross-national Surveys*) two sets of issues are elaborated and reflected on. The first concerns the distribution of stocks of social capital across European (EU) nations. Using conventional proxies like trust and associational involvement based on data from cross-national surveys (EVS/WVS and ESS) the main tentative trends and patterns are outlined. The second issue refers to the quality of the data. Concerning the first issue, it is possible to speak of four groups when it comes to the distribution of social capital at the European level. In contrast to authors who argue there are no large differences in mean scores across the national patterns, this analysis arrives at more differentiated conclusions. Between the first and fourth groups a very clear borderline can be drawn, whereas the differences between the second and third groups are not so pronounced. In the context of thematising and critically reflecting on the validity and comparability of the empirical evidence some errors and inconsistencies are found. It seems they appeared partly due to the inappropriate technical design of cross-national surveys and because of semantic-cultural and institutional factors that were not given much attention in both the stage of preparing and conducting the surveys and in the phase of interpreting and generalising the data.

In the second text (*Matej Makarovič, Angelca Ivančič and Darka Podmenik, Social and Political Participation: Is There a European Convergence?*), the central question is the convergence between the old and new European democracies as far as patterns of social and political participation are concerned. To answer the questions of which features constitute the patterns of participation and their interpretations and if the participation patterns can be related to the availability of social capital, both quantitative (hierarchical cluster analysis) and qualitative methods are used (the triangulation approach). One could argue there are no trends of a pan-European convergence in the sense of reducing differences between the identified patterns (moderate pattern, active democracies and passive democracies) although there are some partial convergence tendencies between some new and old democracies. Those nations with high levels of social capital also seem to have high levels of virtually all forms of socio-political participation, including those that do not seem to be directly related to social capital, such as voting and passive membership.

The starting point of the text *Political Cynicism and Social Cohesion in Europe and the United States by Peggy Schyns and Margreet Nuus* is the following question: does political cynicism lead to a decline in the socially cohesive behaviour and attitudes of individuals? To answer this, five European countries from three different regions and the United States are selected. Several significant negative relationships between political cynicism and indicators of social cohesion are found. The findings show in general that people who are cynical of politics participate less in politics and in volunteer work, are more distrusting of other people, are more xenophobic and portray negative values of citizenship. Yet it should be stressed that these correlations are weak and one cannot speak of strong links between the two phenomena. Further, compared to the other four countries (Italy, Slovenia, Spain and Poland) the Netherlands and the United States show stronger effects of interpersonal trust on political cynicism than the hypothesised reverse effect of political cynicism on interpersonal trust.

The contribution *Quality of Governance in the European Union: Old and New Members in a Comparative Perspective by Matevž Tomšič and Urban Vehovar* deals with the problem of »quality« (stability, inclusiveness and efficiency with transparency) of governance in European Union countries and its relation to the stock of social capital and general socio-economic and institutional performance. Several indicators show that although the 'new' EU members strongly outperform other post-communist countries they still lag behind the majority of the 'old' ones. The authors discern implications of the quality of governance for the creation and maintenance of social capital and economic performance, maintaining that the former is an important generator of the latter two (and not just vice versa), which especially holds for small European countries that usually have fewer resources and thus need an active approach in the sense of skilfully managing their potential and creating their capacities in order to overcome their deficiencies of limited resources and a »critical mass«. The authors also reflect on the relevance of their model for analysing governance at the EU level.

The contribution *Organized Civil Society in the Multilevel System of European Governance by Mateja Re*k focuses on the linkages between local, national and trans-national forms of civic organisations' actions. Some recent research findings, albeit limited in scope, point to the conclusions that transnational civil society interest groups and associations in the EU are not necessarily bridges between the remote EU institutions and the everyday lives of citizens. On the other hand, from the viewpoint of EU institutions, it seems they can only deal effectively with transnational and less so with national civic organisations and they seem too detached to deal with the multiplicity of local concerns. Here, it is important to ensure that local concerns are sufficiently voiced by national and transnational civic organisations.

The following text *Religion and Social Capital: The Diversity of European Regions by Igor Bahovec, Vinko Potočnik and Siniša Zrinščak* raises some aspects of the impact of organised religion on social capital (indicators). In fact, religiosity and church attendance are still a very important generator of associational life and voluntary activities. Voluntary para-church and religiously motivated organisations are among those voluntary organisations with the greatest membership. However, it is important to note that regarding associational culture there are quite significant differences between Catholic, Protestant and Orthodox regions which intersect with cultural and linguistic regions. It is interesting to observe that some highly secularised countries like Sweden, Denmark or the Netherlands have much more membership in religious and church voluntary associations than the more traditional (Catholic or Orthodox) countries.

The second part of the volume presents national case studies. In the contribution *Study Circles in Sweden and Slovenia – Learning for Civic Participation by Petros Gougoulakis and Nevenka Bogataj,* the Swedish and Slovenian experiences with informal adult social learning are compared. An attempt is made here to outline the main characteristics of study circles with a focus on the possible effects and consequences participation and learning in them may have for the creation and maintenance of social capital in the two countries. It is suggested that the pedagogical-philosophical thinking of popular education as outlined in this article, together with the willingness to learn more from non-formal educational traditions in different countries, could form the basis of comprehensive wide-ranging studies at the European Union level. Apparently, we need more profound knowledge of other countries' *folkbildnings,* traditions in the search of common grounds for designing and building up a new European adult education policy, and a policy of a new European '*bildung*' to help create a new identity of active citizenship.

The research findings presented in *The Path Dependency of Civil Society and Social Capital – The Case of Croatia by Gojko Bežovan* suggest, similar to the Polish situation, that social capital is developed more through informal networks at the neighbourhood level than through membership in civil society organisations. Citizens are ever more willing to be involved in activities at that level and they experience the importance of practicing the norm of reciprocity for the sake of a safe neighbourhood. Family and friendship ties still play dominant roles and it is unclear whether this also applies to people from younger generations. The state's paternalistic position, pushing civil society organisations into a marginal position, means they are still not fully legitimised actors in public life. The research findings point to the new ranks of middle-class people who are well-educated, well-off and who represent the new civic culture that is willing to join civil society organisations and to act as a convener of new initiatives.

In the contribution *Polish Traditions of Self-organisation, Social Capital and the Challenge of Europeanisation by Anna Gąsior-Niemiec and Piotr Gliński* it can be seen that in some societies more social capital might be generated than shown by comparative surveys. They argue that the survey data are reductionist and conceal a much more complex picture of phenomena related to the development of civil society, social capital and their linkages with the modern, Europeanised system of governance in Poland. Two other modes or indicators which are not usually fully 'captured' by survey research on social capital – '*ad hoc* actionism' and 'traditional self-organisation' – are identified. It may be claimed these are driven by different participatory logics (solidarity and reciprocity, respectively) and thus function as a supportive informal institutional system that enables (marginalised) individuals and communities to find their way and even to make some progress, despite the deficient economic resources and/or unstable or ineffective formal institutions. However, one needs to be aware that the process of 'catching up' with the West and closing the gap vis-à-vis its type and stocks of social capital should not be seen as automatic and inevitable.

* * *

Political and civic participation, especially associational involvement, are not only a component of the quality of life and social cohesion but they also contribute – directly or indirectly – to good governance. Encouraging civic participation and investing in social capital in the form of incentives for co-operative behaviour means investment in more efficient and responsive governance. However, co-operation is always embedded in a competitive environment and the question is how to balance both principles (so-called co-opetetion). On the other side, this is long-term process in which other (geo-political, historical, economic) factors are also supposed to intervene and determine this process.

At least two lessons emerge from this volume. The first concerns the issue of monitoring social capital developments across European nations while the second is the issue of learning and knowledge sharing. Put differently, two policy implications or proposals seem to arise from the conclusions made by the authors. The issue of monitoring refers to the European research policy which should support the introduction of more appropriate (post-positivist and not positivist or empiricist) methodological tools and approaches in order to come to terms with the cultural and institutional diversity of cross-national surveys. So far, we still know too little about the dynamics and accumulation of social capital on the comparative European level. The second lesson is connected with learning for active citizenship. Although the data on the state-of-the art of civil society and social capital development are in many respects unreliable and inconsistent, it is beyond doubt (and supported by other sources) that informal learning and taking part in knowledge and information sharing is a very important aspect of active civic participation. Investing more in study circles and other forms of informal education and so-called experiential social learning might accelerate the diffusion of the knowledge needed for a competent engagement in civil and political society.

It seems that deliberative democracy is immanently connected with the idea of the knowledge-based society which is a strategic goal of the EU. We have arrived at the intersection of three interconnected concepts – deliberative democracy, the knowledge society and civic participation/social capital – which should define (together with a competitive economy) the EU's present and especially future societal formation and vision. But we have to be moderate in our expectations. It is known that democracy, knowledge and participation may have some paradoxical side-effects and externalities. On the other side, it is not through social (political) top-down engineering that this vision might be implemented but an evolutionary bottom-up medium- or long-term process in which only evolutionary capable options and inventions become part of a new evolving system complexity.

Frane Adam, editor
Ljubljana, October, 2006

Part I
Comparative Studies

1. The Distribution of Social Capital and the Quality of Data from Cross-national Surveys[1]

Frane Adam

Introduction

It is interesting to note that, despite an abundance of empirical research, there are still no systematic overviews providing reliable insights into cross-time and cross-nation differences and similarities regarding the distribution of social capital within Europe or the European Union. A number of partial studies exist yet the question is not truly answered by them. The initial aim of this contribution is to provide a more comprehensive approach to explaining trends and the state of social capital while keeping in mind that only preliminary findings are given and these need to be subsequently completed through a correction process once new data and insights are available. However, it turns out that this aim cannot be satisfied without a methodological reconsideration of the quality and credibility of data that could provide a basis for drawing conclusions about the growth or decline of social capital in European societies.

Social capital research remains in its initial phases. When looking for appropriate conceptualisation and measurement solutions we still find ourselves in the 'pilot' phase.[2] However, it may be argued that some well-elaborated approaches promising the successful continuation of research efforts do exist, while some others have proven to be less productive. There is a wide range of conceptual problems that mainly derive from the statement that social capital is a genotype phenomenon which comprises a se-

---

[1] This paper was prepared during my stay – which proved to be very stimulating regarding my research on social capital and related issues – as a Humboldt Research Fellow at the Scientific Centre in Berlin (WZB) between March and May 2006. I would especially like to thank A. V. Humboldt-Stiftung, the Director of WZB Prof. Kocka and Dr. Thurn.

[2] Recently, one author wrote that social capital's conception and measurement may currently be at the same early stage that human capital theory was thirty years ago (Grootaert/Bastelaer, 2002: 341). From this assessment, we exclude approaches based on empirically more developed network analysis and block modelling (Lin, 2002; Savage et al., 2004).

ries of contextually conditioned phenotypical applications (Adam/Rončevič, 2003). As a consequence, there are several conceptual misunderstandings and oversimplified operational definitions.[3] Four main fields of application connecting older theoretical approaches with the still fluid and ongoing social capital discussion can be distinguished. The first – on which our approach is based – connects macro-level research into civil society and civic participation with social capital indicators like associational involvement and trust. The second proceeds from the notion of human capital and regards social capital as an additional resource which enables the circulation and sharing of knowledge and information (one branch of this mainly micro- or mezzo-oriented field evolved in a macro-level field focused on developmental/non-economic factors). The third field is in fact the implantation of social capital at the informal and micro-level into network analysis, while the fourth joins collective action theory with social capital as a solution to the so-called free-rider problem.

Our point of departure is van Deths' analysis of methodological pitfalls which states that conceptual heterogeneity is much less reflected in operational and empirical realms than expected.[4] The measurement is characterised by several orthodoxies that mainly relate to the dominant position of the survey method and use indicators that measure the stock of social capital only on the basis of respondents' statements and attitudes. While we agree with this observation, our critical assessment is more concrete since it is based on an evaluation of three cross-national comparative surveys, namely the World Values Survey (WVS), the European Values Survey (EVS) and the European Social Survey (ESS). Like Van Deth, we also stress the need for triangulation. Yet, by doing this, we do not merely address the additional use of other methods of data collection like experiments or secondary statistical data analyses but believe a combination of different datasets deriving from cross-national surveys should also be included. When conducting a complex analysis we cannot use and rely on just one set of data, for example, only the data from the WVS (see Norris, 2002) or EVS (see Arts et al.,

---

[3] One author is very critical. He states: 'Empirical social capital literature seems to be particularly plagued by vague definition of concept, poorly measured data, absence of appropriate exchangeability conditions, and lack of information necessary to make identification claims plausible' (Durlauf, 2002: 474).

[4] He points out the following 'pitfalls': the use of proxies from existing data sets due to the unavailability of specific data, using perceptions instead of observations, using aggregate measures deriving from the individual level for investigating collective phenomena, using inverse measures as proxies (the rate of criminality as an indicator of the absence of social capital), using identical indicators in different settings and using single indicators instead of composite measures (Van Deth, 2003).

2003). Instead, a broader context of empirical evidence should be taken into account. More complex research designs should also include a combination of 'deductive' (outsiders') data acquired by the abovementioned cross-national research and 'inductive' (insiders') national and regional case studies.

Based on the existing findings and debates, two circumstances that demonstrate the state of art in the field of social capital research can be underlined. First, the level of reflection and critical assessment of the main theoretical and methodological dilemmas has increased (see Stolle and Hooghe, 2005; Morales, 2002; van Deth, 2003; Schuler/Baron and Field, 2000). This is true of the general level of analysis, however, it does not have a direct impact on the empirical level or problems with operationalisation and measurements.

Second, at the data analysis level the development of increasingly sophisticated statistical multivariate techniques can be observed along with attempts to formalise a theoretical proposition in the form of mathematical models (especially where economists are involved). Yet these exact ('hard') procedures cannot resolve the question of the quality of the input data (data gathered by survey questionnaires). To put it differently, statistics is only a useful tool that by itself does not ensure the quality of input data and consequently high levels of coherent analysis and interpretation. The problem lies in the very old fashioned empiricist 'habitus' of (still) many social scientists who consider each set of quantifiable data as being taken for granted and ready for further statistical operations (see Cicourel, 1964).

Proceeding from these preliminary observations and insights, three sets of questions will be elaborated and reflected on:

1) How are stocks of social capital distributed across European (EU) nations? Using the conventional proxies like trust and associational involvement on the basis of data of cross-national surveys (EVS/WVS and ESS) we will try to show the main tentative trends and patterns.
2) What is the quality of such data? Are the findings and indicators reliable and credible? How do we explain inconsistencies and even contradictory findings when comparing similar or even the same wording of a question? Is the EVS a methodologically problematic source of data?
3) How can the research design be improved in the sense of greater methodological reflexivity and a triangulation strategy? How do we interpret the findings and statistical calculations based on the doubtful validity and reliability of the input data?

The cross-time and cross-nation distribution of social capital: some tentative trends and patterns

Although a number of cross-national researches allowing a comparative analysis of the state of social capital have been conducted in the last five years, a more holistic answer to the questions of whether social capital is growing or shrinking or, in which particular components can we see progress or a decline, still has to be answered.[5] One attempt in this direction is an analysis which studies the index of social capital in 47 countries, albeit it is based on old data from the WVS (data from 1995) and only includes some European countries (Norris, 2002). The comprehensive study of generalised trust and its predictors on the world scale has been undertaken on the basis of WVS data from 1990-1996 (Delhey/Newton, 2005). A much stronger focus on European countries is seen in an anthology written on the basis of the EVS 1999/2000, but even here only social capital in Western European countries was studied (Arts, Hagenaar, Halman, eds., 2003).[6] The same holds for a study focusing on factors that determine social capital in member states of the EU-15 on the basis of a European Community Household Panel conducted in 1999 (Christoforou, 2005).

Very few empirical studies encompass both Western European and Eastern European countries. To the best of our knowledge there are three such studies. One was based on the Eurobarometer surveys (1998-2002) (Fidrmuc and Gerxhani, 2005), while the second one took the European Values Survey from 1999/2000 as its basis and uses the so-called fuzzy-set method in its analysis of the data and indicators (Adam, et al., 2005). The third is also based on the same data set but only takes into account membership and active participation in voluntary associations (Bratkowski and Jasinska-

---

[5] In a recent article, the authors (Stolle/Hooghe, 2005: 157) speak of the lack of long-term empirical sources at the European level as a reason for the absence of the systematic monitoring of social capital dynamics. But in reality the data from the EVS have been available since 2001 (see Halman, 2001), while ESS data from 2002 are also available at least since 2004. Besides these sources, other sources could be utilised like Eurobarometer, New Democracy Barometer, partly the International Social Survey Programme (ISSP) and Political Culture in East-Central Europe. However, it is true that besides the WVS and EVS no other (complete) time-series data are available or they are not appropriate for making generalisations.

[6] One contribution stresses (by referring to Western European countries as an example) the generational aspect. The authors state: 'In reply to Putnam, we may conclude that young generations outside of US, are not less but more involved in participatory life compared to older generations, more instead of less inclined to trust other people, and even more not less politically involved, mostly regardless their levels of involvement in civil society' (Dekker/Ester/Vinken, 2003: 245). Some other authors point out that in a few EU countries the younger generations are less involved in associations (Halpern, 2005).

Kania, 2004). However, only a few cross-time studies at the European level have so far been conducted (Oorschot and Arts, 2005 on the basis of EVS data with only ten Western European countries plus the USA and Canada, and Morales, 2004 on the basis of the EVS and the ESS).

It is also worth mentioning here publications based on national case studies. The first regards social capital in individual Western European countries (van Deth et al., 1999), the second one deals with five Western European countries (Sweden, Spain, France, Germany and Great Britain) as well as Japan, Australia and Canada (Putnam, ed., 2002). There are also some investigations dedicated to Eastern Europe (Badescu/Uslaner, eds., 2003; Mihaylova, 2004; Haerpfer et al., 2005).

In order to study the state of social capital in Europe and its trends, we need to focus on data that allow us to conduct cross-nation as well as longitudinal (over time) comparisons. By doing so, we can gain some insights into distinctions and similarities among countries or groups of countries while, on the other side, it will allow us to make conclusions about the trends and time fluctuations. To establish the stock of social capital we will use standard indicators of generalised trust (Table 1.1), membership (Table 1.2) and the activity or amount of unpaid work in voluntary associations (Table 1.3). We should stress that this is a very approximate way – including where an entirely correct measurement procedure is involved – of investigating the (potential) stock of social capital.

Generalised trust

Although the interpersonal trust – trust in generalised other – is seen as one of the main components of social capital is difficult to agree with the thesis that this component is the best (single) indicator of social capital (notably: Uslaner, 2000; Newton, 2005; Halpern, 2005). While these authors overestimate the significance of trust – and especially its operationalisation and measurement – as being the best predictor of social capital, some others do not include it at all in their analyses (Bratkovski and Jasinska-Kania, 2004). This means that every investigation of social capital should include trust, however to measure it only by using trust is not theoretically justified. The underlying assumption is that generalised, diffused interpersonal trust indicates the readiness of an actor to enter into communication and co-operation with unknown people (strangers). However, serious limitations in the form of either a situational or semantic and cultural (particularist) conditioned understanding of the wording of the question or statement ('most people can be trusted') should not be overlooked.

Table 1.1: Generalised trust – WVS 1981, 1990 and EVS 1999.
% of respondents agreeing that most people can be trusted

	WVS 1981	WVS 1990	EVS 1999***
Austria	N/A	31.8	33.9
Belarus	N/A	25.5	41.9
Belgium	29.2	33.5	30.7
Bulgaria	N/A	30.4	26.9
Croatia	N/A	25.1**	18.4
Czech Republic	N/A	27.4	23.9
Denmark	52.7	57.7	66.5
Estonia	N/A	27.6	22.8
Finland	57.2	62.7	58.0
France	24.8	22.8	22.2
Germany	32.3*	32.9	34.7
Great Britain	43.1	43.7	29.7
Greece	N/A	N/A	23.7
Hungary	33.6	24.6	21.8
Iceland	39.8	43.6	41.1
Ireland	41.1	47.4	35.8
Italy	26.8	35.3	32.6
Latvia	N/A	19.1	17.1
Lithuania	N/A	30.8	24.9
Netherlands	44.8	53.5	59.8
Norway	60.9	65.1	65.3**
Poland	N/A	31.8	18.9
Portugal	N/A	21.7	10.0
Romania	N/A	16.1	10.1
Russia	N/A	37.5	23.7
Slovakia	N/A	22.0	15.7
Slovenia	N/A	17.4	21.7
Spain	35.1	34.2	36.2
Sweden	56.7	66.1	66.3
Switzerland	N/A	42.6	37.0**
Turkey	N/A	10.0	15.7
Ukraine	N/A	31.0**	27.2

Both the WVS and the EVS have the same question on generalised trust: 'Generally speaking, would you say that most people can be trusted or that you can't be too careful in dealing with people?' (1 – Most people can be trusted, 2 – Can't be too careful)
*data only available for West Germany
**data available for 1995 – WVS
***data pertaining to EVS 1999 are weighted
N/A – data not available
Source: World Values Survey: wave 1981, wave 1990, wave 1995, European Values Survey: wave 1999

In these cross-time findings we cannot find a unilinear trend. Comparing the periods between 1981 and 1990, the growth of generalised trust in the majority of countries can be seen; in some cases, the growth is low or stable whereas in others it is a little more pronounced (the Netherlands or Sweden). Besides France where we encounter a slight fall, it is solely in Hungary – the only country from the communist bloc included in the first wave of the WVS – that a considerable decline of trust is to observed. What is intriguing here is the fact this country had relatively high levels of social trust under the communist regime whereas the beginning of the democratic transition saw a reduction of trust, with this negative trend continuing in 1999. Comparing the periods between 1990 and 1999/2000, we can see that the level of generalised trust was reduced in twenty countries, it grew in eight countries while others remained at nearly the same level. What is quite surprising is that the biggest growth in trust took place in Belarus, which is today still the only non-democratic country in this part of the world.[7] In most European countries we find a clear decline in generalised trust. This is a dramatic turnaround. Looking only at the (old) EU-15 members, the picture is as follows: in six member states a fall in trust is registered, in five it increased and in two it is stable. Observing the EU-25 (we have 22 countries included), in 13 countries the trend is negative and only in six is it positive.

Regarding the situation in the new (post-socialist) members of the EU (since 2004), all have a negative trend except Slovenia (which made an improvement but from quite a low starting position in 1990). All of them have a score under 26% and can be placed in the category of low-trust societies (see Delhey and Newton, 2005). In the category of highly trusting societies four (Scandinavian plus the Netherlands) countries can be found, six are medium-trust and the rest (all new members plus Portugal and Greece) are in the lower trust category.

[7] It is quite obvious and surprising again that other ex-Soviet countries (Russia, Ukraine plus Bulgaria but not Romania) also express – despite a decreasing trend – a relatively high level of trust in comparison with more developed Eastern and Central European (and Baltic) countries. This is in clear opposition to the theoretical expectations. We know from the WVS that some authoritarian states show very high levels of trust (like China) but the question is if these data are trustworthy regarding the huge problem with sampling and also the readiness of the respondents to tell the truth in a non-democratic society. The other reservation is that the Chinese but also the Belarus findings can only be understood within the particular cultural and semantic context (meaning that the question of trust evokes on the side of respondents other associations and experiences than in the Western European context).

Membership and participation in voluntary associations

The other indicator of social capital is passive and active membership (participation) in voluntary organisations theoretically elaborated especially in the work of Putnam (but not in Coleman's and Bourdieu's approach or within network analysis). According to the so-called Tocquevillean-Putnamian model, the density of 'horizontal networks of citizen engagement' and vibrant associational life are the core factor of understanding the dynamics and accumulation of social capital. Associational participation is seen as a school of democracy, as an opportunity to learn co-operative behaviour. The strength of voluntary associations – forming an intermediary sphere – is also understood as an indicator of developed civil society and as a sign of self-organising capacity of a given community or society.

Table 1.2: Membership in voluntary organisations – WVS 1981, 1990, EVS 1999.
Index (all memberships per respondent), in brackets percentage of members in least one organisation

	WVS 1981	**WVS 1990**	**EVS 1999**
Austria	N/A	1.1 (53)	1.5 (67)
Belarus	N/A	0.6 (47)**	0.5 (46)
Belgium	0.6 (41)	1.4 (57)	1.6 (65)
Britain	0.9 (52)	1.1 (52)	0.6 (34)
Bulgaria	N/A	0.7 (41)	0.4 (23)
Croatia	N/A	1.1 (67)**	0.7 (43)
Czech R.	N/A	1.1 (62)	1.0 (60)
Denmark	1.0 (64)	1.8 (81)	1.9 (84)
Estonia	N/A	1.2 (73)	0.5 (34)
Finland[8]	N/A	1.8 (77)	1.9 (80)
France	0.4 (27)	0.7 (38)	0.6 (39)
Germany	0.7 (48)*	1.5 (74)	0.7 (47)
Greece	N/A	N/A	1.3 (56)
Hungary	N/A	0.7 (50)	0.5 (31)
Iceland	1.6 (82)	2.4 (90)	2.7 (93)

[8] The data for Finland from the first wave should be regarded with reservation (Morales, 2004). We even recently received (July 2006) from the person responsible for the EVS data at Tilburg University an explanation that Finnish file is no longer available i.e. that it is excluded from the WVS 1981 data set due to 'severe problems with socio-demographic variables'.

The problem is that such errors have been reoccurring, for instance in ESS 2002 when two countries (Switzerland and Czech Republic) were also excluded from the data file because 'their items on associational involvement were incorectly formulated in these countries' questionaires and their data are not comparable to the rest' (Morales, 2004: 10).

Ireland	0.8 (52)	1.0 (49)	1.2 (57)
Italy	0.4 (24)	0.6 (34)	0.8 (42)
Latvia	N/A	1.2 (68)	0.4 (31)
Lithuania	N/A	0.9 (60)	0.3 (19)
Netherlands	1.2 (61)	2.7 (84)	3.1 (92)
Norway	1.1 (63)	2.0 (81)	1.5 (74)**
Poland	N/A	0.6 (41)	0.4 (25)
Portugal	N/A	0.6 (33)	0.4 (28)
Romania	N/A	0.4 (30)	0.3 (21)
Russia	N/A	1.0 (71)	0.4 (31)
Slovakia	N/A	1.0 (56)	1.1 (65)
Slovenia	N/A	0.6 (39)	1.0 (52)
Spain	0.5 (31)	0.4 (23)	0.5 (29)
Sweden	1.1 (67)	2.1 (85)	3.2 (96)
Turkey	N/A	0.2 (18)**	0.1 (8)
Ukraine	N/A	0.5 (41)**	0.5 (34)

Index membership in voluntary organisations: WVS 1981 uses the following question on membership in a voluntary organisation: 'Which, if any, do you belong to?' The types of organisations mentioned were the following: 1. Charities concerned with the welfare of people; 2. Churches or religious organisations; 3. Education or arts groups; 4. Trade unions; 5. Political parties or groups; 6. Organisations concerned with human rights at home or abroad; 7. Conservation, environmentalist or animal welfare groups; 8. Youth work (e.g. scouts, guides, youth clubs etc.); 9. Consumer groups; 10. Professional associations.
WVS 1990 uses the following question: 'Please look carefully at the following list of voluntary organisations and activities and say, which, if any, do you belong to?' In comparison to WVS 1981 the list of organisations was expanded, while one item (consumer groups) was omitted: 1. Social welfare services for elderly, handicapped or deprived people; 2. Religious or church organisations; 3. Education, arts, music or cultural activities; 4. Trade unions; 5. Political parties or groups; 6. Local community action on issues like poverty, housing, racial equality; 7. Third world development or human rights; 8. Conservation, the environment, ecology; 9. Professional association; 10. Youth work (e.g. scouts, guides, youth clubs etc.); 11. Sports or recreation; 12. Women's groups; 13. Peace movement; 14. Animal rights; 15. Voluntary organisations concerned with health; and 16. Other groups.
EVS 1999 uses the same question as WVS 1990; items 8 and 14 were merged into 'Conservation, environment, animal rights groups'; 'Trade unions' was changed into 'Labour unions'.
*data available for West Germany
**data available for WVS 1995 – this survey uses a different question wording: 'Now I am going to read off a list of voluntary organizations; for each one, could you tell me whether you are an active member, an inactive member or not a member of that type of organization?' the question is followed by the list: 1. Church or religious organization; 2. Sport or recreation organization; 3. Art, music or educational organization; 4. Labour union; 5. Political party; 6. Environmental organization, 7. Professional association; 8. Charitable organization; 9. Any other voluntary organization. In the index above only 'inactive' memberships are taken into account.
N/A – data not available
Source: World Values Survey: wave 1981, wave 1990; European Values Survey: wave 1999

Analysing the period between 1981 and 1990 we get a similar picture as in the case of generalised trust, namely an increase of membership in most countries. The period between 1990 and 1999 (with more countries included) shows a different picture, in 14 countries the trend is negative, in eleven it is positive and in five it is unchanged. If we only take the EU-15, we can see a decline in membership in only three cases (the extreme fall in membership in Britain and Germany is a surprise). In the EU-25 we again have mixed evidence, in 13 cases there is an increase or stability and in eight cases a decrease.

Yet the differences are huge between, for instance, Sweden and Lithuania or Portugal. On the other hand, Slovenia, Czech Republic, Slovakia and (especially) Greece have relatively very high scores despite their quite low levels of generalised trust.

Active membership in voluntary associations is especially important for learning skills and attitudes of self-organisation and mutual co-operation. On the structural (societal) level its role in generating social capital in the form of trust, solidarity and participation seems quite obvious, although contradictory empirical evidence has also been presented so far, especially regarding the relationship between (active) membership and trust as well as regarding the impact of associational engagement on political participation (for more information on different findings, see Halpern, 2005: 189-194; Delhey/Newton, 2005: 313-314). On the other hand, it is quite clear that not all associations are equally important and that diverse and multiple active membership is probably more important for the creation of higher levels of social capital (Morales, 2002; Morales, 2004; Halpern, 2005). Most cross-national analyses are still far away from such a selective and sophisticated approach and use very rough indications for detecting the role of associational participation in the creation and diffusion of social capital.[9]

---

[9] There are attempts at a detailed analysis. Some authors use the distinction between Putnam (including more socially-oriented and public good producing associations) and the Olson group (including associations representing special interests), see Fidrmuc and Gerxhani, 2006 and Welzel, Inglehart, Deutsch, 2006 or between mailing list and face-to face associations (Dekker and van Broek, 2005).

Regarding the measure of associational involvement most analyses use the proportion of respondents who are members or doing unpaid work in a least one organisations from the list. A few investigations take as a starting point the sum of members in each organisation, though this procedure is quite unusual and incomparable with others (Raisen et al., 2001; Haerpfer et al., 2005). In this article we use the measure which includes not only the respondents reporting themselves as being a member or active in at least one organisation but also those who have multiple memberships or multiple activities.

Based on conventional and available measures of the active involvement we get the following picture:

Table 1.3: Unpaid work in voluntary organisations – WVS 1981, 1990 and EVS 1999. Index (all unpaid work per respondent), in brackets the percentage of members doing unpaid work for at least one organisation

	WVS 1981	WVS 1990	EVS 1999
Austria	N/A	0.4 (26)	0.5 (30)
Belarus	N/A	0.1 (9)**	0.3 (19)
Belgium	0.3 (21)	0.6 (28)	0.7 (35)
Britain (Great)	0.3 (19)	0.4 (22)	0.8 (42)
Bulgaria	N/A	0.4 (20)	0.3 (19)
Croatia	N/A	0.6 (41)**	0.4 (24)
Czech R.	N/A	0.4 (29)	0.5 (33)
Denmark	0.2 (18)	0.4 (26)	0.6 (37)
Estonia	N/A	0.5 (34)	0.3 (18)
Finland	N/A	0.9 (45)	0.6 (38)
France	0.2 (15)	0.5 (23)	0.4 (27)
Germany	0.3 (21)*	0.5 (34)	0.2 (19)
Greece	N/A	N/A	1.0 (40)
Hungary	N/A	0.2 (16)	0.3 (15)
Iceland	0.7 (28)	0.6 (36)	0.5 (33)
Ireland	0.3 (22)	0.5 (27)	0.6 (33)
Italy	0.2 (17)	0.4 (24)	0.5 (26)
Latvia	N/A	0.7 (36)	0.3 (22)
Lithuania	N/A	0.5 (30)	0.2 (16)
Netherlands	0.3 (24)	0.7 (36)	0.9 (49)
Norway	0.4 (24)	0.6 (37)	1.0 (58)**
Poland	N/A	0.4 (28)	0.2 (14)
Portugal	N/A	0.3 (18)	0.2 (16)
Romania	N/A	0.3 (25)	0.2 (16)
Russia	N/A	0.3 (23)	0.1 (8)
Slovakia	N/A	0.4 (27)	0.8 (51)
Slovenia	N/A	0.3 (15)	0.5 (29)
Spain	0.4 (23)	0.2 (12)	0.2 (16)
Sweden	0.3 (26)	0.7 (39)	1.1 (56)
Turkey	N/A	0.3 (18)**	0.1 (6)
Ukraine	N/A	0.1 (9)**	0.1 (13)

Index unpaid voluntary work in organisations: WVS 1981 used the following question: 'And do you currently do any unpaid work for any of them?' WVS 1990 and EVS 1999 used the wording: 'Please look carefully at the following list of voluntary organisations and activities and say, which, if any, are you currently doing unpaid work for?' For list of organizations see comment under Table 1.2.
*data available for West Germany
**data available for WVS 1995 – see comment under Table 1.2. In the index above only 'active' memberships are taken into account.
N/A – data not available
Source: World Values Survey: wave 1981, wave 1990; European Values Survey: wave 1999

Even in this – in the framework of the Putnam-Tocqueville model – the most relevant and useful indicator of social capital we can see a rise throughout the 1981 to 1990 period while in the period between 1990 and 1999 the situation is more ambivalent. Taking the whole sample into account, in 19 countries we can observe an increase or stability in active membership and in 11 a decrease. In the EU-15 a decrease is registered in only three cases and in the enlarged EU in seven cases. It can be concluded that the prevailing trend is, on average, quite positive. The greatest surprise is Greece where its active membership figure is well above the average of EU countries since only Sweden shows higher scores in this regard. Slovakia's very high position is also difficult to explain (considering its low trust level, this is also true of Greece).

Although the interpretation might not be unanimous, it can be asserted that social capital according to the WVS/EVS data in Europe is generally not eroding. There are signs of decline as well as improvement. While the reduction of generalised trust is quite visible – though not in all countries – the associational involvement shows a more complex but on average positive trend. However, the dynamics and fluctuations of our three main indicators are not in accordance with the theoretical expectations. For instance, the decrease in trust does not result in a reduction of (active) membership and vice versa as projected by Putnam's theory. There are some cases (mainly Nordic countries) which are consistent with this theory, but many cases show an 'erratic' movement. The scores for some countries are difficult to explain (and understand). In some cases, the question remains open of whether the findings reflect a real increase (or decrease) or whether this can be attributed to methodological artefacts, statistical errors or problems relating to cultural-semantic issues arising in the processes of preparing the questionnaire and data collection. Some findings and atypical oscillations are hard to explain. Yet even bigger problems emerge if one conducts a synchronic comparison of the results from two different surveys or datasets, namely the EVS and the ESS.

The quality and credibility of the indicators and data – a comparison of the EVS and ESS findings

By comparing the findings from two different datasets we can establish some kind of logical control. Let us now see what is the result of comparing the data from the EVS and ESS surveys. The latter was conducted three, in some cases two years, after the first one. As far as the measurement instruments are concerned, changes were made to the wording concerning generalised trust. Instead of the dichotomous item, a methodologically more correct eleven-scale ladder was used. However, the problem is that the ESS includes much fewer countries than the EVS/WVS so that we are unable to explain some 'mysterious' cases (like Slovakia or Belarus).

Table 1.4: Comparison Generalised Trust EVS 1999 and ESS 2002

	Generalised trust, in brackets the ranking of countries		
	EVS 1999 (% of respondents expressing trust; on dichotomous scale)	ESS 2002 (% of respondents expressing trust; on a scale from 6-10; 0 = no trust, 10 = full trust)	ESS 2002 (mean score on a scale from 0-10; 0 = no trust, 10 = full trust)
Denmark	66.5 (1)	74.7 (1)	5.1 (7)
Sweden	66.3 (2)	61.1 (3)	6.2 (2)
Netherlands	60.0 (3)	58.4 (4)	5.7 (4)
Finland	57.4 (4)	70.9 (2)	6.3 (1)
Spain	38.6 (5)	40.9 (8)	4.8 (10)
Ireland	36.0 (6)	50.8 (5)	5.8 (3)
Austria	33.4 (7)	41.9 (7)	5.2 (6)
Italy	32.6 (8)	33.7 (10)	4.4 (12)
Belgium	29.2 (9)	40.2 (9)	5.0 (8)
Britain (Great)	28.8 (10)	43.1 (6)	5.3 (5)
Czech R.	24.5 (11)	27.6 (12)	4.5 (11)
Greece	23.7 (12)	21.3 (16)	3.4 (17)
Hungary	22.3 (13)	23.3 (14)	4.3 (15)
Slovenia	21.7 (14)	24.2 (13)	4.3 (14)
France	21.3 (15)	28.1 (11)	4.8 (9)
Poland	18.4 (16)	18.9 (17)	3.9 (16)
Portugal	12.3 (17)	22.9 (15)	4.3 (13)

This table shows that in most cases the values in the ESS (the second column) are higher than the values in the EVS, but these differences can be ascribed to some extent to the fact that the former data set has more differentiated scaling and the calculation is different. If the ranking of an individual country is taken into account, the congruency between both data sets in the majority of countries is quite visible. Put differently, the differences regarding generalised trust between the EVS and ESS data sets are relatively small considering the rank order of countries. However, there are four exceptions whose ranking changed substantially, namely Spain, Greece, France and the Britain. While the first two are better placed in the EVS data set, the other two have a higher position in the ESS. Many more deviations or incongruences are found between the EVS and ESS third column (average value on a scale from 0-10). From a theoretical point of view, it is interesting to note that Finland is better placed in the ESS regarding trust but its position regarding active associational involvement in the same survey is much lower than in the EVS.

Let us now see the results of a comparison of both data sets regarding the patterns of passive and active associational involvement.

Table 1.5: Comparison of the European Social Survey (ESS) and the EVS
Index - memberships and unpaid (voluntary) work per respondent; in brackets the percentage of respondents who are members or doing unpaid work for at least one organisation

	Membership		Unpaid work res. voluntary work	
	EVS 1999	**ESS 2002**	**EVS 1999**	**ESS 2002**
Austria	1.5 (67)	2.0 (74)	0.5 (30)	0.2 (13)
Belgium	1.6 (65)	1.6 (71)	0.7 (35)	0.4 (23)
Britain (Great)	0.6 (34)	1.6 (69)	0.8 (42)	0.4 (23)
Denmark	1.9 (84)	2.5 (92)	0.6 (37)	0.4 (28)
Finland	1.9 (80)	1.6 (76)	0.6 (38)	0.2 (12)
France	0.6 (39)	0.9 (48)	0.4 (27)	0.3 (19)
Germany	0.7 (47)	1.5 (70)	0.2 (19)	0.4 (24)
Greece	1.3 (56)	0.4 (25)	1.0 (40)	0.1 (6)
Hungary	0.5 (31)	0.4 (27)	0.3 (15)	0.1 (9)
Ireland	1.2 (57)	1.6 (68)	0.6 (33)	0.3 (16)
Italy	0.8 (42)	0.6 (34)	0.5 (26)	0.1 (5)
Netherlands	3.1 (92)	2.2 (83)	0.9 (49)	0.4 (29)
Norway	1.5 (74)**	2.4 (84)	1.0 (58)**	0.6 (37)
Poland	0.4 (25)	0.3 (21)	0.2 (14)	0.1 (6)
Portugal	0.4 (28)	0.5 (28)	0.2 (16)	0.1 (5)
Slovenia	1.0 (52)	0. 9 (52)	0.5 (29)	0.3 (19)
Spain	0.5 (29)	0.7 (35)	0.2 (16)	0.1 (6)
Sweden	3.2 (96)	2.5 (90)	1.2 (56)	0.6 (35)

Source: European Values Survey 1999; European Social Survey 2002
** data from WVS 1995

Comparing the data referring to membership and unpaid work in voluntary organisations it seems that we have considerable inconsistencies between both data sets. Concerning membership on the basis of the first measure (all memberships per respondents meaning that some respondents are members in more than one organisation) in nine cases higher values of the ESS data can be observed, while in eight it is the opposite. Regarding unpaid work res. voluntary work, lower scores in all countries except Germany are noticeable. In some countries like Austria, we find with the ESS a higher level of membership but a lower level of active involvement in the form of unpaid work. Regarding the scores for unpaid (voluntary) work the cross-national differences are smaller than what appeared to be in the EVS. What are reasons for these divergent findings? Is it appropriate at all to directly compare the findings from these two data sets?

It has to be stressed that question wording differs in some aspects. First of all, in the ESS the respondents are asked not only to report membership and unpaid res. voluntary work in voluntary organisations (like in the EVS-WVS) but also to distinguish between: 1) membership (belonging); 2) participation in these organisations; 3) doing voluntary work; and 4) donating money. We compared unpaid work and voluntary work, but what about the category of participation?[10] The other difference between the EVS and ESS instruments might be the limitation in the sense of timing, namely the respondents only had to report their involvement within the last twelve months while in the EVS the respondents are required to report if they are 'currently' members or doing unpaid work. In the ESS the time limitation appears more strict at least in a psychological sense. Also concerning the list of organisations there some differences, in the EVS on the list there are 14 organisations (plus 'other'), while in the ESS there are 23 organisations (plus 'other').

These differences in the wording of the question mean that a direct comparison between both data sets is hard to justify. To some extent passive membership is an exception. Despite some differences concerning the list of organisations (which is in the case of the ESS more diversified) one might expect similar or convergent findings. What we can reveal is that only in five countries do such convergent results appear whereas in some of them, especially in Germany, Britain, Greece and Sweden we instead observe very divergent scores. If we calculate the ranking, the picture is in two respects similar to that emanating from the EVS. On the top are again the Nordic countries (minus Finland) plus the Netherlands, on the bottom are Poland, Portugal, Hungary and Greece. Unlike the EVS, the position of Greece is completely different (now at the bottom). The scores for countries

---

[10] Actually it is difficult to imagine what is meant by participation and how respondents understood the difference between these two categories. If we namely count as participation such short-time activities like attending meetings or answering (e-)mail, exchanging information then the question arises of what is meant by membership or belonging to an association. If somebody is a member only formally (cheque-book or mailing list membership) and has nothing to do with the situation in their association, then it is difficult to speak about the generation of social capital or the strength of civil society. However, it is true that in some periods people are more active or more passive.

in-between the top and bottom are in many cases substantially different (Germany, Britain). Put differently, comparing the rank positions in both data sets we encounter some convergent (especially on the top and bottom) and some very divergent findings. Taking into account the other measure – the percentage of respondents being members of at least one organisation – it turns out that that differences between EVS and ESS regarding membership are much smaller (with exception of Great Britain, Germany and Greece).

One possibility to undertake some kind of comparison regarding active membership would be to bring together the scores for participation and voluntary work in the ESS and compare that with unpaid work in the EVS. When doing this, Norway, Sweden, Belgium, Denmark and the Netherlands appear on the top. There is again some similarity with the EVS although Finland is missing here (only in eleventh place). The composition of the bottom is also as expected with the exception of Greece. The position of Belgium and especially Germany and partly also France is far better in the ESS than in the EVS while Finland and Italy are placed worse.

How to explain the divergent findings and generalisations

Our presentation and treatment of social capital indicators like trust and participation in associations on the basis of the EVS and ESS data show that we are dealing with certain findings and oscillations that are difficult to explain. Cross-national researches seem to have serious problems with the provision of credible data (see Jowel, 1998). This in turn raises doubts about the generalisation of findings and theoretical conclusions. These aspects have not been discussed much so far; the prevailing stand is to treat the empirical data as taken-for-granted.

From this point of view it is very interesting to read the volume, edited and (partly) written by the authors who were directly engaged in organising and conducting the EVS project. While carrying out various multivariate analyses, especially those involving the cluster approach, they found 'strange' patterns or blocks of supposedly similar countries. They were surprised with what these statistical operations can bring about, complaining that 'no sensible interpretation of these findings comes to mind' or, in another place, 'this is again a cluster whose connection is unclear' (Arts and Halman, 2004: 42-43).

In their eyes it is not the quality (or poverty) of the input data that is responsible for this cognitive confusion, but the grand theories they used as an interpretive framework of reference. They argue: '*Such patterns are hard to understand and interpret and it seems as if these patterns are not really as strongly related to economic development as Ronald Inglehart, among others, would like us to believe. The only cluster of countries which seem to make sense is the group of Nordic countries*' (ibid, 51).[11] The authors of the quote do not depart from the point that there is something wrong with the data but see the problem in an inappropriate theoretic paradigm functioning as Procrustes' bed. What is frustrating is the very fact that, in this sense, they do not offer any alternative, nor a middle-range theory. However, it is totally impossible that the conceptual confusion they themselves describe would only result from a deficient or inappropriate theory of modernisation or post-materialism. This finding has been confirmed by a growing number of authors (also mentioned below). In fact, theory also plays an important role but in a different context – in the sense of a theoretically well-considered research design. Haller (2002) believes that one of the main weaknesses of cross-national projects (like the WVS/EVS) is that the questionnaires are produced without a design and are not based on (preliminary) theoretical grounds. In this sense, he speaks of inductive post hoc generalisation appearing in the stage of interpreting the data.

The quote mentions Inglehart as a theoretician but not as the author of many studies based on the WVS data. In fact, this author is a true authority in the field of studying changes in values – among which he includes trust and social capital – in the context of global structural and economic processes (Inglehart, 1997; Welzel, Inglehart, Deutsch, 2006). Lately, he has been reproached for interpreting the data from cross-national researches incorrectly and ad hoc and for using inadequate statistical procedures and for confusing the levels of (aggregate) analysis (Seligson, 2002; Haller, 2002).[12]

There is a similar story about Putnam who is considered to be the founder of empirical research into social capital, although mostly he himself does not use the WVS/EVS data. He has also become the target of serious criticism. What is surprising is that he is not reproached partially or for individual weaknesses, but many oppose the essence of his statement about the decrease in social capital in the USA, some even arising from the same

[11] In contrast to this, two other authors in the same book dealing with the same data set (but using different exogenous variables – like the Human Development Index as an indicator of modernisation – and applying regression analysis instead of cluster analysis) arrive at the opposite conclusion, namely that just this (modernisation) theory matters, meaning there is a close connection between socio-economic development and social capital indicators (Bratkovski and Jasinska-Kania, 2004: 124, 134-35).

[12] Haller even says this: 'Since Inglehart had changed neither his approach nor his method, and since his work – despite its evident weaknesses – continues to be quoted around the world, I think it is imperative to review it critically again and again' (Haller, 2002: 154).

databases (e.g. Paxton, 1999). Inglehart's problem is that in his studies on values he almost exclusively draws on the WVS data, i.e. on a certain 'deductive', outsider database while, on the other hand, Putnam is almost exclusively focused on American data from different sources and operates as an insider (national case study) researcher in this sense (Putnam, 2000). At least two researchers who used the WVS data, one from second wave and the other from the fourth wave, showed that these data do not indicate a decrease in social capital in the USA. Further, especially recent data point to an improvement of the situation as far as participation in associations is concerned (Baer, Curtis and Grabb, 2001; Dekker and van den Broek, 2005).

Let us highlight that information which will be surprising to many. It is believed that membership in traditional organisations like church organisations, parties and trade unions is decreasing. However, the results of the EVS/WVS show the opposite trend, with membership and activity increasing (in the 1981-2001 period) and, what is unusual – primarily in the US. In this country, even the number of those belonging to trade unions and political organisations grew and is higher than in most European (EU) countries. Elsewhere in Europe, growth was also registered and a fall was only recorded exceptionally. Certainly, this is in striking contradiction with the information indicating a fall in interest in trade unions and parties, or speaking of extensive secularisation. Some researchers believe that the thesis about declining social capital and civic participation is wrong as it overemphasises the old forms of sociability which are indeed on the decrease, as shown by Inglehart, and pays insufficient attention to new, less formalised forms (Stolle and Hooghe, 2005). However, the figures discredit such opinions and Putnam. Of course, it is possible that the EVS/WVS results paint an inadequate picture. Here, another question is raised, that of why is there such a discrepancy between the American and the WVS data, and which should we trust. Certainly, as far as the American data are concerned other interpretations are possible. One of the most convincing says that the character of voluntary associations itself is changing, that they are organised according to the principles of lobbying, 'advocacy groups', with a professional leadership and increasingly passive members (Skockpol, 2003).

The situation in Europe is also facing many conflicting, controversial findings and interpretations based on supposedly exact statistical calculations. This is especially characteristic of the studying of connections between different variables or indicators of social capital, for instance between generalised trust and membership in associations, or between different components of social capital and exogenous variables (level of economic development, level of democratisation or political culture etc.). We seem to be dealing with an immeasurable mass of conflicting analyses and conclusions, some proving the connections while others are denying the same connections.[13] The spirit of empiricism is identifiable, there is in many cases a distinct absence of any wider contextual and qualitative reflection.

The cultural and institutional context of cross-national findings

When speaking of methodological deficiencies, one should distinguish between two levels. The first concerns weaknesses arising from comparative, cross-national research. The second level is directly connected with the issues of the conceptualisation, operationalisation and measurement of social capital. These two levels overlap in many ways; we will only highlight some characteristic aspects.

We have mentioned the quality (or, in other words, validity and reliability) of input data several times. In this regard, we distinguish between three aspects. The first concerns the question whether the data from cross-national studies reflects the situation and trends in individual countries included in comparative research. This aspect could be called *correspondence*. It is possible to check this by comparing the data from several international researches or – which is more appropriate – by comparing cross-national findings with the findings of national case studies. If there are no major deviations, we can speak of satisfactory correspondence. We have already mentioned the disparity between the American data (or the interpretation by Putnam), indicating a decrease in membership and activities in voluntary organisations, and the WVS data showing that civic participation is growing in the US, even to a greater extent than in Europe (Dekker and van den Broek, 2005). The central question should be why such divergent findings appear. However, it seems that at the moment nobody can answer

[13] For instance, Delhey and Newton (2005) found out (on the broader WVS sampling) that voluntary organisations may not be particularly important for the generation of trust, and a similar opinion is expressed by Uslaner (2000). On the other side, some authors (working with a somewhat different selection of countries) argued differently: 'Belonging to voluntary associations was positively related to social trust in 10 of 12 countries, to political involvement in 11 countries.... No single negative effect was found' (Dekker and van den Broek, 2005: 53-55). Van Deth and other co-authors (Gabriel et al., 2002: 171) argue that political involvement has very little to do with social capital : ' ... ist in keinem einzigen Land ein starkes Zusammenhang zwischen Sozialkapital und politischem Engagement empirisch zu beobachten' , also see van Deth (2000). Of course, this is in contradiction with the above quotation. Sometimes these contradictory findings and calculations are the consequence of a different selection of countries and levels of (statistical) analysis (individual level vs. aggregate or national levels).

this question systematically since it seems that many researchers are not used to working with controversial and contradictory findings or various data sources. This gives a bad name to the ability of sociological analysis – and especially the part researching the dynamics and trends in the accumulation and distribution of social capital – to also address tougher methodological challenges and dilemmas.

The second aspect of data quality is *mutual comparability*; the question is whether the results obtained in one country are comparable (equivalent) to the results obtained in other countries. For instance, did the Swedish respondents in the EVS 1999/2000 understand the question about membership in religious or church organisations (question 5B) in the same way as German or Czech or other respondents. It has already been mentioned that was not the case, with the Swedish respondents probably understanding this question in a considerably different way than the others. What were the reasons for that? In the opinion of two Dutch sociologists, the problem is that Swedish citizens are 'automatically administered as members of the Lutheran Church' (Oorschot and Arts, 2005: 11) and understand this question as confessional adherence and not as membership in quasi-church voluntary organisations (which is the intention of the question). However, this explanation neglects the fact that the EVS questionnaire also contains a special question: 'Do you belong to a religious denomination?' (question 22). Seventy-six percent of Swedish respondents answered this question affirmatively, and only slightly fewer (71%) said they were members of religious or church organisations (of whom 23% declared themselves active members or members doing unpaid work). It is possible that they confused the two questions or understood them in the same way, but in 1990 they gave a completely different answer to the same question. In that year, just 11% said they were members of religious or church organisations. What happened in 1999 to make them answer differently? If we take the data from the ESS 2002 we again see the 'normal' picture, namely it appears that only 15% of Swedish respondents report their membership in this type of voluntary organisation.[14]

Some authors claim that people in Great Britain erroneously or inadequately answered the question about adherence to organisations in the area of sports

[14] A contradiction in EVS can also be established between the question about membership and that of how much time the respondents spend at church (question 6-C). Here, 70% of Swedish respondents – which is more than in many other countries – answered that they do not go to church at all. This also shows they do not have a specific connection – or that this connection is very symbolic and can be understood only in Swedish national - historical and institutional context – with the church and their organisations.

and recreation (or that this question was not asked correctly) (Dekker and van den Broek, 2005: 56, footnote 5). But these are more 'exotic' details, what our analysis comparing the EVS and ESS data revealed is much more critical, namely systematic measurement errors in the case of associational involvement in Greece.[15] The reason for that is supposed to be relatively banal, either errors in translation, biased sampling or errors in data processing (and probably not the failure to deal with country-specific arrangements or semantic-cultural problems). Regarding comparability, there are therefore many unresolved problems in the EVS like an 'implausible low level of volunteering in Germany' (Dekker et al., 2003: 223), a disproportion between membership and unpaid work in the British case (which only appears in the EVS and not in the ESS). What is especially critical is that findings which are difficult to explain or are contradictory do not only appear in post-communist Eastern Europe (like the high trust levels in Belarus) but mainly in Western Europe where both cross-national researches and public opinion surveys have a tradition of many years.

The third aspect is the *theoretical relevance* of data. The question is whether these data form an appropriate basis for the creation of indicators and whether it is based on theoretical starting points (in our case the theory of social capital). There are also certain reservations here. Van Deth (2003) believes there should not be a situation where the data determine the interpretation or definition of social capital. Here, we can reiterate Haller's opinion that this is about post-hoc and ad-hoc generalisations, which means that the problem is in the improvisation involved in the production of a questionnaire or in the fact that the questionnaire is not based on theoretical considerations.

Errors in measurement and inconsistencies – influencing correspondence and comparability as well as theoretical relevance – largely depend on two factors. The first concerns the *technical design* of the research. This refers to the stages of compiling and translating the questionnaire (mostly from English to (other) national languages) – this aspect can only technical but in certain situations is connected with semantic issues – the stage of sampling, and the control of fieldwork in individual countries included in the sample.[16] Such deficiencies can be eliminated relatively easily if there is the will and agreement among the researchers co-ordinating the survey.

---

[15] Also other data sets like Eurobarometer (see Fidrmuc and Gerxhani, 2004) and the European Community Household Panel (Christoforou, 2005) confirm that associational involvement in Greece is very low.

[16] In the last chapter of the EVS report (Halman, 2001; EVS Methodology, pp. 335-378) we find detailed information about the control procedure concerning the whole process of preparing and

A greater problem involves errors in measurement concerning the comparability of results ascribed to *semantic (hermeneutic)* reasons (concerning the issues of understanding and interpreting the 'proper' meaning of a given question's wording in a survey by respondents) stemming from *idiosyncratic cultural* and/or *institutional contexts*.[17] The former is especially connected with the question about generalised trust and the latter with questions asking about membership and activities in voluntary organisations, yet in many cases they are overlapping. There exist both individual and culturally-conditioned variations in the understanding and interpretation of the significance of interpersonal trust (most people can be trusted). What does 'most people' actually mean? For some, this question indeed indicates their trust in strangers while for others that is not the case, especially for those moving within narrow limits of their everyday world (Lebenswelt). We have already mentioned 'Nordic exceptionalism', which is also shown in a high level of trust. Certain authors have a great belief in the classic question about generalised trust and claim that it in fact measures the trust

---

testing the questionnaire (the problem of translation), about compulsory, optional and country-specific questions. Also the issues of sampling, response rate and checking of reliability of data are addressed. The intention to make these aspects transparent must be welcomed. However, it can be discerned from this information that the researchers failed to take into account all relevant control measures in order to ensure reliable and valid findings. It seems that some national teams had too much freedom in deciding to conduct the control or not. For instance, the supervision of interviews was only carried out by half of the national teams, the data were not checked for logic and consistency in seven countries. It seems that national teams could use additional ('country-specific') questions and modalities. For example, we found out that the Slovenian team completed the question relating to membership in local-level organisations by adding (suggesting) the names of such organisations (for instance they added: Red Cross). It is possible that a similar finding could have emerged without such an intervention by the national team, but there are some doubts because we do not know if the other teams also made such local adaptations of the questionnaire. But it seems that this has been generally allowed. If this is associated with an insufficient control procedure, the results cannot be optimal. This also means that we **should be very careful in dealing with such adaptations, they are needed but should be made in a transparent way (each national team is supposed to report such adaptations and the related reasons).** Even bigger questions and doubts arise regarding the WVS, where the control was much more difficult to carry out (also see Haller, 2002).

[17] A very illustrative example of an idiosyncratic institutional context is the already mentioned Swedish 'church and religious organisations'. The same is true for membership in trade unions in the same country which is not entirely voluntary since it brings some very concrete (financial) benefits and this explains why in Sweden union membership is so high. A more detailed analysis of data concerning associational involvement in Belarus shows that a relatively high proportion of membership is actually focused on membership in unions (approximately 70% of all membership) and this is again not entirely voluntary membership. It is a consequence of the still existing communist tradition and social inertia which in some years (if the reforms take place) might completely disappear. For the creation of social capital such a constellation has little significance.

put in strangers (particularly Uslander, 2000). However, Delhey and Newton reached a different conclusion, although their analysis was based on Uslander's thesis at the outset. When they made empirical analyses, they found that '...ethnic homogeneity is strongly associated with generalised trust...' (Delhey and Newton, 2005: 324). This in fact conveys a doubt that this question does measure trust in strangers. As Scandinavian nations are among the most ethnically homogenous in Europe (in addition to the fact that these are small nations with relatively small social differences), it is logical to find that the trust of Nordic respondents concerns the segment of people who – in the sense of an 'imagined community' – are detected as similar, and not as strangers.[18]

The problems of understanding and interpretation also – as we have seen – appear in the questions about membership and activities in voluntary associations. One of the known researchers working with the EVS 1999 data even says the following: '...survey questions seem to be understood differently in different countries' (Anheier et al., 2004: 98). One other author comparing the EVS and Eurobarometer (EB) data sets (as well as the EB cross-time data) states that even equivalent question wordings within the same survey repeated in certain sequences (like the EB) can be problematic since they provide quite different – sometimes also contradictory – findings. Proceeding from a very systematic (statistical) analysis, she comes to the conclusion that '*...our measurement of associational involvement and membership is far from perfect, and scholars should be very cautious with making strong theoretical claims with weak data, especially when doing comparative analyses...however what we can do is to improve the items in the survey to be designed in the future*' (Morales, 2002: 516). Besides the problems with sampling she points out the neglect of cross-national variations in the structure of associational life, concerning the country-idiosyncratic institutional arrangements which consequently means that the question wording is not sufficiently specific for respondents who have problems in understanding or interpreting the proper meaning of the question (ibid.: 515-516). Two other authors recently came to a similar conclusion stating (and hoping) that these unresolved semantic-cultural backgrounds of question wording and/or country-specific institutional context should not substantially change or reverse the validity claim of the main scores and ranking position (Dekker and van den Broek, 2005: 56).

[18] The authors argue: 'In other words, generalised trust is strongest where we have something in common with others, especially where we are from the same ethnic background... It raises the question of how generalised generalised trust actually is' (Delhey and Newton, 2005: 324).

With regard to all errors and deficiencies, one could say that taking into account the EVS/WVS data (or any other individual data set) as the only basis of empirical evidence in the analysis of social capital means exposing oneself to a serious risk of not achieving the cognitive goals set. On the other side, as far as future conduct is concerned, it is appropriate to listen to Haller's proposal (2002) that a team of researchers from different cultural environments should be established for the implementation of European comparative surveys in order to reduce errors occurring for cultural reasons and variable institutional arrangements. These should be researchers who do not blindly follow empiricist principles but have a sense of social hermeneutics, as established in the sociological tradition from Weber to Schutz and beyond (for a more epistemic point of view, see Cicourel, 1972; Habermas, 1971; Luckmann, 1980; and for a more empirical point of view Ruschemeyer, 1992; Alvesson and Skoeldberg, 2000; Ragin, 1987). Regarding the semantic aspects of the question about trust, it is desirable to carry out pilot sondage in the form of discussions in focus groups at the national level as well as in such composed by participants from different countries in order to find out how the trust question is being understood and what meanings are attached to it.

Discussion and conclusion

At the beginning we set ourselves three goals. The first was to determine the structure and distribution of social capital in the European context. Here, we encountered the problem of the quality and credibility of data obtained through comparative surveys, especially concerning the EVS/WVS database. Our starting point was the hypothesis that the use of data from a single database is problematic and that – at least in the stage of interpretation – one should strive towards triangulation, i.e. a combination of different types of data. In the end, we asked ourselves how to improve cross-national surveys, primarily regarding the investigation of social capital.

Concerning the first goal, it would probably be wrong to reach any major conclusions or make additional statistical analyses on the basis of data of questionable quality. In fact, that was not really our task. We believe that a sensible interpretation is one based on a wider contextual (qualitative) insight which, of course, takes into account corrections of errors in measurement (for example, the case of the Greek sample). In this framework, it is possible to speak of four groups with regard to the distribution of social capital at the European level. In fact, the significant differences are only discernible between the first and the fourth group. Some countries are difficult to classify, as they have borderline scores. The first group with the largest stock of social capital of course includes the Nordic countries (but Finland is also a borderline case), and the Netherlands. The fourth group consists of countries with weak social capital. This includes both countries outside the EU and EU members. Namely Poland, Hungary, Latvia, Lithuania, Greece, Portugal, Romania, Bulgaria, Russia, the Ukraine and Turkey. If the high trust levels in Belarus is to be believed, this country could be classified between the fourth and third groups. The differences are large, for instance the ratio of Sweden to Portugal is one to eight in membership in the EVS and one to six in the ESS (if we take all memberships or one to five if we take the share of respondents who are members in at least one organisation) and one to six in active involvement.[19] The southern EU members Portugal and Greece according to both data sets but also Spain and Italy according to ESS actually have relatively undeveloped civil societies. It is the large lagging behind which has not been adequately explained or whose explanations have been unconvincing, for instance in the sense of path dependency (Chrisoforou, 2005).

The second group with a solid level of social capital includes (Western) continental and Anglo-Saxon countries, all of them EU members. However, it is sometimes hard to delineate the border separating the third group. While some countries are close to first group (Belgium), others are closer to the third group. Such a case could be Germany with its low level of active members in voluntary organisations (in the EVS but not in the ESS). Otherwise, besides Slovenia, the Czech Republic and Slovakia, the third group also consists of the Mediterranean countries Italy, France and Spain. All these three economically developed countries have lower or similar scores in active participation than the new three EU members from Eastern and Central Europe (but Italy and Spain show higher level of trust). In contrast to authors who argue that 'there are no large differences in mean scores across the regional patterns' (Oorshot and Arts, 2006: 160) we arrived at more differentiated conclusions. Between the first and fourth groups a very clear borderline can be drawn while differences between the second and third groups are not so pronounced.

[19] One author draws attention to the relatively high proportion of active members (in relation to all members) and argues: 'Nevertheless, these figures hide to a certain extent the fact that in some Southern and Eastern European countries those people who decide to join an association more often do so in an active way' (Morales, 2004:12). This observation can be respected but the fact is that lagging behind in associational involvement is actually increasing in these countries. With respect to the creation of social capital it can be said that a critical mass is needed in the sense of broader participation and not only an active minority.

It is possible to establish that there is no systematic connection between generalised trust and participation in civic organisations. As mentioned, the Scandinavian countries are an exception but the ESS indicates that this exceptionality may be losing ground (the cases of Finland and partly Denmark).

In the longitudinal sense, a fall in generalised trust is perceptible (in some places it is very drastic, in others it is not very significant). Regarding participation in associations, the situation is improving in most countries (particularly in EU members), although certain cases involve a regression.

The second highlight refers to issues concerning cross-national surveys. In connection with them, some errors and inconsistencies were found which appeared due to the inappropriate technical design of such researches and also because of semantic-cultural factors which have not been paid much attention partly in the stage of preparing and conducting the survey as well as in the phase of interpreting and generalizing of the data. A certain role is assumed to be played by country-specific institutional arrangements leading to the poorer comparability of answers concerning participation in voluntary associations.

In addition to the comparison (logical control) of two or more data sets, in the future more attention should be paid to the dialogue between the national databases or national case studies and cross-national data (see Ruschemeyer, 1991). Only such a dialogue can produce a more contextual and 'hermeneutic' view of the quantitative findings. The inclusion of qualitative studies is also desirable.[20]

Concerning social capital research in a narrower sense, let us draw attention to two matters. The first refers to the expansion of the repertoire of indicators; without doubt, less formal and even virtual (internet) forms of interaction and exchange are also important. It is also a fact that different phenotype applications, for instance in studying the co-effect of human and social capital or transfer of knowledge, require different indicators to be available (e.g. co-operation between industry and institutes). Nonetheless, we must be aware that the wider use of indicators would lead to a further dilution of the already loosely-defined ('metaphorical') notion of social capital. This will bring up the need for a theoretical reconsideration of this notion.

On the other side, the high expectations of the explanatory potential of social capital should be eased. We must realise that the research so far con-

[20] Let us cite the following: 'More and more diverse, quantitative data would be helpful to give a better picture of trends, and more qualitative research is needed to disclose the meaning and mechanisms of voluntary involvement in relation to feelings of community and happiness and to the quality of civil society and of politics' (Dekker and van den Broek, 2005: 56).

ducted at best only explores the embryonic and potential aspects of these phenomena. Put differently, we know something about the accumulation and availability of this resource, but we know very little about the mechanisms of exerting an influence (spillover effects) on society and its actual utilisation and reproduction (Torsvik, 2004). This is not just about structural (networks, organisations) and cultural dimensions (norms of reciprocity, altruism, confidence...), but also about the *processual* dimension which has largely not been explored since it is only methodologically accessible by using a more complex research design based on triangulation, qualitative case studies and transdisciplinarity.

For the beginning, instead of quick measurements and routine statistical analyses in the sense of 'hit and run' research, greater attention will have to be paid to more reflexive approach when dealing with existing (secondary) data as well as to considerations about the provision of better quality input data. This is the sole way in which European social sciences can deal with the theoretical challenges brought about by the dynamics of European integration (enlargement of the EU) and the only way they can make their policy-relevant contribution in efforts to create an European knowledge-based area which will not only be more competitive but will also manage to preserve an adequate level of societal cohesion. The same holds from the point of view of multi-level governance where the notion of civil society and its self-organising capabilities depending on the accumulation and reproduction of social capital play a key role in maintaining cohesive and democratic order at both the national and European levels.

Literature

Adam, Frane, et al. (2005) *The Challenges of Sustained Development – The Role of Socio-cultural Factors in East-Central Europe*, CEU Press, Budapest&New York.

Adam, Frane and Rončević, Borut (2003) 'Social Capital: Recent Debates and Research Trends', *Social Science Information/Information sur les sciences sociales*, vol. 42, no.2, 155-184.

Alvesson, Mats and Kaj, Skoeldberg (2000) *Reflexive Methodology*, Sage Publication, London.

Anheier, Helmut, Stares, Sally and Grenier, Paola (2004) 'Social Capital and Life Satisfaction', in, Arts, Will and Halman, Loek (eds), *European Values at the turn of the millennium*, Brill, Leiden and Boston.

Arts, Wil, et al. (2003) 'The Welfare State: Villain or Hero of the Piece', in, Arts W., Hagenaars, J. and Halman, L. (eds), *The Cultural Diversity of European Unity*, Brill, Leiden &Boston.

Arts, Will and Halman, Loek (2004) 'European Values Changes in the Second Age of Modernity', in, Arts Will and Halman Loek (eds), *European Values at the Turn of Millennium*, Brill, Leiden and Boston.

Badescu, Gabriel and Uslaner, Eric (eds) (2003) *Social Capital and Transition to Democracy*, Polity Press, London.

Braer, Douglas, Curtis, James and Grabb, Edward (2001) 'Has Voluntary Association Activity Declined? Cross-national Analyses for Fifteen Countries', *The Canadian Review of Sociology and anthropology*, vol. 38, no.3, 242-274.

Bratkovski, Jerzy and Jasinska-Kania, Aleksandra (2004) 'Voluntary Organisations and Development of Civil Society', in, Arts, Will and Halman, Loek (eds), *European Values at the Turn of the Millennium*, Brill, Leiden and Boston.

Cicourel, Aaron (1964), *Method and Measurement in Sociology*, The Free Press, New York.

Christoforou Asimina (2004) 'Building Social Capital: A Discussion on the Determinants of Social Capital in Countries of the European Union', manuscript, Athens University of Economics and Business.

Dekker, Paul, Ester, Peter and Vinken, Henk, (2003) 'Civil Society, Social Trust and Democratic Involvement', in, Arts, W., Hagenaars, J. and Halman, L. (eds), *The Cultural Diversity of European Unity*, Brill, Leiden&Boston.

Dekker, Paul and van den Broek, Andries (2005) 'Involvement in Voluntary Associations in Nord America and Western Europe: Trends and Correlates 1981-2000', *Journal of Civil Society*, vol.1, no.1, 45-59.

Delhey Jan and Newton, Keneth (2005) 'Predicting Cross-National Levels of Social Trust: Global Patterns or Nordic Exceptionalism', *European Sociological Review*, vol. 21, no.4, 311-327.

van Deth, Jan, et al. (eds) (1999) *Social Capital and European Democracy*, Routledge, London&New York.

van Deth, Jan (2000) 'Interesting but Irrelevant: Social Capital and the Saliency of Politics in Western Europe', *European Journal of Political Research*, vol. 37: 115-147.

van Deth, Jan, (2003) 'Measuring Social Capital: Orthodoxies and Continuing Controversies, *International Journal of Social Research Methodology*, vol. 6, no.1, 79-92.

Fidrmuc, Jan and Gerxhani, Klarita (2004) 'Formation of Social Capital in Eastern Europe: Explaining Gap vis-à-vis Developed Countries', CEPR Discussion Paper No. 5068 (http://cepr.org/Pubs/new-dplist.asp?authorid=135282).

Gabriel Oscar et al. (2002) *Sozialkapital und Demokratie*, Universitaetsverlag, Wien.

Grotaaert, Christian and Bastelaar, Thierry (eds) (2002) *The Role of Social Capital in Development*, Cambridge University Press.

Habermas, Juergen (1971) *Zur Logik der Sozialwissenschaften*, Suhrkamp, Frankfurt/Main.

Haller, Max (2002) 'Theory and Method in the Comparative Study of Values. Critique and Alternative to Inglehard', *European Sociological Review*, vol. 18, no. 2, 139-158.

Halman, Loek, (ed.) (2001) *The European Values Study: A Third Wave. Sourcebook of the 1999/2000 European Values Study Surveys*, WORC, Tilburg University.

Halpern David (2005) *Social Capital*, Polity Press, London.

Haerpfer, Christian et al. (2005) 'Social Capital and Economic Performance in Post-Communist Societies', in, Koniordos, Sokratis (ed.), *Networks, Trust and Social Capital*, Ashgate.

Inglehart, Ronald (1997) *Modernisation and Postmodernisation*, Princeton University Press, Princeton and New Jersey.

Jowell, R. (1998) 'How Comparative is Comparative Research? ', *American Behavioral Scientist*, vol. 42, 168-177.

Lin, Nan (2001) *Social Capital. A Theory of Social Structure and Action*, Cambridge University Press.

Luckmann, Thomas (1980) *Lebenswelt und Gesellschaft*, UTB Schoeningh.

Mihaylova, Dimitrina (2004) *Social Capital in Central and Eastern Europe*, Center for Policy Study, Central European University, Budapest.

Morales, Laura (2002) 'Associational Membership and Social Capital in Comparative Perspective: A Note on the Problem of Measurement', *Politics and Society*, vol.30, no.3, 497-523.

Morales, Laura (2004) 'Changing Patterns of Associational Involvement in Europe', paper presented at the ECPR, Uppsala.

Norris, Pippa (2002) 'Making Democracies Work: Social Capital and Civic Engagement in 47 Societies', in, van Deth, Jan et al., (eds), *Social Capital and Democratic Politics*, Russel Papers - Civic Series 3/2002.

van Oorshot, Wim and Arts, Will (2005), 'Social Capital of European Welfare States: the Crowding Out Hypothesis Revisited', *Journal Of European Social Policy*, vol. 15, no.1: 05-26.

van Oorshot, Wim, Arts, Will and Gelissen, John (2006), 'Social Capital in Europe', *Acta Sociologica*, vol. 49, no.2: 149-167.

Putnam, Robert (2000) *Bowling Alone*, Simon & Schuster, New York.

Putnam, Robert, ed., (2002) *Democracy in Flux, The Evolution of Social Capital in Contemporary Society*, Oxford University Press.

Ragin, Charles C. (1987) *Comparative Method: Moving Beyond Qualitative and Quantitative Strategy*, University of California Press.

Ruschemeyer, Dietrich (1991) 'Different Methods – Contradictory Results? Research on Development and Democracy', *International Journal of Comparative Sociology*, no.1-2, vol. 32, 9-38.

Savage, Mike et al. (2004) 'Social Capital and Political Activism: A Social Network Approach', in, Franklin, J (ed.), *Politics, Trust and Networks: Social Capital in Critical Perspective*, London South Bank University.

Seligson, Mitchell (2002) 'The Renaissance of Political Culture or Renaissance of the Ecological Fallacy?', *Comparative politics*, vol.34, no.3, 273-291.

Schuler, Tom, Baron, Stephen, Field, John (2000) Social Capital: A Review and Critique, in, Baron, S. et al., (eds), *Social Capital. Critical Perspectives,* Oxford University Press.

Stolle, Dietlind and Hooghe, Marc (2005) 'Review Article: Inaccurate, Exceptional, One-Sided or Irrelevant? The Debate about the Alleged Decline of Social Capital and Civic Engagement in Western Societies', *British Journal of Political Science*, 35, 149-167.

Sztompka, Piotr (1999) *Trust. A Sociological Theory*, Cambridge University Press.

Torsvik, Gaute (2004) 'Social Capital and Economic Development: A Plea for Mechanism', in, Prakash, Sanjeev and Selle, Peter (eds), *Investigating Social Capital*, Sage Publications, London.

Uslaner, Eric M. (2000) 'Producing and Consuming Trust', *Political Science Quarterly,* vol. 115, no.4, 569-590.

Welzel, Christian, Inglehart, Ronald and Deutsch, Franciska (2006) 'Social Capital, Voluntary Associations and Collective Action: Which Aspects of Social Capital Have the Greatest 'Civic' Payoff', *Journal of Civil Society*, vol. 1, no.2, 121-146.

2. Social and Political Participation: is there an European Convergence?

Matej Makarovič, Angelca Ivančič, Darka Podmenik

Introduction

The social and political configuration of Europe has changed significantly. Countries with a more or less long established democratic tradition have been joined by the new post-communist democracies of Eastern and Central Europe with different political cultures and contexts. The central question addressed in this chapter is the question of convergence between European democracies, particularly between the old and the new ones concerning patterns of social and political participation. What can be concluded from the existing characteristics and trends in various European democracies? How is the existence or inexistence of convergence related to social capital?

Although clearly one cannot simply equate participation and democracy, the issue of convergence in social and political participation is particularly relevant as far as participation is understood as a major dimension of democracy. Here, one may refer to Dahl's concept of the polyarchy, consisting of participation and competitiveness (Dahl, 1971). Convergence or divergence between nations or groups of nations in patterns of socio-political participation may thus hold significant implications for democratic European governance from the local to the transnational level.

A variety of theories may suggest convergence by emphasising the exposure of contemporary European societies to some common trends. Many studies point out that, when considering classical criteria of political participation (i.e. voting, membership in political parties and trade unions, trust in democratic institutions), late modern societies are characterised by a serious decline of participation in democratic institutions (evidence in Norris, 2002). On the other hand, these societies are also characterised by a variety of transformations that challenge the established patterns of citizens' participation in democratic processes. While classic democratic institutions and structures are being reshaped, new, more individualised forms are emerging which enable different kinds of participation – less elite-directed and more shaped by individuals' values and political skills (cf. Holford and van der Veen, 2003: 14).

Some authors argue that globalisation emphasises the importance of civil action, which gives rise to non-governmental organisations capable of challenging the authority of the state, international institutions and even global substructures. In the global society, interest associations at various levels may become agents of active citizenship and democracy; civic global action may be a way of transforming situations of inequality so as to create better opportunities for more egalitarian participation (cf. Castells, 1997; Held et al., 1999: 449; Delanty, 2000).

Beck (1994: 20), on the other hand, suggested that whatever in the traditional understanding of 'political' appears to be an 'apolitical retreat to private life' may in fact represent an individual striving for a new dimension of the political, a striving for the formation of subpolitics and thus for shaping society in a bottom-up manner. Sub-politicisation increases the opportunity for the voices of groups abstaining from politics to be heard and to participate in the regulation of society. Further, some courageous individuals can seize the opportunity to pursue their own projects.

Both old and new European democracies are subject to change, and this change is not necessarily some kind of normatively defined 'development'. Instead, it may – at least according to some classic social capital approaches (especially Putnam) – even mean divergence from some classical normative ideals of wide and active participation. Here, one may especially mention the shift from 'secondary' to 'tertiary' associations (Wollebæk/Selle, 2004 etc.) with the decreasing active membership and decline in voting turnout in several Western democracies.

These trends may also reflect some older contradictions within the very concept of modernity. Representative democracy that includes (the right of equal) political participation has been strongly related to the modernisation processes of functional differentiation and specialisation (on this, see the classical functionalist theory of Talcott Parsons as well as the more recent systems theoretical approaches developed by Niklas Luhmann). On the other hand, the very same growth of societal structural-functional differentiation may make any authentic political participation increasingly complicated and hardly compatible with truly face-to-face and/or all-inclusive forms of political interactions. Institutions at the national and trans-national levels (e.g. the European Commission), for instance, may be highly responsive to a wide variety of NGOs (Majone, 1996; Richardson, 1996), but only as far as the latter are able to apply quite sophisticated forms of communication with those institutions, provide a high level of expertise, operate within very complex sets of rules etc. These facts imply that when participating within NGOs citizens normally have to rely on their professional activists, experts, even classical bureaucrats ('contracting out' the participation function may become necessary according to Maloney, 1999). With regard to these fragmentation and professionalisation processes, the 'lower' levels of the highly structured participation networks and mediating ('intermediary') institutions are gaining in importance. Local democracy, civil society and NGOs have been the subjects of the constantly increasing endeavours of theoreticians as well as researchers dealing with modern representative democracies in the last decade. Taking into account the so-called dynamic, or 'activation', dimensions of participation 'active citizenship' has been reanimated as a concept with multiple meanings. Active citizenship should bridge the gaps between the global, local and individual levels of participation; contribute to a re-evaluation of the individual's contribution to the democratic process, expose the importance of self-learning and learning by acting, and trace the inventions of grass-roots and innovative modes of (self)organisation and participation.

Two preconditions which not only enable the citizens' participation but also significantly influence the participation intensity and modes –civil society and social capital – should be exposed in this context. Both are of great importance for activating individuals at different levels of democratic societies. But they have had quite different roles with regard to two different socio-political frameworks – old and new democracies – during the last few decades. While in developed Western democracies civil society has been treated as an 'inclusive umbrella' for different forms of 'cooperative social relationships that created bonds of trust, public opinion, legal rights' (Alexander, 2001) and, as such, includes the wide spectrum of institutions from political parties, NGOs to churches. With the diminishing importance of the state, in the old democracies with a more or less successful devaluation of the welfare state; in the new, post-socialist democracies with pluralisation, privatisation, re-structuration, civil society is becoming an acronym for 'informal ties, intimate relationships, trust, cultural and symbolic processes and the institutions of public life' (ibid.) Alexander recognises that the present notions of civil society are, on one hand, turning back to the roots of democratic theory and, on the other, to the mezzo and micro levels of society; to the life-world ties, local culture and community. Both of the emphases ascribed to civil society could be understood as indicators of the diminishing trust in the existing national institutions, as well as the search for new or undiscovered sources of social capital.

Besides across civil society, social capital is directly related to socio-political participation, no matter whether it is mostly understood as (generalised) trust or as the actual existence of networks, and irrespective of whether it is studied at the societal or individual level. High levels of social capital may imply high levels of socio-political participation and vice versa within a complex mutual causality thus creating either virtuous or vicious circles (see Adam et al., 2005: 105).

Voting remains the most indicative form of political participation and, on the other hand, a very questionable one in terms of its factual relevance. Voting is one of the rare ways for citizens to really adopt binding decisions (using power instead of just influence); it seems to be the most egalitarian and inclusive form of participation and it is a major source of political legitimacy. However, it may often be understood to be more of a ritual than a true decision-making process; it may be relatively isolated from any social interaction (questionable relevance from the classical social capital perspectives), though it also may be encouraged by interactions; it seems to be based on some relatively simple (mostly class-based) identities – making simple decisions between 'us' and 'them', which hardly correspond to the complex features such as increasing class fragmentation (Dahrendorf, Lipset etc.), individualisation within the risk society (Beck) and post-modernisation (Inglehart). However, despite all of the problems one can also hardly identify any viable alternatives to voting and general elections. Consequently, it may be argued that voting turnout remains one of the central features of participation within democratic political systems.

Despite several seemingly universal trends of the late modernity, the empirical reality reveals a variety of patterns of social and political participation. Our task is to identify these patterns and to attempt to understand to what extent they support the convergence hypothesis.

Identifying patterns of social and political participation

After the works of Verba and Nie (1972, 1978), the multidimensionality of participation has been stressed by nearly all studies since the different modes of taking part in politics – from voting to protesting – affect political outcomes and eventually the democratic order. With regard to this, not only should different modes of citizens' actions be taken into account but also the meanings they seem to attribute to them. What may seem to be the same behaviour may, in fact, be based on very different circumstances, motives and meanings. Voting, for instance, may be based on the voter's true desire to express their will, support a certain political option or participate in decision-making processes. On the other hand, it may be aimless ritualistic behaviour based on habit (or simply obeying the law where voting is mandatory). The same amount of caution is required, for instance, when observing unconventional participation in protest movements. Such participation may mean both the regrettable lack and/or inefficiency of formal/conventional channels of social and political participation. On the other hand, it may imply the existence of highly active citizens engaged in a wide variety of participation forms.

Indicators of socio-political participation within European societies should thus take into account the dimensions based both on behaviour (reported socio-political participation) and on some relevant values and attitudes. Our approach to identify and understand the patterns of socio-political participation consists of two steps:

1) quantitative analysis of survey and other quantitative data to identify the basic patterns; and
2) illustrating the main patterns with data from qualitative research.

Towards patterns of participation: cluster analysis

The main source of survey data is provided by the World/European Values Studies (esp. from 1990-3, 1995, 1999-2000). The main advantage of using this data is both the ability to analyse certain – albeit mostly short-term – trends and the ability to provide cross-national comparisons of patterns of political participation. In addition, the more recent data from the European Social Survey and some other databases may be of use. The method chosen to perform this test at the most basic level is hierarchical cluster analysis.[1] This method has been chosen mostly to avoid taking some groups or categories of countries for granted (e.g. Eastern vs. Northern Europe etc). We have used data from the last European Values Study (1999/2000) since this has been the last truly all-European social survey in this field that provides the standardised data required for our analysis.[2]

On the basis of some theoretical considerations and the available empirical data we have selected 10 different variables that may be used as proxy indicators for five different dimensions that characterise the major patterns of socio-political participation. There is a particular focus on political participation, although 'political' should be understood here in a very broad sense, namely as any active concern for a public issue. The dimen-

[1] Using the squared Euclidean distances method and standardised z-scores of the selected variables.

[2] The European Social Survey data from 2002/2003 are more recent but they do not provide figures for several European countries (especially the new democracies).

sions of political participation that have been included as one or more variables in the cluster analysis are the following:

1) <u>Attitudes</u> to participation, self-organisation and democracy (rejection of an authoritarian leader,[3] rejection of the belief that democracies are not good for maintaining order, generalised trust, confidence in parliament). This four-variable dimension is intended to measure people's beliefs as required to understand their actions and statuses. It is of crucial importance whether people's actions and belongings are led by truly democratic attitudes or not. A high level of NGOs or party membership, for instance, is a questionable sign of democratic participation when not supported by firm democratic values. Moreover, a high level of membership and activity in a variety of associations may have quite different implications when combined with high or low levels of *generalised* trust: similar *structural dimensions* (associational membership) may have considerably different effects when combined with different *cultural dimensions* (generalised trust) (on this issue in relation to social capital, see: Norris, 2002).

2) The <u>associations</u> dimension consists of two summarised variables concerning: (a) membership in political parties, local community actions, third world and human rights movements, environmental movements and peace movements; and (b) current non-paid work for the associations mentioned above as well as social welfare services, cultural activities, trade unions, professional associations, youth work, sports or recreation, women's groups and voluntary organisations concerned with health.[4] Both variables have been constructed as the average numbers of associations per individual.

3) The <u>voting</u> dimension includes one variable measuring a country's average voters' turnout during the last three parliamentary elections.

4) The <u>actions</u> dimension consists of a single summarised variable indicating actual participation (at least once) in the following actions: signing

---

[3] Support for democracy can be measured in the most suitable way when democracy is confronted with an alternative, or when a question suggests some problem with democracy.

[4] The selection of associations may be a matter of discussion. Though all associations may be relevant, not all of them are equally relevant when we consider their concern for public issues. Sports, recreation and cultural clubs, for instance, are mostly intended to satisfy the needs of their members and are much less oriented towards the others. Moreover, the work-related protective interest groups such as trade unions and professional associations have also not been included within this dimension since they usually have very broad membership, but it is quite questionable what in fact this membership means. It may be based on 'privatised instrumentalism' in the sense of Lockwood and Goldthorpe that again means a lack of *public* concern. Or it may even be a result of inertia: in some new democracies such as in Slovenia many workers have simply formally re-established memberships in a trade union that developed out of the old socialist trade union (with virtually mandatory membership). Consequently, only non-paid work in such organisations is taken into account, not membership.

petitions, joining boycotts, attending lawful demonstrations, joining unofficial strikes and occupying buildings or factories. The actions range from the most clearly conventional (signing petitions) to the most unconventional or even illegal but are nevertheless summarised within a single variable.

5) The inclusion dimension comprises two variables indicating the level of inclusion/exclusion in/from political participation. The first is the proportion of women in parliament. The second is the proportion of people who would not vote, are not included in any way in political parties, local community actions, third world and human rights movements, environmental movements and peace movements, and have never participated in any of the actions specified above.

The results of the cluster analysis (see the Appendix) clearly question some (overly) simple assumptions about convergence. Though the old European democracies seem to have shared similar democratic institutions and have been exposed to similar processes of globalisation and European integration for a considerable period of time, the most significant difference exists not between the old and the new democracies but between the three north European countries and the remaining both old and new democracies. The seemingly same general processes clearly do not always lead to the same results. Instead, they may significantly depend on the specific socio-cultural, political and economic settings found at the national and regional levels, even in the long run.

Following from the hierarchical cluster analysis of the survey data, three major patterns of socio-political participation may be identified:

1) the moderate pattern that can be subdivided into two subcategories, namely: (a) the moderate classical pattern (Austria, Germany, Belgium, Luxemburg, Spain, Finland, Malta)[5]; and (b) a moderate sceptical pattern (Czech Republic, Italy, the UK, Ireland, France, Slovenia, Slovakia, Croatia, Greece)[6];
2) active democracies (Denmark, the Netherlands, Sweden)[7]; and

[5] Characteristics: medium (except Finland) and stable trust, quite high confidence in parliament, high satisfaction with democracy, strong support for democracy, high and stable voter turnouts, modest participation in associations and in non-conventional actions, solid parliamentary representation of women, medium trust in politicians.

[6] Characteristics: medium trust, medium confidence in parliament, medium trust in politicians, signing petitions is quite common, medium satisfaction with democracy, low proportions of party membership, medium but significantly declining voter turnouts, medium level of participation in associations, low level of women representation.

[7] Characteristics: politics is considered highly important and interesting and is often discussed;

3) passive democracies (Bulgaria, Hungary, Latvia, Lithuania, Poland, Portugal, Romania)[8].

The active democracies are all characterised by intensive social and political participation of all types. They share some typical northern European characteristics including strong Protestant traditions, early modernisation, a strong democratic tradition, long periods of social, political and economic stability.

The passive democracies share some clear characteristics as well. They are characterised by a relative lack of all types of active participation. All of them are young democracies that share late modernisation, a lack of democratic traditions, and the presence of authoritarian regimes for most of the 20th century.

The remaining European countries belong to what we have called the moderate pattern. This is a significantly bigger and more heterogeneous category. They are all characterised by medium levels of all types of socio-political participation but they differ significantly from each other as well. Some of them, such as Finland or Belgium, are characterised by dense membership and activity in a variety of associations while others, such as Spain or France, are significantly less so. However, the clearest distinction that prevailed in the cluster analysis is between those with stronger and those with weaker classical political participation. The former – moderate classical – implies considerable confidence in parliament, high satisfaction with and strong support for democracy, along with high and stable voting turnouts.

Germany and Austria are perhaps the most typical representatives of this group. Finland, on the other hand, is also close to the active pattern. It is grouped in the moderate category, however, because its classical political

trust is high and slightly increasing, confidence in parliament is high, politicians are trusted, politics is not considered as too complicated for ordinary people, satisfaction with democracy is high, there is strong support for democracy, high proportions of the population belong to political parties, participate at the local level, in human rights and environmental movements, membership and non-paid work in associations is increasing, voter turnouts are high and quite stable, women's representation is high, the proportion of people excluded from all kinds of political participation is insignificant, non-conventional participation is relatively high.

[8] Characteristics: low general trust, low trust in politicians, low confidence in parliament, petitions and unconventional actions are rare, low satisfaction with democracy, comparatively weak support for democracy when confronted with alternatives (strong leader, more order), party membership is rare, low participation at the local level, in human rights and environmental movements, low and mostly declining voter turnouts, low representation of women, significant proportions of population excluded from all forms of political participation, low levels of membership and non-paid work in associations, strong belief that politics is too complicated for ordinary people.

participation it is lower when compared to the active pattern. Belgium and Luxembourg may also be somewhat special cases since their classical political participation may be inflated because of the mandatory voting. With its high level of citizens' involvement in associations and protest actions Belgium may also be approaching the active pattern, although it also has very relevant specifics of its own.

The moderate-sceptical pattern is a combination of the Western European, Mediterranean and Central European countries that share a (moderate) scepticism of classical forms of democracy, perhaps either because of the underdevelopment of their new democratic institutions (the new democracies) or because of a lack of proper adaptation of the old democratic institutions (Great Britain and France). This very mixture may be an interesting sign of partial convergence between the new and the old democracies – convergence in scepticism of classical forms of participation. However, even these signs of convergence may only be accepted with great caution because:

1) the scepticism regarding the old patterns does not necessary mean the rise of new patterns: the new socio-political associations are much stronger in Great Britain than in post-communist democracies;
2) the same actions do not necessarily have the same meanings in various socio-cultural settings: the very intensive political associational life reported by the Greeks is in striking contrast with their prevailingly negative attitudes to politics; and
3) there may also be significant differences between Slovenia (and perhaps Croatia) and, on the other hand, the other post-communist countries especially due to the *relatively* higher openness of (especially the North-western parts of) former Yugoslavia to the West when compared with the remaining post-communist countries.

To contribute to further understanding of the complex relationships between convergence and divergence in socio-political participation, a description of the exemplary cases will be introduced.

Towards illuminating the patterns: a presentation of cases

As stated above, cluster analysis confirmed the participation patterns but not without exceptions. Consequently, the assumptions on convergence could not be verified simply nor generalised for all countries grouped as having the same patterns. On the other hand, the differences among them are not so intense that the divergence hypothesis should be taken into account. The possibility of divergence becomes more significant at the intra-pattern level where the modes of participation in countries with different patterns are compared.

To gain a deeper insight into the mezzo and micro levels of participation resources, samples of cases are presented for each pattern. The goal of presenting the cases is to illuminate those characteristics about which it can be presupposed that they influence the participation mode, content and intensity in specific national surroundings. For the presentation quantitative but mainly qualitative data have been used, as taken from the project Education and Training for Active Citizenship and Governance in Europe (ETGACE and RE-ETGACE, 2000-2003 and 2003-2004). The project was conducted in eight European countries: the United Kingdom, the Netherlands, Belgium, Finland, Spain, Slovenia, Hungary and Romania. The selected results used as additional explanatory materials are based on data gathered by applying three qualitative methods: documentation analysis to analyse national literature and policy documents dealing with the issue of governance and active citizenship, focus group discussions and life history interviews. The analysis of national literature sheds light on specific cultural, political and historical backgrounds creating the broader socio-political frameworks for citizens' participation in the observed countries. The focus groups and life histories analyses, on the other hand, enable deeper insights into value orientations, 'giving meaning' and (self) reflective processes to the group and individual levels of participation. Since the data gained with these methods are not directly comparable with the patterns' indicators based on quantitative data, they will be presented as the illustrations supportive of the patterns.[9]

Moderate - Classical Pattern

As already stressed, the moderate classical pattern consists of countries which are quite diverse in terms of the democratic participation of their citizens. The three countries – Belgium, Finland and Spain – selected as the cases additionally highlighting the characteristics of this pattern point out more, we would argue, their divergences than their convergences, mostly in connection with their historical developments.

[9] The qualitative approach is also used here to compensate for the likely limitations – or sometimes even validity problems – of the quantitative EVS data.

Belgium

Belgium has only been independent since 1830[10] when the northern (Flemish) and southern (Walloon) elites joined in a common fight against the Dutch protestant king. This also reveals the crucial role religion has played in the socio-political participation of Belgians (Snick, Wildemerch and Cellis, 2000: 164). The Christian-democrats, socialists and liberals not only dominated the political scene but through a whole network of organisations in civil society they played a central role in social and cultural life at large, dividing civil society into so-called pillars. This political and social pillarisation strongly marked citizens' identities as well as the values and norms in which they were socialised. Belgian politics have always been the politics of compromise and of 'armed peace'. The pillars had to maintain the difficult balance between the workers' and employers' classes, between the Flemish and the Walloons and between Catholicism and liberality.

An analysis of the life histories of socially and politically active citizens indicates that up until the late 1950s even families belonged to a certain 'pillar' that affected many aspects of their life course, ranging from belonging to political parties, unions, socio-cultural organisations, health insurance funds, schools etc. Living in a certain village or neighbourhood or attending a certain school was automatically connected with membership in the local youth movement. Moreover, family members passed their activism on to their offspring. *'My dad, my mom, were both part of a youth movement, took on leadership. {...} And we've sucked it in with our mother's milk. I find it very determining - still'* (Mieke; in Snick, A. et al. 2001: 216).

Having a personal experience with the working man's environment was another important drive facilitating socio-political activism. '*...I was really proud when all his work buddies and union colleagues sang the Internationale at the cemetery... I didn't want to cry at that moment, I wanted to convince them with my youth 'look at me, the times, they are a changing'* (Patricia; ibid.: 214).

According to the EVS, politics is important in the lives of one-third of Belgians.[11] Given the ESS data, however, the associational dimension is

---

[10] In a sense 'government' still is burdened with this connotation of something external, opposed to the freedom and free will of the people. This has been reflected in the so-called Belgian 'disease' of the tendency of citizens to look for ways of 'cheating the government', a spirit of conspiracy against regulations imposed by government (Snick, Wildemerch and Cellis, 2000: 164).

[11] According to the ESS, the importance of politics in life received an average score of 4.03 (on the scale from 1 to 10), which is somewhat below the European average as measured by the ESS. There is not a very high rejection of undemocratic alternatives since only 68% reject the idea of »a strong leader« as an alternative to democratic institutions (EVS data).

considerably strong: 28% of the respondents are trade union members, 7% are political party members[12], and 9% are in business and farmers' organisations, which is also above the European average. The same may be argued for membership in humanitarian organisations (6.5%). The readiness for voluntary work for the variety of associations is quite high as well: the index calculated for the purpose of our cluster analysis according to the EVS data is 15.27 (the average value is 10.26). Some people join political parties because they believe that a group is more powerful than an individual and that they can have a greater influence on societal structures, an influence that is not strictly local. For Patricia '*...politics is about servitude, you feel called upon. One should have a dream, something from which you know 'this is a heart of my story, this is what I want to achieve', servitude for the people is part of that...*' (ibid. 238). Although in recent decades the pillars have lost their coherence and their binding power, their structures are still seen as meaningful and necessary especially in coping with the problems which exceed one's immediate control and need structural answers. Participation in civil society organisations, on the other hand, gives some people a sense of being able to contribute personally to an improvement of the situation or life circumstances of people in their immediate environment: *'We are exhausting the natural resources, we are driving cars and poisoning the air etc. In the story of the environment I can see clearly and I know what my contribution could be. (...)'* (Gerda; ibid. 228).

Today, however, with the process of fragmentation and individualisation both a weakening of the traditional political power structures as well as more opportunities for alternative, less formal ways of the democratic participation of citizens may be identified. Eight percent of Belgian citizens belong to more 'post-modern' associations. This is somewhat above the European average, but still less than in *active* democracies. There is also a significant readiness for unconventional activities in socio-political participation that is strongly above the European average. For instance, in the EVS 39% of respondents expressed a readiness to join demonstrations, 9% to strike and 6% to occupy buildings, while 2.4% had even participated in an illegal protest during the last 12 months.

In response to new late-modern developments characterised by new risks, new NGOs have been set up to address these risks.[13] Since the 1990s NGOs

---

[12] Only the Scandinavian nations display higher percentages.

[13] Examples are: Gaia, Greenpeace, groups contesting the power of international financial institutions, organisations promoting fair trade, socially acceptable working conditions or ethical investments.

have also changed the definition of their own role from ‘contestants’ to ‘proposers’. They see it as their task to offer suggestions rather than just contesting government decisions (ibid. 2000: 169).

The findings further reveal that the relationship between socio-political structures and individual citizens has changed. People seem to approach socio-cultural and political organisations more like consumers and to make their choices on a more restricted and individually motivated basis. While searching for the options most in line with their personal value systems and commitments they may shift organisations and structures but remain fateful to their own conviction: *‘I have retained the Flemish conviction from home but I made an explicit choice for a pluralistic organisation. {...}. For me nothing is fixed and people always evolve along with societal changes and trends’* (Hans; in Snick, A. et al. 2001: 224).

A key notion in the present discourse on policy and citizenship is that of the ‘active welfare state’ (ibid.: 165-166). Since the 1990s an important concern of Belgian discourse has been to find a new political culture and to make a new pact with the citizens. The trust of Belgians in democratic institutions is slightly higher than the European average: the parliament received 4.99 (on a scale of trust from 1 - 10 according to the ESS), while 39% of the population expressed their confidence in parliament, which is close to the European average (EVS). This confidence, however, declined slightly during the 1990s according to the EVS. The trust in politicians is above-average (4.28 on the scale from 1 - 10) and the same can be said for the belief that politicians care about people (although the scores on this scale are quite low for all European countries) according to the ESS.[14]

Finland

Finnish national history is significant for its specific geopolitical role among European countries – the role of a mediator between the so-called Eastern and Western blocs, symbolically between Western democracy and Eastern communism. After the rough period of national history (an attempt of a communist turnover in 1917; the Winter War with the Soviet Union; settle-

[14] Due to the mandatory voting, voter turnout cannot be measured for Belgium in a way comparable to most other European countries. The belief, however, that voting is important for being a good citizen (6.56 on the scale from 1 to 10) is significantly below the European average. This result cannot simply be explained only by mandatory voting itself (that may make voting too self-evident to be able to generate »a good citizen«), since Luxembourg with its similar mandatory system has a significantly higher score on this issue (8.04).

ment with the German 'influence' during the Second World War), Finnish foreign policy has been characterised by a permanent balancing between Scandinavian countries and the Soviet Union. During the 1970-1990 period, Finland developed its welfare systems to such a level that it became the so-called 'Japan of the North'; the rich post-modern social democratic state imitating the Swedish example (Laitinen and Nurmi, 2001: 71). But this rapid development ended in a deep recession accompanied by a high rate of unemployment, the restructuring of the economic system and citizens' general distrust of the main political institutions. In 1995, when Finland entered the EU the recession was already over with the exception of the public sector, which was heavily in debt. The preoccupations of the Finnish political multi-party system did not change significantly since it had to cope with Soviet pressures and worked for Western alliances after the EU entrance as well. Social movements established after the Second World War have persisted in the new millennium with major additions: the greens with ecological and developmental co-operation ideas and the animal liberation front anarchists (ibid.: 72). 'Finland offers its citizens a law-abiding social environment, excellent educational opportunities and a real albeit expensive welfare system' (Laitinen et al., 2000: 10).

It could be presupposed that this agitating national history is one of the influences which determines the positioning of Finland in the pattern of moderate democracy and not in the active one. In spite of some indicators which show the significant democratic orientation of Finnish citizens – a high level of trust in political institutions, government and politicians[15], a strong rejection of undemocratic alternatives[16], participation in election and associations[17]; some other indices of democratisation seem to be below the EU average[18]. With regard to qualitative data the results of interviews in the

---

[15] 42% of Finnish citizens expressed confidence in parliament according to the EVS. This figure is well above the European average and even increased during the 1990s and is confirmed by the ESS data. Trust in parliament scored 5.79 (only the Danish parliament received a higher score in the survey) and trust in politicians is comparatively high (4.78 on the 1-10 scale).

[16] The rejection of undemocratic alternatives ('a strong leader') of 75% is close to the European average according to the EVS.

[17] The turnout figure of 67% for the last three parliamentary elections is close to the European average but remains quite stable and activity in the associations is close to the European average. Moreover, the density of trade union membership (46%) remains one of the highest in Europe (ESS).

[18] The importance attributed to politics in one's life is below the European average for both EVS (19% consider it important) and ESS (3.85 on the scale from 1-10); the associational dimension was in significant decline with regard to the classical forms of political participation during the 1990s from - 14% to 6% of respondents recorded by the EVS data. The party membership of 7% according

Finnish sample show that the citizens' involvement in governance and politics is significantly influenced by different and polarised dimensions, such as: the old Russian Tsarist bureaucratic tradition; the Nordic welfare state model, characterised by growing plurality; neo-liberal market forces; participation in the EU which brought about new kinds of governance characterised by elite-driven politics, as well as participative sub-politics (Laitinen, et al., 2001).

The militarily and politically turbulent national history accompanied by the 'protestant ethics' value orientation also determined the relatively strong tradition of the people's activation in political and social affairs, which is illustrated by examples of Finnish interviewees who argued they have 'always' been active and engaged in social and political events. As stated in the Finnish Report on active citizenship: 'In Finland active citizenship is instigated by home. Even a non-bourgeois home has been able to somehow mediate to the activist a core of protestant ethics: to value work, liberty and some form of solidarity. Christian, entrepreneurial and labour values are all there, so there is always a choice of alternative commitments' (Laitinen and Nurmi, 2001: 112).

Besides the citizens' activism which is rooted in 'home and tradition' a 'pattern of relatively sudden change of direction' proved to be important among the Finnish interviewees.[19] In respect of the participation modes polarity was also exposed; on one hand the formal participation modes and smooth change by education whereas, on the other, direct citizens' participation, like demonstrations and other forms of protest. The shift in the participation contents and modes is clearer when groups of older and younger respondents are compared: the younger ones were more concerned about nature, animal rights and developing countries; they had less trust in conventional strategies and were keener to use various new technologies like the Internet. Among them, new forms of participatory democracy were also

---

to more recent ESS data, however, still places Finland well above the 'sceptical' democracies but below the 'active' ones. The developmental levels of the 'post-modern' associations are close to or even below the European average and are hardly comparable to its Scandinavian counterparts.

[19] Jukka, for example, realised in his 30s that despite his disability he was able to contribute to society and joined the local association of the disabled promoting social equality: According to him, *'many disabled people undergo this kind of development... When you are young you get through different kind of things... you want to communicate more with your healthy peers. Only at a later age when the process of defining things for yourself is going on you want to join the association of the disabled, people of the same background with same problems'* (ibid., p. 74). Leo, on the other hand, entered politics in late 1994 as his conscience did not allow him to continue complaining without offering an alternative. This alternative presented itself as a new party, the Young Finns Party (*Nuorsuomalainen puolue*). He participated in the process of collecting 5,000 names in order to establish the new political party. After dismantling the party in 1999 he found a new political home in the Green League.

indicated such as learning partnerships, e-activism, although these were short-term actions. But in spite of these 'innovations', the present day Finnish activism is based firmly on the established forms and is not directed at radical change agendas except when they are firmly grounded in UN, EU or OECD programmes.[20]

'Multi activity' – participation in different social domains – was shown to be significant for the Finnish sample of active citizens. Most of them were members of groups or organisations acting in very different fields – from politics to science fiction. Participation in different socio-political domains with the internalisation of activism in the sense of '*habitus*' (Bourdieu), as well as the openness to education (mainly informal) and innovative participation forms/contents compounding with the general dimension of the high level of trust in democratic institutions could be presupposed to be indicators of the relatively high social capital stores with which Finland's actively participating citizens are equipped.

Spain

Franco's dictatorship in Spain lasted from 1939 to 1975 and imposed strong political, social and cultural repression on Spanish citizens. The country was isolated from external influence. Cultural repression was seen as an important element to achieve the unity of the country.[21]

The main form of citizens' action under such repressive conditions was resistance. The resistance was sustained by different underground initiatives and organisations (political parties, unions, progressive Christian sectors, neighbourhood associations etc.). As Franco's regime was especially repressive as regards women, they organised to fight against the regime in different domains. This meant the beginning of the feminist movement in Spain (see Gomez et al. 2001: 187).[22]

---

[20] In Finland 27% of respondents claimed to have used a boycott as a protest action during the last 12 months according to the ESS, while other protest activities are significantly less likely than in most other European countries.

[21] Education was seen as an important element to indoctrinate children in the new national-Catholic morality. Education institutions and contents were subjected to strict control. In many of these institutions, co-ed classes were suppressed and boys and girls received a differentiated education corresponding with their differentiated gender roles in the Francoist society. Language became another important cultural symbol. Spanish was imposed as the only official language across all of Spain and in all educational, professional, and administrative activities. Other regional languages were banned (Galician, Catalan, Basque) and their use became restricted to the private sphere.

[22] Today Spain is characterised by a very high level of representation of women in parliament (36%).

Franco's death in 1975 meant the beginning of the transition to a democracy and the start of a period of political, social and cultural opening up. During the time of the socialist government (PSOE) a series of steps was taken to lead the country towards some form of welfare state.[23] However, this was combined with economic liberalisation and the opening up of the economy that finally led to Spain's entry to the EU.

According to the results of the EVS, Spanish citizens appear to be firmly against undemocratic alternatives (79% are against a strong leader). The average voter turnout for the last three elections to the national parliament (75%) has shown its stability in the long run. It is typical that the percentage trusting the parliament is above the European average (45%). More recent data (ESS), however, imply a comparatively lower level of trust (4.85 on the 1-10 scale, which is below the European average). According to the same data source, trust in politicians is as high as 3.41 on the 1-10 scale (ESS).

The EVS also shows that 55% of Spanish citizens discuss politics but only 22% believe that politics is important. The ESS results seem to support such a conviction. The associational dimension is somewhat below the European average: 5% are trade union members, 3% belong to political parties while only 2% belong to environmental, peace or animal rights associations.

The findings from the life histories of socially and politically engaged Spanish citizens imply that the main dimensions of the identification processes driving their social and political activism continue to display the strong emancipatory nature characteristic of the period of Franco's dictatorship (see Gomez et al. 2001). Oppression and solidarity were the two most powerful motives for most interviewees to join social movements. Some people occupying more responsible positions within democratic structures, like Luisa, see this 'as an opportunity to voice people's views and fight for their rights in the development of a more egalitarian society'. Namely, the top governmental positions provide 'the best opportunities for promotion of social changes' (ibid. 194).

Several interviewees asserted they became members of unions in the first place out of their identification with the problems of workers in general, especially at the time of Franco's repression: '*I started to participate because of the situation of dictatorship, in 1964 we started to organise in a clandestine committee within the enterprises...*' (Antonio; ibid. 193). For others, values and beliefs may be the drivers: *'When I entered the Commu-*

[23] The so-called 'Pactos de la Moncloa' in 1977, the definition of Spain as a 'social state' in the 1978 Constitution, the advancement of social policy implementation during the PSOE government.

nist Youth I didn't do it because they were Marxist or because I had a very definite ideology in mind, but simply because I knew I was a leftist and I felt I had a series of values in mind that have not changed in the least' (Enrique; ibid. 192).

The Spanish civil society was strengthened by the democratic transition process but it is still considerably weaker than the civil societies of other countries e.g., the UK (Rubinstein 1994). The activity of citizens in a variety of associations in civil society is somewhat below the European average. Typical protest activities are boycotts (a willingness to undertake them was expressed by 34%) and demonstrations (26%) (EVS). The fragmentation of associations and organisations makes Spanish civil society have little impact on the development of social policy. With the advent of democracy, grassroots associations started to assume an important role in promoting basic rights.

On joining the EU, Spain also entered the new information, global type of society. In addition to the existing economic and social problems – above all high unemployment – it has been facing new challenges such as increased mobility and multiculturalism. According to some researchers, the importance of associationalism among minorities in Spain, such as the Roma people and different North African national groups, has been growing. Special attention is paid to the integration of excluded sectors such as women, adults who have or do not have initial levels of schooling, ethnic minorities and immigrants both in society and in the labour market. Today, the adult education movement acts in the role of including excluded groups by empowering them for dialogic egalitarian participation (Gomez et al., 2001).[24]

Sceptical pattern

As illustrative examples of this pattern **Slovenia and the UK** will be presented. These two countries have significant divergent democratic histories, as well as broader social and political contexts, which have been influencing the modes and intensity of their participation. However, both countries underwent significant changes in political, economic and social domains during the final decades of the last century.

[24] 'In the dialogic literacy circle participants choose a book... well,... various are proposed and one is chosen between all. Then every Monday we meet to comment on. Everyone gives their opinion always being respectful with others, in everything we listen... not matter one has an university degree, one has a certificate in basic education or other is in literacy classes, all learn from others because all can bring their experience' (Theresa and Gomez et al., 2001: 196).

The greatest change in the UK's short-term history was the devaluation of the welfare state after a period of nearly 40 years of an unchallenged post-war welfare state and economic prosperity. In this prosperous period, the trade union had unprecedented strength, marked by militancy and the engagement of leaders in 'corporatist' management. In national politics the approaches of Conservative and Labour governments were not significantly different. Society was structured on the basis of social classes, not in a Marxist sense, but in that of a strong awareness about belonging to a specific social stratum, linked to income, occupational status, education etc. Social classes determined political identity, networks of social institutions and voting patterns. Driven by the changing of industrial organisation, this social structuration was breaking down by the 1970s yet neither classes nor inequality disappeared. In the 1970s rapid inflation, industrial decline and funding pressures on the public sector caused economic stresses. Links between government and labour were interrupted by trade union resistance. The Thatcher government 'kicked over' the traces of the 'post-war' consensus and replaced compromises and committees with management and the market. The so-called 'laissez faire' liberalism was encouraged by the national military victory in the Falklands War and with defeat of the mineworkers' union strike. (Eridisingha et al., 2000) Demolishing of the welfare state was accompanied with the transferring of public burdens to civil society (Gamarnikow and Green, 1999). The political identity and structure as well as voting patterns were changing and citizens' political loyalties became unstable. Participation in political organisation and in civil society eroded and shifted from active engagement to observation; belonging to Labour or Conservative political streams eroded and 'where individuals do engage in political activity, they appear often to do so through engagement with "single-issue" movements' (Eridisingha, et al., 2000).

These shifts can be observed through the EES and EVS data: there was a clear decline in classical modes of citizens' participation such as participation in elections[25], trade unions and political parties during the 1990s. On the other hand, there was significant membership and activity reported for those associations with the more 'post-modern' contents, such as environmentalist, peace and human rights movements.[26] With regard to the results of the life history interviews on the UK sample of active citizens the (re)engagement in social 'class' activity prevailed, which did not represent

[25] Voter turnout is below the European average and declining; it was just 59% in the 2001 parliamentary elections.

[26] 6% membership claimed for the ESS.

innovations in participation. Besides trade union activism, individual engagements in voluntary, local community and educational institutions appeared to be very popular. Among these classical modes of participation, the 'single-issue' initiatives may be evaluated as more innovative, but only in respect of their contents. For example, gay/lesbian engagements or women's rights activities were carried out differently and in more favourable social circumstances by individuals from the younger age groups (25-40 years) than by those from older ones (55-70).

Slovenia had not experienced any long traditions of the nation-state, political pluralism and participation since before the Second World War it had formed part of the Kingdom of Yugoslavia and after the war part of the Socialist Federative Republic of Yugoslavia. As far as ownership rights and arrangements of capitalist societies, market competition and trade unions were concerned, the situation was quite the same. After nearly fifty years of a socialist authoritarian regime, democratic governance, political pluralism, participation patterns, civil rights, a market economy and private ownership had to be established and reinforced *ad novum.* 'Apart from the predominantly ritualistic ways of activism, which took place in institutions of the so-called 'socialist' and 'integral self-management', spontaneous public activism was carried out occasionally by Slovenian intellectuals, during the whole era of socialism, only to be suppressed by the monopoly power-holding elite' (Vehovar, et al., 2000). In the 1980s, public debates on the enduring economic crisis of the socialist regime were launched, while some newspapers and magazines openly challenged the dominant views of the power holders. The undertakings of the Slovenian cultural and intellectual elite compounded with the outburst of civil society activities, which demanded the reconsideration of the status of the Slovenian nation in the Socialist Federative Republic Yugoslavia as well as the establishment of a sovereign nation-state, political pluralism with civil rights and economic independence. By the end of the 1980s the so-called 'triple transition' (Offe) had begun. During the transition period new possibilities for socio-political involvement have been opened up to Slovenian citizens.

The results of the ETGACE project show that those from the sample of active citizens who were already active in the previous socialistic regime changed the modes and/or contents of their activities. The younger ones who were activated just before or during the transition were attracted by the innovative contents and possibilities of participation. The most frequent forms of socio-political participation among Slovenian respondents were: taking part in establishing or organising political parties and non-governmental, professional, interest organisations (associations); establishing private firms; becoming a candidate at local or national elections; establishing a branch of an international association, a (non-governmental) organisation. Since all of them were very effective and successful in reaching their goals, the pragmatic component became one of the generally accepted characteristics of Slovenian active citizenship. These engagements could be summed up in the statement that (very) active Slovenian citizens have 'ridden the wave of transition'.

Besides changes at the national level changes at the international level, i.e. globalisation with the accompanying individualisation process, shifted the modes and contents of citizens' participation; in the UK to individually important subjects but in Slovenia to those connected with the effectiveness of the transition and consequently successful accession to the EU. In these contexts, the countries are hardly comparable; participatory modes and contents, which were completely new for the young Slovenian democracy should be evaluated as classical, if not traditional, from the point of view of the 'old democracies'. So, in comparison with the data for the UK which exposed a shift from classical to post-modern and the so-called 'single issue' in the case of participation, the Slovenian data show that participation in classical modes is quite close to the European average[27], but the typical 'post-modern' activities such as environmental, peace etc. ones are significantly weaker.[28]

In spite of these relatively favourable results on the diversification of participative modes and contents, and the fact that Slovenian and UK citizens excluded the possibilities of undemocratic alternatives, the indices of the sceptical value orientation to national democratic institutions can be traced in statistical data as well as in the interviews from both countries. In Slovenia, politics is considered to be significantly less important to the respondents' lives than in all the rest of the European countries studied by both the EVS and ESS social surveys. Only a quarter of Slovenian respondents expressed confidence in their national parliament. The figure decreased during the 1990s according to the EVS. The low level of trust in parliament is also confirmed by the ESS data (4.04 on the 1-10 scale). Trust in politicians is among the lowest in Europe (3.07 on the scale from 1 to 10). In the UK the spread of the belief that politics is important in one's life is quite

[27] The average turnout for the last three elections to the national parliament is 68%, which is somewhat close to the European average (the figure has been steadily and consistently declining); trade union membership is 20% (according to the ESS) and political party membership is 5% (according to the ESS).

[28] Only 1.2% of Slovenian respondents claim that they belong to such organisations according to the ESS data, which is below the European average.

close to the European average according to the EVS, but clearly below it according to the more recent ESS data. Confidence in parliament is closer to the European average and higher than in Slovenia, but it seems to be affected by similar declining trends. Trust in parliament measured by the ESS is not high (4.64 on the 1-10 scale). Trust in politicians (3.77 in the ESS) is lower than the European average.

As shown by examples from the Slovenian sample of active citizens, political scepticism can be negative or positive. One respondent, a senior civil servant, who on one hand firmly advocated democratic civil rights and legislation on the other became a professional politician to avoid losing a job and public respect. His comment was: *I had no other choice, when information about (...) came to the public* (O. in: Working material, ETGACE, ACS). 'Healthy' scepticism is expressed in the personal story of a middle-aged Slovenian intellectual who was engaged in establishing democracy in Slovenia, but who refused to join the new political elite in order to retain his intellectual integrity and personal autonomy by keeping his distance from the political turmoil at that time.

Scepticism among active participants from the UK sample may be ascribed to the erosion of political loyalties to Labour and Conservative, to the devaluation of the social state and to the diminishing autonomy of civil society. Namely, the shift of confidence in balanced political power leads to criticism of the socio-political environment. Criticism and 'healthy' scepticism emerged in the statements of some interviewees who were engaged in 'class roots' activities and in so-called single-issue movements. Three female interviewees from the UK are good examples of active endeavours undertaken to overcome social injustice by engagement in trade unions. After developing critical and 'healthy' sceptical standpoints (for example, Charleen claimed this about her workplace: *Lots of changes going on, lots of contracting out and privatisation*, and people *feeling vulnerable and insecure* (Eridisingha et al., 2001: 30), they became politically activated. Martha, a local politician, was motivated by the social injustice experienced in her family: *...because you were trying to help yourself you can't have any help. If you are living in a council house you got everything done for you...People in other parts of society were getting help...* (ibid. 29).

Scepticism expressed in some of the Slovenian active citizens' stories can be partially explained by the pragmatic value orientation towards democracy which prevailed among Slovenian citizens during the transition period (Bernik, 1995). Pragmatism is also documented in some life stories of Slovenian active citizens; one of them, the Mayor of one Slovenian municipality, explained that he has always been *sceptical in regard to the po-*

litical parties as the means to do something 'real'. As a member of a political party he was aware that *party politics at the local level was very problematic* (Jure in: Podmenik et al., 2001: 154). But in spite of this insight, he was appointed a candidate at the local elections and became elected. He explained this decision: *'...Then (the 1994 elections,* note by D.P.*) we were unable to find candidates for the mayor's office...I said O.K., then I'll give my name, since we can't give away an incomplete list; then it just happened that I was elected...'* (Jure, ibid.) Scepticism regarding politics could be defined as the prevailing attitude among the majority of Slovenian 'well informed citizens' (Schutz) since it has been strengthened during the long historical periods of foreign or domestic political oppression, and not abolished with the shift to democracy. The interference of politics in civil society and NGOs can be observed as one of the remainders which stirs up the scepticism of civil society activists and NGO participants. Urša, a middle-aged NGO activist, who felt herself and her association threatened by pressures of governmental and oppositional political parties, stated:

Since I became publicly recognisable with my work in the association here and abroad, as well, I became useful for them...The Slovenian political parties exert pressure to subordinate the association, they wish that I should belong to them, but these different political parties' interests then start to crash over your head (Urša in: Podmenik et al., 2001).

For the majority of interviewees from the UK, as well as from Slovenia a multi-agency was identified, which means they actively participated simultaneously in organisations from different social domains: politic and governance, the economy and civil society. In Slovenia almost all respondents gained experience and skills from participating in institutions and organisations in the previous regime and were well equipped for (re)starting the engagements in new democratic institutional circumstances. The respondents from the UK 'had knowledge, skills, and the enterprise to organise and mobilise resources'. The majority of them acquired these skills at work and, since they live in more than one social domain, they transferred their knowledge and experiences of one domain to the others (Eridisingha et al. 2001: 34).

Characteristics of the active citizens from the UK and Slovenian demonstrated by the ETGACE project results as e.g. engagement in institutions from different social domains, accumulation of skills and knowledge, appreciation of formal education, openness to informal education and 'learning by doing' practices could lead to the conclusion that actively participating citizens from both countries have great amounts of social capital at their disposal. Namely, cross-domain participation enables inclusion in social networks, the employment of 'bridging' and 'bonding' social capital and social reciprocity; and the accumulation of different sorts of knowledge, skills and experiences means a high level of educational and cultural capital (Bourdieu). Nevertheless, it is questionable whether these individual provisions with social capital could be invested in the democratic restructuration of Slovenian and British society since the social trust in democratic institutions among UK citizens and even more among Slovenian ones is relatively low – as shown by the data presented above; it is below the EU average.

The passive democracies

The democratic deficit characteristic of the new CEE democracies is, in addition to the lack of democratic structures, largely explained by the communist 'mental heritage' demonstrated in the culture of citizens' passivity or 'uncitizenship' learned in former communist regimes (see RE-ETGACE, 2003c: 19-20). To illustrate these characteristics we present two cases, Hungary and Romania.

In Hungary, the transition to democracy can be seen as a very long and turbulent process that has spanned over two centuries. Prior to 1989 there was a long history of economic and partly also political reformist openings. But they were initiated and performed by the ruling party and economic elite and not by any mass opposition movement (Elster et al. 1997).[29] As stated by an activist, '*In Hungary civil participation is missing from the process of the transition to a democracy. Transition is conducted by the elite. So, it is no wonder that there is a shortage of real experience in active citizenship' (RE-ETGAC, 2003: 32).*

The functionality of civil society in the period before the transition was strongly influenced by 'adaptation through opposition' (Frenzel-Zagorska 1990). Connected with adaptation through opposition was the withdrawal from the system to the private sphere – family and the close circle of friends – not only and not mainly in overt behaviour but in the sphere of values and identification. Hankiss (1988) concluded that in Hungary in the late 1980s there was no civil society.

From the very beginning of the transition there was a distinctive feature of some CEE countries, including Hungary: a strong anti-party approach by their democratic oppositions based on the concept of 'anti-politics' with

[29] In the years of János Kádár's leadership (1956-1988), the regime was consolidated (1962-1989) and from the beginning of the 1960s a more pragmatic and more liberal practice of communist dictatorship – the so-called kadarism – was in operation.

its central concern for an autonomous civil society. The idea of the forum-party became the model.[30] In 1989 forum-parties were transformed into legal political parties and have had permanent parliamentary representation up till now (RE-ETGACE, 2003a: 25).

Today political parties, the state administration and political ideologies do not appear to act either as sources of identification or structures providing spaces for social and political actions of 'common' citizens.[31] However, Hungarians strongly reject undemocratic alternatives: 80% decided against a 'strong leader' (EVS). Average turnout at the last three elections to the national parliament has remained quite stable: 66%, which is somewhat below the European average. The Hungarians' level of trust in the parliament and in politicians is close to the European average (average scores of 5.00 and 3.88, respectively, on the 1-10 scale). Given the EVS findings, 33% of Hungarians do express trust in parliament. On the other hand, 57% discuss politics but only 18% consider politics to be important[32].

The associational dimension of Hungarian citizens is quite weak for both classical modern and post-modern associations: 6% claim to be trade union members (below the European average); 1.6% belong to political parties; only 0.4% belong to environmental, peace or animal rights groups – the figures for both parties and these groups are lower than for any other European country studied by the ESS.

The omnipresence of hierarchically organised institutions is perceived to be the main obstacle to learning democratic participation. A Hungarian expert in community development asserts: '*Although after 1989 hard political walls disappeared, soft barriers did not generate strong resistance or there was not a lot at stake. Unfortunately, the transition to democracy has not finished, and authoritarianism continues existing in lighter forms*' (RE-ETGACE, 2004: 70). Another person explicitly pointed out that, '*in Hungary every democratic forum exists on paper but none works in real life*'

---

[30] Although political parties could be established legally after 1989 in Hungary, the seeds of prospective parties started to sprout as associations in 1987-1988 arising from different socio-political movements. The Forum of Hungarian Democrats was formed in 1987 in Lakitelek; the Association of Young Democrats was founded by students and the Association of Free Democrats was founded mainly by the democratic opposition and were formed in 1988. In 1989 all of them transformed into legal political parties and have had a permanent parliamentary representation to date (RE-ETGACE, 2003a: 25)..

[31] Some participants in the Hungarian focus group discussions suggested that active citizenship seems 'to be in contradiction with politics'. The argument goes that the political party binds its members to party interests, therefore they cannot act as independent responsible persons (RE-ETGACE 2003b: 27).

[32] The average importance of politics in one's life is 3.75 (the 1-10 scale, ESS).

(ibid.: 70). Some activists suggest that '...citizens' activity or mobilisation is accepted and appreciated only when it is within the field of power, when it's outside, they call it subversive. The leading political power perceives initiatives made by others as an attack' (RE-ETGACE, 2003c: 20).

The whole process of the democratic participation of citizens in the new CEE democracies has been built on the development of civil society. NGOs are seen more as agents creating civil society (Osborne and Kapuvári 1997). However, there are numerous problems affecting citizens' opportunities for participation in civil society. A Hungarian activist in civil society is distrustful of the possibilities of partnership with the state and political domains: *'The partnership concept does not work in practice; it remains more an issue of rhetoric. The former practice of imposing power hasn't changed much' (RE-ETGACE 2003c: 20).* Another observation is that: *'politics and civil society cannot really co-operate (i.e. in Hungary) because the civil organisations with an interface role which exist in the reports - don't actually deliver the goods in the reality' (RE-ETGACE, 2003c: 20).*

Most recently the Hungarian government launched a new policy on civil society organisations based on partnership.[33]

Unlike in Hungary, the totalitarian communist dictatorship in Romania was not interrupted by any democratic period till 1989 when it was brought down by a revolution accompanied by a strong mass movement. The lack of political activism in Romania after 1989 seems to be in contrast with the mass movements in the 1989 revolution.[34] This situation is accounted for by ineffective and derisory changes, the time-consuming process of democratisation and social, economic and political difficulties. Economic growth in Romania was sharply interrupted by the serious macroeconomic crises brought on by insufficient structural reforms in the mid-1990s, and GDP in 2000 stood at four-fifths of its 1990 level. De-industrialisation, the changes in opportunity structures and the drop in social contributions from the state have made poverty a mass problem. In addition, the totalitarian dictatorship destroyed social capital and even stimulated negative social capital embodied in the creation of problematic networks based on corruption (RE-ETGACE, 2003a). The post-socialist transition of political institutions extended until the first democratic power shift that occurred in 1996.

---

[33] In 2003 the 'Government Strategy on Civil Issues' was passed by the Hungarian Parliament. The core concept of this strategy can be expressed with the slogan, 'Partnership, Dialogue, and Money' (the Hungarian abbreviation forms 3Ps). One of the most remarkable outcomes of this strategic programme is the introduction of the National Civil Fund Programme (NCFP) in June 2003.

[34] The EVS data show that 62% of Romanians discuss politics but only 25% consider it important, while voter turnout amounts to 66% with a consistent and significant declining trend.

As a young nation, Romania still has a strong national movement. It can be stated that since 1989 nationalism has been the only coherent legitimate ideology. It has been manifested in policies especially in the first half of the 1990s by promoting 'national sovereignty' and unity with a discourse that is specific for the ideologies of ethnic nationalism (RE-ETGACE, 2003a).

Romania is among those countries with the lowest associative participation: 2.27% belong to political parties, 1.1% to environmental movements, and an insignificant number (0.08%) to the peace movement (EVS).

The high level of expressed mistrust in political institutions and the state administration – only 19% have confidence in national parliament, moreover, only 33% reject undemocratic alternatives such as a 'strong leader' (EVS) – is above all rooted in negative experiences from the communist regime but also in outcomes of the reform processes after the transition carried out by the reformed political elites. Disappointment, frustration and alienation have turned people away from these structures. As observed by some authors, instead of growing the already low post-communist social capital deteriorated to become negative (Paldam and Svendsen, 2001).

Democratic civil society in Romania encounters more problems than in most transition countries of the region. The average activity in civil society associations is quite low. There is not much readiness to engage in protest actions: boycotts (2%), demonstrations (15%). Some have gone so far as to speak of the existence of civil society as a virtual one, *'a space of symbols for which many actors compete but in which no one truly accepts to embark on cooperation with others'* (Dungaciu, 2001; cited in RE-ETGACE 2003a: 51).

It appears that there is a common denominator of the many of those who seized the opportunity to participate in democratic governance as opened to them by the transition to democracy: the instrumental nature of participation in democratic structures enables access to resources: *'The children were always ill: allergy, connected with the bad air. I read a bill of the Air Team in the bus and then I phoned them. I visited their sessions for two or three years regularly. Then, as I was fed up with the troubles of 'no work, lets get a job, take up one I don't know about, or I hate'; it was too much. I asked the leader of the team I already knew for two or three years, doesn't he have a job I could do? And then I began work'* (RE-ETGACE, 2003b: 23). The same findings also point to the phenomenon of the development of professional activists in NGOs, which makes people also distrust civil society structures (ibid. 21).

Active democracies – the Netherlands

Discussing citizens' participation and governance in the Netherlands is best understood within the tradition of 'negotiating harmony' since Dutch society could be called the 'debating society' and an example of the 'harmony model'. This historical and cultural pattern of policy-making was introduced in the first half of the 20th century to the so-called *pillarised* Dutch society. The need to survive in tough circumstances and to protect the sovereignty had built up an awareness about interdependence and responsibility for political and economic welfare among the leaders – at that time mostly religious ones who started to negotiate to ensure equality among different dimensions. The second half of the 20th century was characterised by gradual secularisation and *de-pillarisation*, followed by the search for new forms of settling societal conflicts, which led to a corporative economy and social peace. In the 1970s and 1980s political and cultural movements such as those of feminists, the environment, peace etc. gained in socio-political power. But the 1990s 'became famous for what seems to be at first glance a contradictory movement, a new habit of reconciliatory politics' (Basten, van der Veen, in ETGACE, 2001: 116) It started with an agreement between representatives of employers and unions in the early 1980s about the reduction of wage growth in exchange for reduced working hours with the common goal of cutting unemployment. This spirit of the so-called *poldermodel*, characterised by collaboration, spread to other domains of Dutch society and replaced social action with negotiation. This habit of seeking harmony has also had negative results such as the exclusion of non-traditional pillar groups like women and newcomers from the negotiations. 'Recent comparative researches confirm the Dutch blend of progressive thinking and a tendency towards collaboration' (ibid.).

With regard to citizens' participation, the results of this national attitude to governance and politics could not be evaluated as unfavourable.[35] 57% of Dutch citizens consider politics to be important in their lives and 80% discuss it, according to the EVS data. These figures, just like the 5.04 achieved on the ESS scale of the importance of politics, are significantly above the European average and clearly imply an 'active pattern'.[36] The

[35] Dutch authors argued (*Sociaal en Cultureel Rapport 2000* in Basten, van der Veen, ibid) that, because of the tendency towards collaboration, the 'Netherlands turned out to be the country with comparatively very low participation in traditional organisations (political parties, unions and churches). On the other hand, the Netherlands has by far the highest participation in modern political organisations'.

[36] There is also a clear rejection, which is revealed by Dutch authors as well, of undemocratic

associational dimension is strong. There seem to be some inconsistencies between the EVS and ESS data concerning the classical (modern) aspects of participation. Party membership is close to the average (5%) according to the ESS but somewhat above it according to the EVS (9%). Likewise, the average voter turnout for the last three parliamentary elections of 77% is significantly above the European average and remains quite stable in the long run. 22% of Dutch respondents claim to be trade union members according to the ESS. But the strength of post-modern associations cannot be overemphasised in the Netherlands since 20% claim (according to the ESS data) that they belong to an environmental, peace or animal rights organisation.

The results of the life history interviews of the Dutch sample reflect a specific historical and cultural environment. The majority of Dutch respondents were engaged in policies and politics, some of them in traditional political institutions. Others were disappointed with this area for different reasons, for example 'by the culture of power play and infighting', or 'by the immobility of politics', but the distrust in state politics which they expressed did not mean that they had stopped worrying about state politics. 'If they cannot negotiate a meaningful position within the political system, they may choose for extra-parliamentary political action' (ibid. 122). Respondent Ronald, for example, was active in the 1970s and 1980s in the anti-nuclear movement but later he started to live a quieter life and became a member of a cultural foundation board. Or Charlotte, who had been an ecological activist for two decades later, as the mother of a handicapped child, became an active member of a parent organisation. In the interview she described the connection between personal development and shifts in her social surroundings: in the 1970s and 1980s the environmental movement was quite militant but gradually both the movement and herself individually learned to think more strategically.

For Dutch respondents, the national 'debating culture' brought some specific experiences and the overwhelming impression is that most active citizens obtain their information just through endless *discussions*, or as the respondent Ronald described: *Well, in fact I learned a lot. At least I learned the skill to discuss (...) (our) power was not based on authority but was based on arguments and the fact that people listened to us. If you put a lot of energy into it, you know to parry and possible argument there is, in discussions with outsiders but also in integral strategy discussions* (ibid. 127).

All Dutch respondents were, in one way or another, connected with the organisations and learned by engagement in working in an organisation.

---

alternatives and a firm belief that democracy is good for maintaining order (shared by 79% according to the EVS data).

Most of them had tried out different kinds of associations and institutions and expressed a high level of belonging and identification with an organisation in which they 'feel at home'. Strictly individual forms of active participation were not expressed among the Dutch sample. Respondent Antoine said: *...Being on your own as an entrepreneur, you have the inclination to think individualistically, but I have learned also to talk with people in the group at crucial points, to learn about their ideas and to build support ...Yes, that's what you learned, the human side of the company* (ibid. 130).

As shown by the quantitative data, working for a variety of associations is significantly more common among Dutch citizens than among citizens of other European countries. Political institutions and actors are relatively trusted; 54% of the respondents expressed confidence in their national parliament, which is the highest proportion in Europe according to the EVS (except Luxembourg). This confidence remained stable during the 1990s and is confirmed by the ESS data (5.19 on the 1-10 scale). The average trust in politicians is 4.83 (ranked second in the ESS survey).

The role of social capital in sustaining classic and fostering innovative forms of participation

It is not surprising that patterns of socio-political participation are clearly related to the various levels of social capital when the latter is measured as a combination of generalised trust, active involvement in voluntary associations and spending time in various social clubs and associations (see Adam et al. 2005). High participation corresponds to high levels of social capital, namely:

1) all countries characterised by the active pattern have very high levels of social capital;
2) all countries characterised by the moderate pattern have high or medium levels of social capital;
3) all countries characterised by the passive pattern have low levels of social capital;
4) all countries with the classical pattern, except for Spain, have high levels of social capital; and
5) all countries with the sceptical pattern, except for the UK and Ireland, have medium levels of social capital[37] (for the levels of social capital, see Adam et al. 2005).

[37] These conclusions do not necessarily apply to Croatia and Malta.

To some extent, there is a certain tautology in the establishment of these relationships since some aspects of socio-political participation, especially activity in civil society's associations, are themselves partial indicators of social capital (they are actually part of Putnam's more complex measurement instrument). The same may be argued for the generalised trust dimension. Certain connections between some aspects of political participation and some aspects of social capital are therefore quite obvious.

However, several questions do require some further clarification. Certain aspects of political participation do not seem to be very close to what was originally defined as social capital by authors like Putnam or Coleman. The most typical of them are voting and passive membership in political organisations and movements. On the other hand, these are also the most common types of political participation and are far from irrelevant (on passive membership relative to social capital see e.g. Maloney (1999) on 'chequebook participation' or Wollebaek and Selle (2004)).

Comparing these common types with the new flexible ones, the latter could be perceived as a way for the accumulation of all sorts of social capital.

Taking into account some of the previous discussions on these issues and the comparative data on socio-political participation mentioned above, the relationships between voting turnout, political organisations/movements membership (both active and passive) and social capital will now be discussed. Several existing analyses have already demonstrated correlations between voting and other types of political (and social) participation (van Deth, 1997 etc.). On the individual level, the relationship between voting and other types of participation is not completely clear since they may be used either as supplements or alternatives to each other. The relations become clearer when the analysis is shifted from the individual to the national level: nations with a high level of involvement in political organisations/movements also seem to have high voter turnouts. Moreover, nations with high levels of social capital also seem to have high levels of virtually all forms of political participation, including those that do not seem to be indicating high levels of social capital, such as voting and passive membership. Such relationships, however, are not completely straightforward. For instance, all European societies with high generalised trust seem to have high voting turnouts though there are some exceptions due to the specific national traditions and/or regulations.

This is additionally supported by the available qualitative data. The stories of socially and politically active citizens in the countries participating in the ETGACE and RE-ETGACE projects clearly emphasise the significance of social capital in the shaping and reshaping of their social/political agency regardless of the pattern of democracy they belong to according to the quantitative data. Indeed, we may identify differences among the forms and sorts of the social capital used by active citizens from different patterns. People from old and new democracies who actively participate in social and political affairs reveal the significant role of formal and non-formal networks at the local level – families, peer groups but also leisure time activities, important others, voluntary work. However, one has to be especially cautious when discussing the differences in participation in voluntary work since new democracies have just started to develop this kind of social capital formation, while it has a strong tradition in long-lasting democracies. As underlined in the Hungarian national literacy review, the low level of trust in these countries – not just in political structures but also in other people – led the citizens to turn to private life and consumerism (RE-ETGACE, 2003a).

The support of these networks and social relations has proved crucial in building their identities as well as their efficiency as activists. They seem especially supportive in developing the personal capacities (skills and competencies) needed for effective social and political action. Social learning may be revealed as an extremely important form of learning for active democratic participation.

Moreover, universal norms and values such as equality, solidarity, social justice are among the important motivating forces behind the individual decision to take an active part in building and furthering democracy. These values seem to be most powerful drivers in the building the social and political commitment of Spanish citizens. The Spanish experience from the period of the dictatorship may even indicate that not just high trust (i.e. in parliament) but also low trust may, in certain circumstances, trigger the social and political mobilisation of people (resistance).

Multi-agency – another important characteristic of the socially and politically active people participating in the ETGACE project – seems to indicate the ability to combine networks and social trust across domains. Social capital built in one domain (e.g. work/profession) often leads to participation in another domain (e.g. politics).

Within the sceptical pattern, the establishment of democratic institutions and organisations in independent Slovenia, as well as the individual accumulation of some important sorts of capital before independence, could explain the fact that the Slovenian representatives have above-average amounts of social capital. Multi-agency; a high level of formal and non-formal education: horizontal and vertical networks across the different domains (private, professional, political, non-governmental); a straight value orientation – to contribute to the shaping of the new democracy – are significant characteristics of the majority of the Slovenian sample. It could be said they are well equipped with different resources of social capital which they are able to use in *bridging and bonding ties.* This is not the case for the UK sample. The majority of persons from this sample are: active in one specialised domain; in educational, social and non-governmental organisations or institutions; oriented more toward identity-building and reshaping the existing social relations; and their upward mobility is not relatively high.

The low social trust – at the individual and institutional levels – combined with the few possibilities for the networking characteristic of most CEE countries on the other hand is evident through the instrumental approach to the participatory structures and is most obvious in the pragmatic and incidental reasons for participating in NGOs in these countries. But in these countries people committed to social change also rely on their local communities and primary groups.

Discussion: can we speak of convergence?

To what extent can we speak of convergence when looking at both the survey and qualitative data? Clearly, one may identify some common European (or even global) trends, especially in the long run. The economical, political and cultural aspects of globalisation have affected all European countries, while EU members and candidates have been additionally affected by the institutional convergence required by the EU. Levels of education, as one of the significant conditions for social and political participation, have been increasing – though to very different extents – in virtually all European countries. The old social divisions and identities, mostly based on class, have decreased in significance, participation forms have become more individualised, while new issues and new forms of organisations have received growing interest. Yet the extent to which these trends have taken place varies significantly.

Voter turnouts as perhaps the most typical indicator of classical political participation was decreasing almost universally in European democracies before 1990. Nevertheless, in the 1990s signs of divergence appeared when voter turnouts stabilised in active and classical democracies, while the decline mostly continued in the sceptical and passive democracies. The declining trust in political leaders is far from being a universal trend of postmodernisation in Inglehart's sense. During the 1990s, for instance, confidence in parliament remained high and stable in all northern active democracies, which also belong to the most advanced group of 'post-scarcity' societies. The rise of the new forms of social and political participation has ranged from very high levels (especially within the north active pattern) to their virtual insignificance (within the passive pattern). It is clear that their development requires much more than institutional convergence with developed European democracies.

This is related to the central question of convergence between the old and the new European democracies. The case of Spain shows that high levels of convergence are possible since today this country clearly belongs to the classical democratic model, in spite of the lack of any longer democratic traditions and its recent authoritarian history. The Spanish case may demonstrate to the younger, post-communist new democracies that convergence is possible, perhaps not in a single decade but in a few decades. Moreover, after the first ten years of democracy the Czech Republic, Slovakia, Slovenia and Croatia already seem to belong to the common pattern along with some of the old Western democracies.

Nevertheless, it is questionable whether these cases actually confirm any kind of overall convergence. The Spanish data indicate strong classical but weak (though rising) new forms of participation. As far as the latter are concerned, Spain still clearly differs from almost all of the older democracies. The most converging post-communist new democracies also maintain their specifics, such as anti-political attitudes, close to the passive pattern.[38] Moreover, the most converging post-communist nations seem to have some characteristics that are not shared by the others. The Czech Republic and Slovakia had already experienced a well-developed democracy before WW II, while Slovenia and Croatia have been relatively open to the West for a considerable time both due to their geo-political and historical positions and the relative openness – compared to other communist countries – of the north-western Yugoslav borders.

The extent to which the Spanish case may provide a hint as to the future development of the new democracies in the forthcoming years is also quite questionable. In response to the former regime of Franco in Spain significant resistance movements and organisations emerged, while this was mostly not the case of the former communist regimes, where a passive attitude was

[38] For example, less than 15% of Slovenians consider politics as important, according to the EVS/WVS (1999/2000), which is the lowest proportion in Europe. Virtually identical results are provided by the ESS (2003), where Slovenians were again those in Europe who considered politics as being the least important.

much more typical and civil society movements have only emerged in recent years. Therefore, the Spanish case – despite the obvious similarity of a recent authoritarian experience – may be based on a tradition that differs from the communist one.

Social capital may represent specific socio-cultural features linked to a variety of traditions that cannot be simply 'imported' by globalisation and institutional Europeanisation, and may significantly contribute to divergence in patterns of socio-political participation.

References:

Adam, F., Makarovič, M., Rončević, B., Tomšič, M. (2005) *The Challenges of Sustained Development: The role of socio-cultural factors in East-Central Europe*. Budapest, New York: Central European University Press.

Alexander, J. (2001) 'The Past, Present, and the Future of Civil Society', in: Bron, A. & Schemmann, M. (eds), *Civil Society, Citizenship and Learning*. Münster: Bochum Studies in International Adult Education.

Arato, A. (2000) *Civil Society, Constitution and Legitimation.* Lanham: Rowman & Littlefield Publishers.

Basten, F., van der Veen, R. (2001) 'Life Histories of Active Citizens in the Netherlands', in: Snick, A., Stroobants, I., Wildemeersch, D. (eds), *Learning citizenship and governance in Europe: overall review and analysis: analysis of life histories*, (Education and training for governance and active citizenship in Europe). Leuven: Catholic University of Leuven, Unit of Social Pedagogy.

Beck, U., Beck-Gernsheim, E. (2002) *Individualization*. London, Thousand Oaks, New Delhi: SAGE Publications.

Castells, M. (1996) *The Power of Identity*. Oxford: Blackwell.

Dahl, R., A. (1971) *Polyarchy: Participation and Opposition.* New Haven, London: Yale University Press.

Delanty, G. (2000) *Citizenship in a global age: society, culture, politics*. Buckingham (England), Philadelphia, PA: Open University Press.

Elster J., C., Offe, U., Preuss, K. (1997) *Institutional Design in Post-communist Societies. Rebuilding the Ship at Sea.* Cambridge: Cambridge University Press.

Edirisingha, P., Holford, J. (2000) 'The United Kingdom', in: Holford, J. and Edirisingha, P. (eds) (2000), *Citizenship and Governance Education in Europe: A Critical Review of Literature*. Unpublished Framework 5 funded Project Report submitted to the Commission of the European Communities, Guildford: University of Surrey, UK.

Edirisingha, P., Holford, J., Merricks, L., Preece, J., Everson, P. (2001) 'Learning Active Citizenship and Governance: Insights from British Lifehistories', in: Snick, A., Stroobants, V., Wildemeersch, D. (eds.), *Learning citizenship and governance in*

Europe: overall review and analysis: analysis of life histories (Education and training for governance and active citizenship in Europe). Leuven: Catholic University of Leuven, Unit of Social Pedagogy.

European Social Survey (2002/3).

European Values Study/World Values Study (1990-93, 1995, 1999/2000).

Final Report of the EGACE Research Project. (2003) University of Surrey, Guildford, UK.

Frenzel- Zagorska, J. (1990) 'Civil Society in Poland and Hungary'. *Soviet Studies.* Vol. 42. No. 4, 1990: 759-778.

Gamarnikow, E., Green, A. (1999) 'Social Capital and the Educated Citizen', in: *The School Field.* Vol. 10. No. 33-4.

Geraint, P., Moyser, G. (1999) 'More participation, More Democracy?', in: Bentham, D. (ed.), *Defining and Measuring Democracy.* London: SAGE.

Gomez, J. Oliver, E. and Purgvit, L. (2001) 'Life Histories Horizontal Analysis – Spain', in: Snick, A., Stroobantsand, V., Wildemeersch, D. (eds) (2001), *ETGACE: Learning Citizenship and Governance in Europe: Analysis of Life Histories.* Report to European Commission, DG Research; Leuven: Catholic University of Leuven, Unit of Social Pedagogy; pp. 186-213.

Hankiss, E. (1988) 'The Second Society. Is There An Alternative Model Emerging in Contemporary Hungary?', in: *Social Research.* Vol. 55. No. 1-2.

Held, D., McGrew, A., Goldblatt, D., Peraton, J. (1999) *Global Transformations.* Cambridge: Polity.

Holford, J., van der Veen, R. (eds) (2003) *Lifelong Learning, Governance & Citizenship in Europe.* Final Report of the ETGACE Research Project. Guildford: University of Surrey.

Inglehart, R. (1997) *Modernization and Postmodernization: Cultural, Economic and Political Change in 43 Societies.* Princeton: Princeton University Press.

Ivancic, A., Podmenik, D., Novak, D., Mohorcic Spolar, V., with the assistance of Vehovar, U. (2001) 'Focus Groups in Slovenia', in: van der Veen, R., van Raak, J. (eds), *Intervention Strategies for Citizenship and Governance Education: Analysis of Focus Groups*, Unpublished Framework 5 funded Project Report submitted to the Commission of the European Communities. Nijmegen: Catholic University of Nijmegen, the Netherlands.

Kaldor, M., Vejdova, I. (eds) (2002) *Democratization in Central and Eastern Europe.* London: Continuum.

Körösényi, A. (1991) 'Revival of the Past or New Beginning? The Nature of Post-communist Politics', in: Szoboszlai, G. (ed.), *Democracy and Political Transformation. Theories and East-Central Realities.* Budapest: Hungarian Political Science association, 155-92.

Laitinen, M., Nurmi, E., K. (2000) 'Finnist Literature on Active Citizenship and Governance'. in: *Literature Reviews*, ETGACE.

Lattinen, M., Nurmi, K. E. (2001) 'Life Histories Analysis of Active Citizens in Finland', in Snick, A., Stroobantsand, V., Wildemeersch, D. (eds.) (2001), *ETGACE: Learning Citizenship and Governance in Europe: Analysis of Life Histories.* Report to European Commission, DG Research; Leuven: Catholic University of Leuven, Unit of Social Pedagogy; pp. 71-115.

Literature Reviews. ETGACE. (2000) ACS, Ljubljana, Slovenia. (working materials)

Luhmann, N. (1990) *Political Theory in the Welfare State.* Berlin, New York: Walter de Gruyter.

Majone, G. (ed.) (1996) *Regulating Europe.* Routledge, London; New York.

Maloney, W., A. (1999) 'Contracting out the participation function: social capital and chequebook participation', in: van Deth, W., J., Maraffi, M., Newton, K., Whiteley, F., P. (eds), *Social Capital and European Democracy*, London and New York: Routledge.

Norris, P. (2002) *Democratic Phoenix: Reinventing Political Activism.* New York: Cambridge University Press.

Osborne, S., Kapuvári, A. (1997) 'Towards a Civil Society? Exploring its meanings in the context of Post-Communist Hungary'. *Journal of European Social Policy.* 1997. vol.7 (3). 209-222.

Paldam, M., Swendsen, G., T. (2001) 'Missing Social Capital in the Transition in Eastern Europe'. *Journal for Institutional innovation, Development and Transition*, Vol. 5, 21-34.

Parsons, T. (1977) *Social Systems and the Evolution of the Action Theory.* The Free Press, New York.

Podmenik, D., Ivancic, A., Novak, D., Mohorcic-Spolar, V. (2001) 'Life Histories of Active Citizens in the Slovenia', in: Snick, A., Stroobantsand, V., Wildemeersch, D. (eds) (2001), *ETGACE: Learning Citizenship and Governance in Europe: Analysis of Life Histories.* Unpublished Framework 5 funded Project Report submitted to the Commission of the European Communities, Leuven: Catholic University of Leuven, Belgium.

Putnam, R. (2000) *Bowling Alone.* New York: Simon and Schuster.

RE-ETGACE (2003a) *Active Citizenship and Governance in the Central and Eastern European Context. Report on critical review of the national literature and policy analysis.* Nijmegen: University of Nijmegen; Ljubljana: Slovenian Institute for Adult Education.

RE-ETGACE (2003b) *Learning Governance and Citizenship in Central and Eastern Europe. Report on Life Histories.* Leuven: University of Luven, Oradea: University of Oradea.

RE-ETGACE (2003c) *Similar or Different Learning Strategies for Active Citizenship and Governance in Europe? - Report on Focus Groups.* Nijmegen: University of Nijmegen.

RE-ETGACE (2004) *Reviewing Education and Training for Governance and Active Citizenship in Europe – A Central and Eastern European Perspective. The Implica-*

tions of the Research for Central and Eastern European Policy Design on Active Citizenship and Governance. Nijmegen: University of Nijmegen.

Richardson, J. (1996) 'Actor-Based Models of National and EU Policy Making', in: Kassim; Mennon (eds.), *The European Union and National Industrial Policy.* Routledge, London; New York, pp. 26-51.

Rubinstein, J., C. (1994) *Sociedad civil y participation ciudadana.* Madrid: Ed. Pablo Iglesias.

Snick, A., Stroobants, V., Wildemeersch, D., Celis, R. (2001) 'Governance and Active Citizenship in Belgium', in: Snick, A., Stroobantsand, V., Wildemeersch, D. (eds), *ETGACE: Learning Citizenship and Governance in Europe: Analysis of Life Histories.* Report to the European Commission, DG Research; Leuven: Catholic University of Leuven, Unit of Social Pedagogy. (Leuven: Catholic University of Leuven, Unit of Social Pedagogy, pp. 214-250.

Snick, A., Stroobants, V., Wildemeersch, D., (eds) (2001) *Learning Citizenship and Governance in Europe: Overall Review and Analysis. Analysis of Life Histories.* ETGACE. Unit of Social Pedagogy, Catholic University of Leuven, Belgium.

van Deth, J., W. (1997) 'Introduction: Social involvement and democratic politics' In van Deth,, J., W. (ed.), *Private Groups and Public Life: Social Participation, Voluntary Associations and Political Involvement in Representative Democracies.* London and New York: Routledge.

Vehovar, U., Ivancic, A. (2000) *Citizenship and Governance Education in Europe: A Critical Review of Literature.* Unpublished Framework 5 funded Project Report submitted to the Commission of the European Communities, Guildford: University of Surrey, UK.

Wightman, G. (1995) 'Conclusions', in: Wightman, G. (ed.), *Party Formation in East-Central Europe – Post-communist Politics in Czechoslovakia, Hungary, Poland and Bulgaria.* Aldershot: Edward Elgar, 238-51.

Wollebæk, D., Selle, P. (2004) 'Passive membership in voluntary organizations: Implications for civil society, integration and democracy', in Saanjev, P., Selle, P.(eds): *Investigating Social Capital: Comparative Perspectives on Civil Society, Participation and Governance.* New Delhi etc.: SAGE Publications.

Appendix: Graph 2.1: Dendrogram for the hierarchical cluster analysis

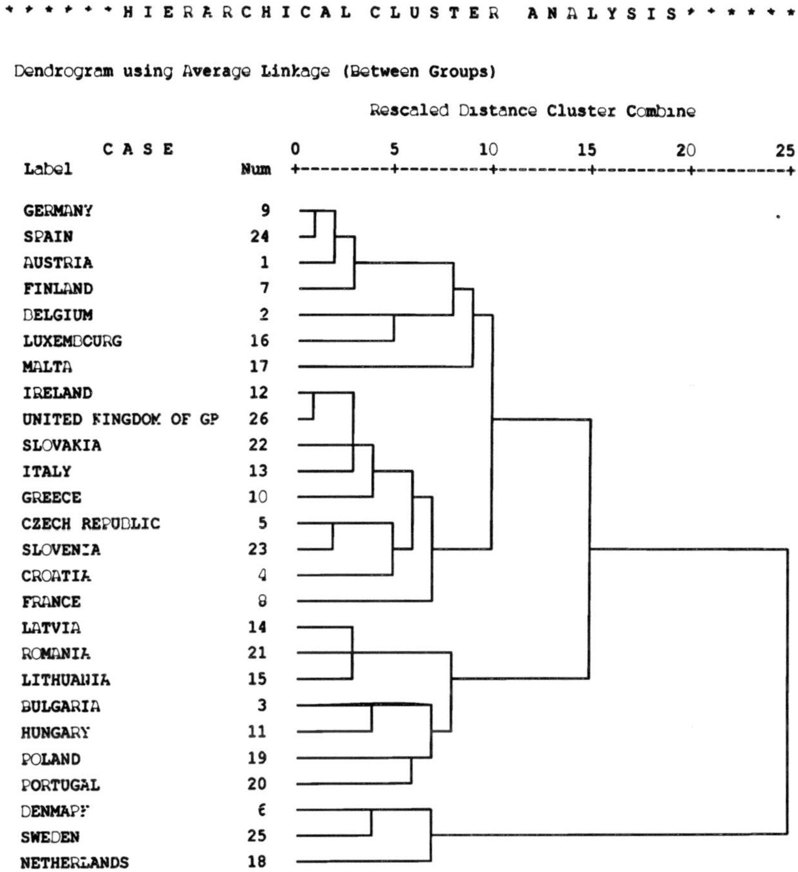

3. Political Cynicism and Social Cohesion in Europe and the United States

Peggy Schyns and Margreet Nuus

Introduction

The Dutch Prime Minister declared in an interview with the Dutch newspaper *de Volkskrant* that he was fed up with the cynicism permeating Dutch society. He called for 'a new positivism' among Dutch citizens (de Volkskrant, 2005). In Europe, politicians seem to be increasingly worried about growing Euroscepticism. A study which focused on the Dutch referendum on the European constitution reveals that most countries became more sceptical of European integration over the 1999-2004 period, and that the Dutch have shown the steepest increase in scepticism (Thomassen, 2005). In addition, predominantly in the American political science literature a waning level of political trust is being pointed out – a concept often used interchangeably with political cynicism (Hibbing and Theiss Morse, 1995; Newton, 1999; Norris, 1999; Pharr and Putnam, 2000; Dalton, 2005).

The topic of political cynicism has been studied in the political science literature from the 1950s onwards. While still on the research agenda up until approximately the 1970s, it reappeared again in the 1990s when declining levels of political trust were noticed in the United States and other Western democracies (Putnam, 2000). It then also permeated the discourse of politicians and the media. One of the fears which has not yet been investigated in depth in empirical studies is that political cynicism will lead to less social cohesion in society. The reasoning is that if people are convinced that politics is a dirty business, there are no compelling incentives to invest in political and social participation any longer, and this cynicism about politics may even spillover to a cynicism towards other people in general and a disdain towards one's country (Rothstein, 2000; 2003).

The concept of social cohesion has an even older tradition. Dating back to de Tocqueville and Durkheim, it gained renewed attention in the 1990s in the social science literature when problems regarding a shift in economic and social policy towards neo-liberalism in the 1980s and 1990s became the most visible (Jenson, 1998). In addition, social cohesion became one of the main policy concerns of Europe and was as such declared in the Treaty on European Union in 1993 (Berger-Schmitt, 2002) and in the Lisbon Summit of the EU in 2000 (ibid.).

In this paper, we explore the empirical relationship between political cynicism on the one hand and social cohesion on the other. We test the popular hypothesis that political cynicism leads to less social cohesion using individual-level data.

We studied this relationship in five countries in Europe and in the United States. Within Europe, we selected the Netherlands as a case study from the group of Western European countries, Italy and Spain as examples of Southern European countries, and Poland and Slovenia as examples of Eastern European countries. We compared the relationship in these countries with the one in the United States since the United States is one of the most studied nations in this field.

A second research question relates to this diverse group of nations: is the relationship between political cynicism and social cohesion different in these six countries? Can we, for example, find differences between Europe on the one hand and the United States on the other, or between different regions of Europe? For example, we found in the literature that social cohesion is typically low in Eastern European countries, moderate in Southern European countries and high in Northern European countries (Adam, 2005), whereas political cynicism is low in Northern European countries, moderate in Southern European countries (except for Italy), and high in Eastern European countries (see Section 5). Does this varying context affect the relationship, or does the relationship between political cynicism and social cohesion follow a similar pattern across all countries?

First, in Section 2 we discuss some theoretical notions that exist about the relationship between political cynicism and social cohesion. Since the concepts of political cynicism and social cohesion are not undisputed, we next reflect upon their meaning and measurement in Section 3. We shortly present the data, indicators and method we used in Section 4. The results are presented separately for each group of countries in Section 5. Finally, we discuss the implications of the results for a theory of political cynicism and social cohesion in our last section.

Theoretical notions of the relationship between political cynicism and social cohesion

Before answering the question of whether political cynicism leads to diminished social cohesive behaviour and attitudes, we have to deal with one issue first: political cynicism is an attribute of an individual whereas social cohesion is, by definition, a group's attribute. How can we deal with this 'multilevel' problem?

First, one could look at the national level and compare levels of national political cynicism with social cohesion levels. We would need many countries to make some statements about this cross-national relationship. Still it would not settle the causality issue: maybe social cohesion is causing a rise or decline in the average level of political cynicism of a country instead of the reverse.

A second option would be to look at time series of one or several countries and draw conclusions based on several measurement points in time. Unfortunately, concerning this relationship we still do not have much data that go back in time more than 10 to 20 years, certainly not for the Eastern European countries.

Since we are interested in citizens' attitudes and behaviour, we opted for a third possibility, which is to look at the relationship from the individual-level perspective. We can investigate the degree of political cynicism of citizens and relate it to their degree of social cohesive attitudes and actions. Thus we treat social cohesion as a characteristic of a group attributed to an individual in the sense that we look at the social cohesive attitudes and behaviour of an individual. This option is usually followed in social cohesion research in the Netherlands (see, e.g., De Hart, 2002a; 2002b).

Now let us turn to the literature. Most studies we found focus either on the relationship between political distrust and political participation (see, e.g., Aberbach, 1969; Olsen, 1969; Norris, 1999; Luks and Citrin, 2001), or on the relationship between a trustworthy government and social trust (for an overview, see Putnam, 1993; 1995; 2000; Newton, 1999; Levi and Stoker, 2000; Rothstein, 2000; 2003). The relationship between political cynicism and social cohesion *including* both generalised trust as well as participation components is, however, less studied.[1]

We summarise some of the main findings of studies addressing either of the components of social cohesion. All studies focused on the individual level. First, we look at the relationship between political cynicism and various forms of political and social participation. Olsen (1969) found that political discontentment (cynicism) was not associated with a voting participation index (i.e., whether or not a person had voted in three previous presidential elections, and frequency voted in past local elections), and only very weakly with a political involvement index (e.g., reading party litera-

[1] See the next section for the conceptualisation and operationalisation of social cohesion.

ture, giving money to a political party, doing volunteer political work). Norris (1999) found only a very modest relationship between trust in government and protest potential (signing a petition, joining in boycotts, attending lawful demonstrations, joining unofficial strikes, occupying buildings or factories). According to Luks and Citrin (2001), there is no relationship between trust and voter turnout at the individual level.

Second, we look at the relationship between political cynicism and generalised trust. Zonis (1968) found, for example, that cynicism of the political elite in Iran led to greater xenophobia (items on foreigners residing in Iran, foreign military assistance, foreign films and television programmes etc.). Newton (1999) reported that social trust and political trust were not closely associated. Rothstein (2003) also found weak, but positive, correlations between generalised trust and trust in institutions. Levi and Stoker asked themselves in their review study whether authors can argue that there is a relationship between political and social trust: '... it is an empirical question whether a trustworthy government helps promote social trust and the cooperative behaviors that support democracy, or whether social trust is a necessary condition for democracy' (Levi and Stoker, 2000: 493).

So far, we only found a limited amount of studies which empirically addressed the relationship between both components of social cohesion and political cynicism, which we discuss next. Brehm and Rahn (1997) looked at the relationship between civic engagement, interpersonal trust and confidence in government. Civic engagement and interpersonal trust can be viewed as components of social cohesion and low confidence in institutions as a proxy for political cynicism. They found that the effect of having confidence in the government on civic engagement was only small: .05 (standardised coefficient), but that the effect of confidence in institutions on interpersonal trust was .60, which was the highest effect in their LISREL model (Brehm and Rahn, 1997). When they looked at it from the other angle, they found that interpersonal trust positively influences confidence in government (.10), but that civic engagement actually lowered confidence in government (-.08). They concluded that the relationship between civic engagement and interpersonal trust is reciprocal and has counteracting effects on trust in government.

Kaase (1999) studied the relationship between interpersonal trust, political trust and noninstitutionalised political participation in Western Europe. He found that the relationship between interpersonal trust and political trust is small, but generally positive. The relationship between interpersonal trust and participation is, on the contrary, negative: the lower the political trust the higher the probability of engaging in political action.

Although the literature appears somewhat mixed in its empirical results, following the generally expressed fear in the introduction and Rothstein's (2000; 2003) and della Porta's (2000) line of arguing, our hypothesis is that political cynicism causes a decline in social cohesion at the individual level. The reasoning behind this hypothesis is that citizens who are cynical about politics, who for example believe that politics is a dirty business, have no incentive to be politically and socially active, nor will this lead to a general trust in other people. Put differently, if people believe that the institutions which are responsible for handling matters act in a fair and competent way, they will also trust other people (Rothstein, 2000; 2003; della Porta, 2000), and they are inclined to participate in politics and society as well.

The concepts of political cynicism and social cohesion

Political cynicism

Growing political cynicism is a concern shared by politicians, journalists and lay people. Before we can assess whether political cynicism has actually increased in society or not, we need to ascertain what political cynicism is, and how it can be measured.

In a literature review, we found that the concept is used interchangeably with other related concepts such as scepticism, political distrust and alienation (Schyns and Nuus, 2003). This has not led to much conceptual clarity. Let us have a look at these related, but – in our view – distinct concepts.

In accordance with Kanter and Mirvis (1989), we state that cynicism entails more than scepticism. The difference between a sceptic and a cynic lies in the former's potential to be convinced of the good intentions of politicians, whereas the latter has lost this potential.

Political trust is seen as 'a basic evaluative orientation toward government' (Stokes, 1962, in Aberbach and Walker, 1970: 1203). Distrust can be seen as a negative evaluative orientation. However, we think that cynicism is more than just distrusting a system. Distrust is to a certain degree healthy for the political system since democracies may not want naive, passive citizens who can be easily misled (for a discussion, see Hardin, 1999). Cynicism on the other hand is in the end not healthy for a system. For example, Eisinger (2000) argues that cynicism, more than distrust, entails intense, antagonistic distrust of or contempt for humanity. Captious anger and hostility is also endemic to what constitutes cynicism. Selfishness and hostility are core elements of cynicism (Eisinger, 2000: 55 and 57). These characteristics can hardly be called beneficial for society.

The difference between alienation and political cynicism is that the latter concept is usually seen as a dimension of the former. Finifter (1970), for example, distinguished between four possible dimensions of alienation toward the polity: political powerlessness, political meaningless, perceived political normlessness and political isolation. Perceived political normlessness is related to political cynicism. Reef and Knoke (1993) stated that political alienation and political distrust are conceptually orthogonal, and that nowadays a conceptual separation between the two concepts is common practice. We also argue that political cynicism does not have a simple one-on-one relationship with estrangement like political alienation has. Cynical people may still be highly involved in politics, whereas estranged people are, by definition, not involved.

In sum, cynicism is different from several other concepts because of its more acid-like and intense temperament. In addition, it may have more negative consequences for society than scepticism and distrust (alienation is another story) since it may eventually make people less trusting of others and make them less active to some extent.

Based on a thorough examination of the literature, we further distinguished three elements of political cynicism: 1. its subject; 2. its object and; 3. its orientation. We decided that the subject of political cynicism is the individual, who can be either a citizen or politician. Most research focuses on the citizen but politicians may of course also display cynical attitudes to politics. The objects of political cynicism are politicians (the micro level), political institutions (the meso level), and the political system as a whole (the macro level). Furthermore, we distinguish between two types of characteristics these objects have: their (in)competence and their (im)morality. Not only do we judge, for example, politicians on how well they cope with the tasks they should perform, but also – and even more so – whether they are ethical in their actions. For political institutions and the political system it is perhaps more difficult to discern between these two dimensions, nonetheless, political parties and the system as a whole also have to perform certain tasks, and the culture or setting in which these tasks are performed can be morally right or wrong. We consider a political culture to be more than just the sum of individuals acting. Finally, the orientation of political cynicism is an attitude which consists of a mixture of cognitive and emotional evaluations of the performance of political actors. It is difficult to disentangle these two types of evaluations, but evidence from the literature in other fields suggests people have both thoughts and feelings about politics (Ajzen, 1994; Dean, Brandes and Dharwadkar, 1998).

Based on our literature review and several expert meetings, we propose the following definition of political cynicism: it is *an individual's attitude, consisting of a conviction of the incompetence and immorality of politicians, political institutions and/or the political system as a whole.*

The next question is how to measure political cynicism. In a previous paper, we examined the measurability of political cynicism items as used in American and Dutch election studies (Schyns, Nuus and Dekker, 2005). We concluded that in terms of the scales' validity and reliability, they performed moderately to adequately. Therefore, we are currently designing and testing new items to measure political cynicism since we believe the existing scales are not fully appropriate to meet our definition. However, for the time being we have to work with the scales which are available in the existing data sets. We are aware that this is a suboptimal solution with implications for our results, such as a possible underestimation of our coefficients. For an overview of the political cynicism items we used in the study, we refer to the data section.

Social cohesion

The discussion concerning the concept of social cohesion may be even more blurred than the one political cynicism (for an overview see, for example, Jenson, 1998; Berger-Schmitt, 2002; Chan, To and Chan, 2006). In the literature we encountered several definitions. According to Maxwell, social cohesion 'involves building shared values and communities of interpretation, reducing disparities in wealth and income, and generally enabling people to have a sense that they are engaged in common enterprise, facing shared challengers, and that they are members of the same community' (cited in Jenson, 1998: 3). The Government of Canada's Policy Research Subcommittee on Social Cohesion defines it as: 'the ongoing process of developing a community of shared values, shared challenges and equal opportunity within Canada, based on a sense of trust, hope and reciprocity among all Canadians' (cited in Jenson, 1998: 4). According to Dekker, social cohesion concerns 'the reciprocal relationship of citizens, their networks and their actual and normative integration into society' (Dekker, 2003: 10). Chan et al. (2006: 290), after having evaluated the literature in the fields of sociology and policy-analysis, introduce their own definition: 'Social cohesion is a state of affairs concerning both the vertical and the horizontal interactions among members of society as characterized by a set of attitudes and norms that includes trust, a sense of belonging and the willingness to participate and help, as well as their behavioral manifestations.' Finally, according to Putnam, who focused more on the concept of social capital, social capital is 'social networks and the norms of reciprocity and trustworthiness that arise from them' (Putnam, 2000: 19). Social capital is usually seen as the positive side of social cohesion.

Certain elements can be discerned from these definitions: social cohesion has to do with organised, voluntary interrelationships between citizens, which are 'good' for society, and it is based on a feeling of (interpersonal) trust and belonging. Usually, social cohesion is placed on the policy and research agenda if there is a shortage of it in society (Beauvais and Jenson, 2002).

We do not want to engage in another definition struggle; therefore we choose Hirschman's terminology of Exit, Voice and Loyalty to operationalise social cohesion at the individual level. With these concepts he tried to combine the sciences of economics, political science and sociology in one theory (Hirschman, 1970; Hemerijck, 2002). This terminology is also adopted by the Dutch Scientific Council (NWO) in their Social Cohesion Programme (Korver, 2003).

The Exit option is quite difficult in political systems since it would imply leaving the country one lives in.[2] Therefore, we will not include Exit in our conceptualisation and operationalisation of social cohesion.

Instead, we focus on the Voice and Loyalty components which also correspond with the participation and trust elements found in other social cohesion definitions. With Voice we touch upon the political science angle of the theory. Voice refers to public debate, discussion and dialogue (Hemerijk, 2002). It includes all sorts of political and social activities ranging from

[2] The Exit option in Hirschman's theory was originally designed to account for the fact that people opt out of certain markets whenever they felt dissatisfied with certain products. To put it simply, in economics, Exit means not buying a specific product anymore, Voice means trying to improve this specific product by lobbying for improvements, and Loyalty means sticking to the product and hoping it will improve. In political systems, it is much more difficult to opt out of the system or change to another system. According to us, in politics Exit is more than just the absence of Voice or Loyalty; it is deciding that you do not want to be part of a political system anymore. It would mean leaving the country to find a more suitable political system (also see Dowding et al., 2000). The problem then arises that if we decide that Exit means a withdrawal *from* the political system but remaining *within* the political system (that is, staying in the country) – which would mean some form of alienation – then it becomes extremely difficult to distinguish Exit from (Non)Voice or (Non)Loyalty. For example, if a person does not vote does this mean they are dissatisfied with the political system and are thus exiting the system, or does it 'just' mean they are not participating and have a low Voice (for whatever reason)? Another difficulty is that Exit in the sense of alienation comes too close to our concept of political cynicism, which would lead us to have circular arguments.

voting to discussing politics with friends, from joining a demonstration, to being a volunteer. Throughout this paper, we will also employ the term Participation for the Voice component. Loyalty refers to a mixture of attitudes of interpersonal trust, solidarity and pride in one's nation, which is a field mostly studied by sociologists (ibid.). We propose an operational definition of social cohesion at the individual level: it is the amount of Voice and Loyalty an individual expresses. The more people participate in society and politics and the more they feel involved in their society, the more 'socially cohesive' an individual is.

For the Voice component, we looked at indicators of electoral participation and political participation ('conventional' and 'unconventional'). In addition, we think it is important to include measures of social participation since the political repertoire of people is not the only way to express Voice in society. Therefore, we included measures of memberships of organisations, of doing volunteer work, and donating money to organisations as well. For the Loyalty component we looked at indicators of pride in one's nation, patriotism, xenophobia and citizenship values. The specific indicators used for political cynicism and social cohesion are discussed next.

Data, indicators and method

In this paper, we used the Dutch Parliamentary Election Studies (DPES) for the Netherlands, the European Social Survey (ESS) for Italy, Spain, Poland and Slovenia, and the National Election Studies (NES) for the United States. We summarise the main aspects of each dataset, the indicators used and method employed below.

DPES

The Dutch Parliamentary Election Studies (DPES) consist of a representative sample of eligible voters in the Netherlands. Respondents are selected from municipal registers. The dataset consists of a pre- and post-election survey. The political cynicism items are used in the 2002 post-election survey (Irwin, Van Holsteyn and Den Ridder, 2005).

Political cynicism encompasses the following three statements:

- Although they know better, politicians promise more than they can deliver (Fully agree/Agree/Disagree/Fully disagree/Don't know).
- Ministers and state secretaries are primarily concerned about their personal interests (Fully agree/Agree/Disagree/Fully disagree/Don't know).

- One is more likely to become a member of parliament because of one's political friends than because of one's abilities (Fully agree/ Agree/Disagree/Fully disagree/Don't know).

Cronbach's alpha for the three-items political cynicism scale was .61. We constructed an index by adding the answer categories for the three separate statements. The index runs from a minimum of 3 (lowest level of political cynicism) to a maximum of 12 (highest level of political cynicism).

As stated before, social cohesion was operationalised with two of Hirschman's concepts, namely, Voice and Loyalty (Hirschman, 1970). The social cohesion indicators were all coded from less social cohesive to more social cohesive.

Concerning the Voice option, we included indicators of social participation, such as being a member or supporter of organisations, and being a volunteer at the local and national level. Examples of these organisations are: environmental, traffic, housing, third world/human rights/peace, cultural/ artistic, hobby, neighbourhood, women's, sports, professional, and trade union organisations.[3] Next, we looked at measures of political participation such as being a member of a political party, voting, contacting the radio, television or newspaper, involving political parties or organisations, participating in political meetings/debates, contacting a politician or civil servant, joining a civic action group, joining a demonstration, and using the Internet, email or SMS. In addition, four campaign activity variables were included: displaying window posters, trying to convince others about politics, contributing money to political parties, and attending election rallies.

The Loyalty component was subdivided into two dimensions. The first dimension is the patriotism/xenophobia dimension. Since the DPES 2002 did not contain any questions concerning this dimension, we used the DPES 1998 data instead. This dataset contains eight questions on patriotism and xenophobia. The items are: an important job is to teach children patriotism, our social provisions are not meant for foreigners, every Dutchman should observe our national symbols, foreigners are a threat to our culture, youngsters should learn self-control and determination, foreigners abuse social provisions more than Dutchmen, children should learn obedience and respect for authorities, and differences between ethnic groups are natural. The second dimension contains one item on general trust in people, which is measured by the question of whether people can be trusted or one cannot be too careful.

[3] We constructed indices by adding the number of organisations per category.

ESS

The European Social Survey (ESS) is a new biennial survey in which 22 countries participated in its first round, held in 2002.[4] The dataset for each country is a random (probability) sample consisting of the eligible population aged 15 years and over. The goal of the survey is mentioned on their website: 'Academically driven but designed to feed into key European policy debates, the ESS hopes to measure and explain how people's social values, cultural norms and behaviour patterns are distributed, the way in which they differ within and between nations, and the direction and speed at which they are changing' (ESS, 2005).

In the ESS survey, we did not find any political cynicism items. We had to use two 'trust in institution' variables, namely trust in parliament and trust in politicians. The items were worded as follows:

- Please tell me on a score of 0-10 how much you personally trust each of the institutions I read out. 0 means you do not trust an institution at all, and 10 means you have complete trust...
  - [country's] parliament? (0 No trust at all, 10 Complete trust, 88 Don't know)
  - politicians? (0 No trust at all, 10 Complete trust, 88 Don't know).

Cronbach's alpha for the two-items scale ranged from .74 in Poland to .77 in Slovenia. An index of these two variables was constructed by adding the answer categories of the two variables, and recoding the scale from 0 (lowest political distrust) to 10 (highest political distrust).

The Voice component consisted of social participation indicators, measured by membership/volunteer work items, that is, being a member of organisations, participating in organisations, donating money to organisations, doing volunteer work,[5] the probability of taking an active role in a political group, and helping others on a voluntary basis. Next, we looked at measures of political participation such as being a member of a political party, voting, displaying a campaign button/sticker, contacting a politician or government official, working in a political party or action group, giving money to a party organisation or group, taking part in a lawful demonstration, signing a petition, boycotting certain products, and participating in illegal protest activities.

[4] At the time of finishing this paper, the second round of data was being released. Unfortunately, the data on Italy were not yet available.

[5] We constructed four indices, running from 0 'no member/participant/donor/volunteer', to 1 '... of one organisation', to 2 '... of two or more organisations'.

The Loyalty component consisted first of all of xenophobia/citizenship items.[6] The following (11-point) scales were used to measure it: allow few/many immigrants to live here, immigrants take/don't take jobs away in the country, cultural life is/is not undermined by immigrants, immigration is bad/good for the economy and (dis)agreeing with the statements in order to be a good citizen it is important to vote, and in order to be a good citizen it is important to act in politics. Second, we included general trust in people items, which were measured by the following three (11-point) scales: you can't be too careful/most people can be trusted, most people try to take advantage of me/most people would try to be fair, and people mostly look out for themselves/people mostly try to be helpful. Also here, answer categories were coded from less cohesive to more cohesive.

We preferred using the ESS data over the European Values Survey since in the ESS two instead of only one political distrust items were included. Moreover, it contained more items on the loyalty dimension (several xenophobia and citizenship values items instead of only one national pride question).

NES

The goal of the American National Election Studies (NES) is to produce data on 'voting, public opinion, and political participation that serve the research needs of social scientists, teachers, students, policy makers and journalists concerned with the theoretical and empirical foundations of mass politics in a democratic society' (NES, 2005). Data are obtained from in-person interviews with citizens of voting age living in households within the United States, exclusive of those on military reservations. The American data consist of pre- and post-election surveys. For this paper, we used the post-election surveys which were conducted in November-December 2002. The samples involve multistage area probability designs (ibid.).

The political cynicism scale of the American data has been used since the 1950s. The scale has been given various names: the most often used is the 'trust (in government)' scale (Citrin and Muste, 1999). The scale has also been referred to as the 'political trust' scale (e.g., Aberbach and Walker, 1970; Citrin and Luks, 2001), or the 'political cynicism' scale (e.g. Jennings and Niemi, 1968; Lyons, 1970), or both (e.g. Miller, 1974). The scale consists of four questions:[7]

[6] The ESS data did not contain items on patriotism; instead, we used two items on citizenship values.

[7] Up until the 1980s, a fifth item was included, namely, 'Do you feel that almost all of the people

- How much of the time do you think can you trust the government in Washington to do what is right? (Just about always/Most of the time/ Only some of the time/Don't know).
- Do you think that people in the government waste a lot of the money we pay in taxes, waste some of it, or don't waste very much of it? (Waste a lot/Waste some/Don't waste very much/Don't know).
- Would you say that the government is pretty much run by a few big interests looking out for themselves or that it is run for the benefit of all people? (Government run by a few big interests/Government run for the benefit of all/Don't know).
- Do you think that quite a few of the people running the government are a little crooked, not very many are, or do you think hardly any of them are crooked? (Quite a few are crooked/Not very many are crooked/Hardly any are crooked/Don't know).

Cronbach's alpha for the four-item scale was .60. From these four items, we constructed a political distrust/cynicism index. We first made a dichotomy of the tax variable (collapsing the 'waste some' and 'don't waste very much' categories into one category), next, we made a trichotomy of the trust in government variable (collapsing the 'only some of the time' and 'never' categories into one category) and, third, we recoded the variables to form a political cynicism index, which ranges from 4 (least politically cynical) to 11 (most politically cynical).

The Voice component included several variables on social and political participation. Social participation measures were: being a member of an organisation, attending a meeting on a school or community issue, working with others on a community issue in the past year, working with neighbours on a common issue, and doing volunteer work in the last year. Political participation included items on being a member of a party, voting, trying to influence the vote of others, displaying a campaign button/sticker, attending candidate meetings/rallies, having done other work for party/candidates, giving money to a candidate, giving money to a party, having taken part in a protest/march on a national/local issue.

For the Loyalty component, the NES survey included one question on feeling good when seeing the American flag, one on the strength of one's

---

running the government are smart people who usually know what they are doing, or do you think that quite a few of them don't seem to know what they are doing?' (Hardly any/Not many/Quite a lot/ Don't know). From the 1990s onwards, this item was no longer included in the questionnaires because of its low individual reliability found in a LISREL confirmatory factor analysis (Citrin and Muste, 1999).

love for the country (indicators of patriotism), and three questions on interpersonal trust identical to the ESS questions. Again, items were coded from less cohesive to more cohesive attitudes and behaviour.

Method

In this study, we used two measures to establish the bivariate relationship between political cynicism and social cohesion. The relationship is bivariate since we only have one independent variable (political cynicism) and one dependent variable (social cohesion; subdivided in components and indicators within components). Since most variables were ordinal, we computed Spearman's rho and Somers' d for the bivariate relationships. Spearman's rho is a symmetrical measure, whereas Somers' d is a non-symmetrical one. This last measure can be used to see whether political cynicism influences social cohesion, and/or whether social cohesion influences political cynicism.

Results

In this section, we focus on the empirical relationship between political cynicism and social cohesion at the individual level within five European nations and the United States. First we summarise trends in political cynicism and social cohesion.

Trends in political cynicism and social cohesion

Let us first look at developments over time of political cynicism in the six countries. We used data from the World Values Survey for this purpose, which cover the 1981-1999 period. The following question, which can be seen as a proxy for political cynicism, is asked in all countries in most years:

- I am going to name a number of organisations. For each one, could you tell me how much confidence you have in them: is it a great deal of confidence, quite a lot of confidence, not very much confidence or none at all?
  - Parliament (A great deal of confidence/Quite a lot of confidence/Not very much confidence/None at all/Don't know).

If we take the answer category 'None at all' as a proxy for political cynicism, we can see in Table 3.1 (Appendix 1) the following trends: two countries show declining percentages of people who have no confidence at all in the parliament – or political cynicism – namely Italy and the Netherlands, Spain first shows an increase and then a decrease, and three countries show increasing percentages of political cynicism, namely Slovenia, Poland and the USA.[8] Other studies confirm the finding of an erosion of trust in parliament in the USA (Putnam, Pharr and Dalton, 2000; Dalton, 2004).

Concerning levels of political cynicism, for 1999, the countries can be arranged from lower level cynicism countries such as the Netherlands, followed by medium-ranged levels in Spain and the USA, to countries with higher levels of political cynicism in Italy, Poland and Slovenia.

If we look at social cohesion trends in the literature, we generally find stable or even increasing levels of civic involvement, political participation and social trust in the five European countries (Adam, 2005; Dekker and Van den Broek, 2005).[9] The claim that in European countries, analogous to developments in the United States, social cohesion is waning cannot be upheld by the empirical data.

In terms of the absolute level of social cohesion, Adam (2005) found that the Netherlands together with the Scandinavian countries belong to those countries with the highest social cohesion in terms of associational life and generalised trust, Anglo-Saxon and Continental Western European countries to the second highest, Slovenia together with Italy and Spain in the third group, while Poland together with, among others, Hungary, Romania and Russia were in the group of lowest social cohesion.

Although according to Putnam (1995) social capital in the USA has eroded, Dekker and Van den Broek (2005) found increasing trends in civic involvement and political participation in the USA, except for social trust which first showed a decline over the 1981-1990 period and then an increase over the 1990-1999 period. Newton (2000) also reported increases in social trust in the USA, contrary to national studies in the USA.

In sum, whereas trends in political cynicism reveal different pictures for the six countries, developments in social cohesion seem to be more uniform across these countries.

Political Cynicism and Social Cohesion in the West: the Netherlands

As mentioned before, the political cynicism index was constructed, ranging from low cynicism to high cynicism, and the social cohesion variables

---

[8] If we in addition decide to include the answer category 'Not very much' as a cynical response, the same trends as described above emerge.

[9] Spain may be an exception with some declining levels.

range from low social cohesive attitudes and behaviour to high cohesive attitudes and behaviour.

Let us first look at the Voice component (see Table 3.2). In the Netherlands, political cynicism had a weak negative association with being a member or supporter of civic organisations, and being active for these organisations. Active involvement in national or world issues was also negatively related to political cynicism, whereas being active at the local level was not. Political cynicism was weakly negatively related to being a member of a political party and to voting. The same applied to other political participation variables. Participation in a meeting organised by the government, joining a demonstration, and contributing money were the only items that showed significant, but weak, associations with political cynicism.

It is interesting to see that when political cynicism was considered as the dependent variable, the strength of the association with the Voice variables increased. For example, a moderate association of -.32 appeared when the act of voting was considered to explain political cynicism rather than the other way around.

The strongest coefficients were found in the Loyalty component. All items of the patriotism/xenophobia dimensions showed weak to moderate associations with political cynicism. An interesting finding is that political cynicism is positively related to the two patriotism items (which we coded as a positive social cohesive attitude): the more cynical about politics a citizen is, the more patriotic. The xenophobia indicators, such as 'our social security provisions are not meant for foreigners', 'foreigners are a threat to our culture' and 'foreigners abuse social security provisions more than Dutchmen', showed the strongest associations. Politically cynical people are less loyal, or more specifically: less loyal to foreigners, than non-cynical people. This conclusion applies to 1998 since these items were not taken into account in 2002. According to the Somers' d coefficients, the relationship between political cynicism and the patriotism/xenophobia issues was bi-directional. Finally, political cynicism was negatively associated with general trust in other people. We can see that the effect of general trust on political cynicism was stronger than the opposite effect.

Table 3.2 The relationship between Political Cynicism (PC) and Social Cohesion (SC) in the Netherlands

Component	Dependent variable Social Cohesion	Correlation with Political Cynicism Spearman's rho	Correlation with Political Cynicism Somers' d Dep. SC (Dep. PC)
Voice/ Participation	*Membership organisations/ Volunteer work*		
	Member or supporter of organisations	**-.109****	**-.090** (-.084**)**
	Intensity of activism for organisations	**-.075****	**-.047** (-.090**)**
	Active role in issue related to (part of) municipality or neighbourhood	-.034	-.015 (-.034)
	Active role in issue related to national interest or world problems	**-.068***	**-.030* (-.130*)**
	Member political party and voting		
	Membership political party	**-.068****	**-.029** (-.161**)**
	Voted	**-.109****	**-.025** (-.315**)**
	Political participation		
	Get radio, television or newspaper involved	.027	.006 (.022)
	Get political party or organisation involved	.011	.001 (.003)
	Participated in organised meeting/debate by the government	**-.063***	**-.029* (-.089*)**
	Contacted a politician or civil servant	-.039	-.020 (-.065)
	Joined a civic action group	-.029	-.013 (-.078)
	Joined a demonstration	**-.068****	**-.037** (-.169**)**
	Used the Internet/email/SMS for pol. action	-.018	-.009 (-.040)
	Display window poster/ campaign material	.010	-.001 (-.009)
	Try to convince others	-.022	-.011 (-.040)
	Contribute money	**-.077****	**-.021** (-.260**)**
	Attend rallies	-.029	-.008 (-.152)
Loyalty	*Patriotism/Xenophobia **1998***		
	An important job is to teach children patriotism	**.165****	**.145** (.153**)**
	Every Dutchman should observe our national symbols	**.098****	**.099** (.116**)**
	Our social provisions are not meant for foreigners	**-.260****	**-.178** (-.220**)**
	Foreigners are a threat to our culture	**-.303****	**-.235** (-.243**)**
	Youngsters should learn self-control and determination	**-.177***	**-.135** (-.164**)**
	Foreigners abuse social provisions more than Dutchmen	**-.286****	**-.218** (-.225**)**
	Children should learn obedience and respect for authorities	**-.203****	**-.166** (-.181**)**
	Differences between ethnic groups are natural	**-.144****	**-.107** (-.116**)**
	General trust in people		
	You can't be too careful/People can be trusted	**-.257****	**-173** (-.303**)**

Source: DPES data, 2002 and 1998; * $p < 0.05$; ** $p < 0.01$ bold.

Political Cynicism and Social Cohesion in the South: Italy and Spain

The social capital of Italy was studied in depth by Putnam in his book *Making Democracy Work: Civic Traditions in Modern Italy* (Putnam, 1993). In this section, we compare the relationship between political cynicism and social cohesion in Italy with the relationship in Spain. We can see in Table 3.3 (Appendix 2) that social participation indicators such as being a member of organisations, having participated in organisations and the possibility of taking an active role in a political group are significantly negatively related to political cynicism in Italy, whereas in Spain only the latter factor and helping others is negatively related to political cynicism. In Italy, more political participation indicators matter than in Spain: Italian people who are less politically cynical are more often a member of a political party, vote more often, contact politicians and give money to a party or political group. In Spain, a small negative relationship exists between being politically cynical and voting and boycotting certain products.

As was the case in the Netherlands, being active as a participant in politics and society has a stronger negative effect on political cynicism than political cynicism has on being a participant.

The Loyalty indicators are, except for one, all significant in both countries. Coefficients range between -.061 and -.295. This means that people who are more cynical about politics tend to have lower social cohesive attitudes, that is, they have more anti-immigrant sentiments, are less citizenship-minded, and portray less trust in other people. The effects are quite symmetrical: people who display trust towards other people in general tend to show less distrust towards politics, and people who have trust in politics in general also trust other people more.

Political Cynicism and Social Cohesion in the East: Poland and Slovenia

For the Eastern European countries, we get a picture much the same as the other European countries. If we first look at the Voice component of social cohesion in Table 3.4 (Appendix 3), we see a small negative correlation between being a member of several organisations and political cynicism, between voting and political cynicism, and several forms of conventional political participation such as contacting politicians or government officials, working in a political party or action group, and giving money to a party or group and political cynicism in both countries. Moreover, in Slovenia, actually having participated in and donated money to organisations also appears to be significantly negatively correlated to cynicism. In Poland these correlations are not significant.

Again, the coefficient of the relationship between participation and political cynicism is stronger when participation is causing political cynicism than vice versa. This means that participating in social and political activities has a stronger negative influence on political cynicism than political cynicism has a negative effect on social and political participation.

For the Loyalty component of social cohesion we find again stronger relationships with political cynicism than for the Voice component. Indicators of xenophobia and citizenship show somewhat stronger negative correlations with political distrust: most coefficients range between -.10 and -.30. Indicators of general trust in people have the highest coefficients: between -.22 and -.29. Somers' d is approximately of the same size in either direction, which means the relationship is reciprocal.

Political Cynicism and Social Cohesion in the United States

Now let us look at the American data. When we look at Table 3.5, the overall picture is that most coefficients are relatively weak: compared with the European countries, overall wc see less significant effects. Concerning the Voice or Participation component of social cohesion, membership of an organisation and having done volunteer work is negatively correlated with political cynicism (that is, if people are a member and are doing volunteer work they are less politically cynical).

The act of voting is only very weakly related to political cynicism: -.06 (Spearman's rho), as is the displaying of campaign buttons or stickers: -.07 (Spearman's rho). It is interesting to see that Somers' d shows us that the direction of influence is stronger going from social cohesion to political cynicism than vice versa. For example, whether or not one is a member of any organisation appears to be a stronger predictor of cynicism (-.11) than cynicism is a predictor of whether or not one becomes a member of an organisation (-.06).

Also in the USA, the strongest coefficients are found in the Loyalty component of social cohesion. Contrary to the findings in the Netherlands, political cynicism and patriotism are negatively related in the United States, that is, the more cynical a person is the less proud one feels about the flag and the less love one has for the country. Concerning interpersonal trust, we also see a negative relationship with political cynicism. Two of the three coefficients on interpersonal trust are somewhat lower in the United States than in the European countries; still, their size is bigger than the participation coefficients.

Table 3.5 The relationship between Political Cynicism (PC) and Social Cohesion (SC) in the United States, 2002

Component	Dependent variable Social Cohesion	Correlation with Political Cynicism Spearman's rho	Correlation with Political Cynicism Somers' d Dep. SC (Dep. PC)
Voice/ Participation	*Membership organisations/Volunteer work*		
	Member of any organisation	**-.095****	**-.064** (-.109**)**
	Attend school/comm. issue meeting	-.011	-.007 (-.013)
	Worked with others on comm. issue	-.035	-.023 (-.042)
	Worked with neighbours on issue	-.043	-.027 (-.052)
	Volunteer work in last year	**-.078****	**-.052** (-.090**)**
	Member political party and voting		
	Member political party	-	-
	Voting	**-.057***	**-.035* (-.072*)**
	Political participation		
	Try to influence vote of others	.013	.008 (.016)
	Display campaign button/sticker	**-.067***	**-.027* (-.125*)**
	Attend candidate meetings/rallies	-.028	-.009 (-.066)
	Other work for party/candidates	-.046	-.012 (-.132)
	Give money to candidate	-.035	-.012 (-.079)
	Give money to party	-.043	-.017 (-.086)
	Taken part in protest	.026	.006 (.083)
Loyalty	*Patriotism*		
	How does US flag make resp. feel	**-.186****	**-.131** (-.182**)**
	How strong is resp.'s love for country	**-.136****	**-.093** (-.141**)**
	Interpersonal Trust		
	You can't be too careful/People can be trusted	**-.180****	**-.120** (-.207**)**
	People take advantage/are fair	**-.130****	**-.075** (-.172**)**
	Most people selfish/helpful	**-.238****	**-.143** (-.303**)**

Source: NES data, 2002; * $p < 0.05$; ** $p < 0.01$ bold.

Contrary to the findings in the previous five countries, Somers' d tells us for all significant coefficients that the direction of influence is stronger going from social cohesion to political cynicism than vice versa, even for the Loyalty component of social cohesion.

Conclusion

Does political cynicism lead to a decline in socially cohesive behaviour and attitudes of individuals? To answer this question, we selected five European countries from three different regions and the United States to study the empirical relationship between the two phenomena. Even though it is a common fear that people who are cynical about politics tend to withdraw themselves from politics and society, and tend to develop lower trust towards other people, empirical proof on this matter has been scarce.

We therefore put the hypothesis that political cynicism lowers social cohesion at the individual level to the test. Although not all coefficients were significant, we found several significant negative relationships between political cynicism and indicators of social cohesion in the six countries. In general, people who are cynical towards politics participate less in politics and in volunteer work, are more distrusting of other people, are more xenophobic and portray negative values of citizenship. It should be stressed though that these correlations are weak and that we cannot speak of strong linkages between the two phenomena. Moreover, political cynicism was more strongly related to the Loyalty variables than to the Participation or Voice variables. One relatively obvious reason could be that attitudes usually correlate stronger with other attitudes than with behaviour. Nevertheless, it may also indicate that political cynicism is mediated through attitudes such as interpersonal trust, pride in one's nation and xenophobia, which in turn affect levels of participation. This would be in line with Hirschman (1970), who stated that Loyalty precedes Voice. In addition, we found that the negative effect of the Voice/Participation component on political cynicism was stronger in all countries than the hypothesised negative effect of political cynicism on socially cohesive behaviour.

What about differences between (blocs of) countries? If one recalls the different levels of social cohesion and political cynicism for each country and the different data we used, it was quite surprising to find no major differences between the countries. Roughly speaking, the same patterns as described above emerged in each country. However, this does not mean that the countries were mutually exchangeable concerning the relationship between political cynicism and social cohesion. We also found some interesting deviations from the general pattern. For example, in the United States, compared to the European countries, less indicators of social and political activity correlated significantly with political cynicism. Moreover, in the USA effects of social cohesion on political cynicism were stronger than vice versa, which is more in line with Putnam's theory of social capital influencing political cynicism. Second, in Italy and Slovenia more conventional political participation variables were significantly related to political cynicism than in their respective counterparts, Spain and Poland. One possible explanation could be that in the former countries political activity is generally higher than in the latter countries. Furthermore, compared to the other four countries, the Netherlands and the United States showed stronger effects of interpersonal trust on political cynicism than the hypothesised reverse effect of political cynicism on interpersonal trust. Finally, another interesting finding was that political cynicism was positively correlated to patriotism in the Netherlands, whereas it was negatively related to patriotism in the United States. This difference may be due to different connotations of the concept in the two countries.

This study was a first step in exploring the bivariate relationship between political cynicism and social cohesion. In the future, the model could be extended to include control variables such as cynical personality structure, political literacy and social status. Other studies have, for example, found interesting interaction effects with race and social status (e.g. Levi and Stoker, 2000; Southwell and Pirch, 2003).

Although our main focus was on the concept of political cynicism in relation to social cohesion, unfortunately the data did not always contain valid and/or reliable measures of political cynicism. In the ESS and NES surveys we were restricted to the use of political distrust variables which, in our view, are milder expressions of a negative political attitude than are political cynicism variables. We have therefore probably underestimated our effects. Another caveat concerns the causal order of variables. We only used cross-sectional data on cynicism and cohesion and, even though Somers' d is a non-symmetrical measure, drawing causal inferences is still precarious. Longitudinal data and/or SEM techniques are needed to test the robustness of our findings.

In conclusion, the hypothesis that political cynicism leads to less social cohesion cannot be refuted by the empirical evidence found in the six countries. Nevertheless, the coefficients were not very strong. This finding is in line with the results of Olsen (1969), Newton (1999), and Norris (1999), who all found similar weak associations. However, claiming that political cynicism actually *causes* socially cohesive behaviour and attitudes would, in our view, be one step too far. To make such a claim would at least require stronger coefficients between the two phenomena. Moreover, since we found in all countries preliminary evidence of stronger effects of social cohesion on political cynicism than vice versa – in line with Putnam's theory – the theoretical causal order as proclaimed by Rothstein (2003) and della Porta (2000) remains somewhat questionable and in need of further scrutiny. At this point we can, at best, state that political cynicism at the individual level has a small negative association with socially cohesive attitudes and behaviour in the six countries.

References

Aberbach, J.D. and J.L. Walker (1970) 'Political Trust and Racial Ideology', *American Political Science Review*, December, 1199-1219.

Adam, F. (2005) *Social capital in Europe – Findings, trends and Methodological Disputes*, paper presented at the CONNEX Academic Workshop RG5, Social capital as catalyst of civic engagement and quality of governance, Bled, Slovenia, May 20-22.

Ajzen, I. (1994) 'Attitudes', in R.J. Corsini (ed.), *Encyclopedia of psychology* (2nd edition) (pp.114-116). New York: Wiley.

Beauvais, C. and J. Jenson (2002) 'Social Cohesion: Updating the State of the Research', *CPRN Discussion Paper*, Ottawa.

Berger-Schmitt, R. (2002) 'Considering Social Cohesion in Quality of Life Assessments: Concept and Measurement', *Social Indicators Research*, 58, 403-428.

Brehm, J. and W. Rahn (1997) 'Individual-Level Evidence for the Causes and Consequences of Social Capital', *American Journal of Political Science*, 3, 999-1023.

Bureau Sociale Cohesie (2000) *Stimuleringsprogramma Sociale Cohesie. Brochure*, The Hague, March.

Chan, J., H.-P. To and E. Chan (2006) 'Reconsidering Social Cohesion: Developing a definition and analytical framework for empirical research', *Social Indicators Research*, 75, 273-302.

Citrin, J. and S. Luks (2001) 'Political Trust Revisited: Déjà vu All Over Again?', in: J.R. Hibbing and E. Theiss-Morse, *What is it About Government that Americans Dislike?*, New York: Cambridge University Press, 9-27.

Citrin, J., and C. Muste (1999) 'Trust in Government', in J.P. Robinson, P.R. Shaver, L.S. Wrightsman (eds), *Measures of Political Attitudes. Volume 2 in Measures of Social Psychological Attitudes Series*, San Diego: Academic Press, 465-530.

Council of Europe (2001) *Trends in social cohesion, no. 1: Promoting the policy debate on social cohesion from a comparative perspective*, Council of Europe Publishing, Germany, December.

Dalton, R.J. (2004) *Democratic challenges. Democratic choices. The Erosion of Political Support in Advanced Industrial Democracies*, Oxford: Oxford University Press.

Dalton, R.J. (2005) 'The Social Transformation of Trust in Government', forthcoming in the *International Review of Sociology*, January.

Dean, Jr. J.W., P. Brandes, and R. Dharwadkar (1998) 'Organizational Cynicism', Academy *of Management Review*, 2, 341-352.

De Hart, J. (2002a) 'Theoretische uitgangspunten, conceptualisering en doelstellingen', in: Hart, J. de (ed.), *Zekere Banden. Sociale cohesie, leefbaarheid en veiligheid*, The Hague: Sociaal en Cultureel Planbureau, 3-32.

De Hart, J. (2002b) 'Sociale cohesie bij individuele burgers', in: Hart, J. de (ed.), *Zekere Banden. Sociale cohesie, leefbaarheid en veiligheid*, The Hague: Sociaal en Cultureel Planbureau, 33-74.

Dekker, P. (2003) 'Tussen sociale cohesie en politieke democratie', *Economisch-statistische berichten*, 4398, D9-D11.

Dekker, P., M. Lampert and F. Spangenberg (2004) De politieke onvrede van 2002, in: F. Bronner (ed.), *Jaarboek marktonderzoek 2004*, Haarlem: Vrieseborch, 67-83.

Della Porta, D. (2000) 'Social Capital, Beliefs in Government, and Political Corruption', in S.J. Pharr and R.D. Putnam (eds) *Disaffected Democracies. What's Troubling the Trilateral Countries?*, Princeton: Princeton University Press, 202-228.

De Volkskrant, (2005) *Balkenende heeft genoeg van cynisme*, March 18.

Dijkstra, A. B., J. P. van Oudenhoven and J. Peschar (2000), 'Competenties als sleutel? Op zoek naar aangrijpingspunten voor bevordering van sociale cohesie', *Sociale Interventie*, 2, 4-10.

Dowding, K., P. John, T. Mergoupis and M. Van Vught (2000), 'Exit, Voice and Loyalty: Analytic and Empirical Developments', *European Journal of Political Research*, 37, 469-495.

Eisinger, R.M. (2000) 'Questioning Cynicism', *Society*, vol. 37, no. 5, July-August, 55-60.

European Social Survey (2005, May 12), *http://www.europeansocialsurvey.org*, (last updated: 2005, April 26).

Finifter, A.W. (1970) 'Dimensions of Political Alienation', *American Political Science Review*, vol. 64, June, 389-410.

Hardin, R. (1999), 'Do we want trust in government?', in M.E. Warren (ed.) *Democracy & Trust*, Cambridge: Cambridge University Press, 22-41.

Hemerijck, A. (2002) 'Over institutionele aanpassing en sociaal leren – een verhandeling geïnspireerd door Albert Hirschmans trits van Exit, Voice and Loyalty', In T. Jaspers and J. Outshoorn (eds), *De bindende werking van concepten. Reflecties over participatie, binding en betrokkenheid in opvoeding & onderwijs, arbeid en zorg*, Amsterdam: Aksant, 4-48.

Hibbing, J.R. and E. Theiss-Morse (1995) *Congress as Public Enemy: Public Attitudes Toward American Political Institutions*, New York: Cambridge University.

Hirschman, A.O. (1970) *Exit, voice, and loyalty: responses to decline in firms, organizations, and states*, Cambridge: Harvard University Press.

Hooghe, M. (2001) 'Het einde van de sociale cohesie? Een kritisch overzicht van de postmoderne argumenten tegen het communautaristisch pessimisme', *Sociologische Gids*, jaargang 48, afl. 1, 8-30.

Irwin, G.A., J.J.M. van Holsteyn and J.M den Ridder (2005), *Dutch Parliamentary Election Study 2002-2003*, Amsterdam: Rozenberg Publishers.

Jeannotte, M. S. (2003) 'Social Cohesion: Insights from Canadian Research', *Presented at the Conference on Social Cohesion*, Hong Kong, November 29.

Jennings, M.K. and R.E., Niemi (1968) 'The Transmission of Political Values from Parent to Child', *The American Political Science Review*, March, 169-184.

Jenson J. (1998) 'Mapping Social Cohesion: The State of Canadian Research', *Canadian Policy Research Networks Inc.*, Ottawa: Renouf Publishing Co. Ltd.

Kaase, M. (1999) 'Interpersonal Trust, Political Trust and Non-institutionalised Political Participation in Western Europe', *West European Politics*, 22, 3 (July), 1-21.

Korver, T., in opdracht van NWO (2003) *NWO Strategische notitie Sociale Cohesie*, Maart.

Levi, M. and L. Stoker (2000) 'Political trust and trustworthiness', *Annual Review of Political Science*, 3, 475-507.

Lyons, S.R. (1970) 'The Political Socialization of Ghetto Children: Efficacy and Cynicism', *The Journal of Politics*, 2, 288-304.

Miller, A.H. (1974) 'Political Issues and Trust in Government: 1964-1970', *The American Political Science Review*, 3, 951-972.

National Election Studies (2005, May 12) *http://www.umich.edu/~nes*.

Newton, K. (1999) 'Social and Political Trust', in P. Norris (ed.) *Critical citizens. Global support for democratic governance*. New York: Oxford University Press, 169-187.

Noll, H.-H. (2002) 'Towards a European System of Social Indicators: Theoretical Framework and System Architecture', *Social Indicators Research*, 58, 47-87.

Norris, P. (1999) 'Conclusions: The Growth of Critical Citizens and its Consequences', in Norris, P. (ed.), *Critical citizens. Global support for democratic governance*, New York: Oxford University Press, 257-272.

Pharr, S.J. and R.D. Putnam (eds) (2000) *Disaffected Democracies. What's Troubling the Trilateral Countries?*, Princeton: Princeton University Press.

Putnam, R.D. (1993) *Making Democracy Work: Civic Traditions in Modern Italy*, Princeton: Princeton University Press.

Putnam, R.D. (1995) Bowling Alone: America's Declining Social Capital, *Journal of Democracy*, 6, 1, 65-78.

Putnam, R.D. (2000) *Bowling Alone: The Collapse and Revival of American Community*, New York: Simon & Schuster.

Putnam, R.D, S.J. Pharr and R.J. Dalton (2000) 'Introduction: What's Troubling the Trilateral Democracies?', in Pharr, S.J. and R.D. Putnam (eds), *Disaffected Democracies. What's Troubling the Trilateral Countries?*, Princeton: Princeton University Press.

Reef, M.J. and D. Knoke (1993) 'Political Alienation and Efficacy', in J.P. Robinson, P.R. Shaver and L.S. Wrightsman (eds), *Measures of Political Attitudes, Volume 2 in Measures of Social Psychological Attitudes Series*, San Diego: Academic Press, 413-464.

Rothstein, B. (2000) 'Trust, Social Dilemmas and Collective Memories', *Journal of Theoretical Politics*, 12 (4), 477-501.

Rothstein, B. (2003) 'Social Capital, Economic Growth and Quality of Government: The Causal Mechanism', *New Political Economy*, Vol. 8, No. 1, 49-71.

Schyns, P. and M. Nuus (2003) *Political Cynicism: Definitions and Operationalizations*, Paper presented at the expert meeting about political cynicism and populism, Amsterdam: Free University.

Schyns, P., M. Nuus and H. Dekker (2005) *Political Cynicism: the Measurability of a Disputed Concept*, Working paper, Leiden University: Department of Political Science.

Southwell, P.L. and K.D. Pirch (2003) 'Political cynicism and the mobilization of black voters', *Social Science Quarterly*, 4, 906-917.

Thomassen, J.J.A. (2005) 'Nederlanders en Europa. Een bekoelde relatie?' in K. Aarts and H. van der Kolk (eds), *Nederlanders en Europa, Het referendum over de Europese Grondwet*, Amsterdam: Bert Bakker Uitgeverij.

Appendix 1

Table 3.1 Frequencies of Political Confidence in Parliament across 6 Nations, 1981-1999, in percentages

Political Confidence									
	Neth (1981)	*Neth (1990)*	*Neth (1999)*	*Italy (1981)*	*Italy (1990)*	*Italy (1999)*	*Spain (1990)*	*Spain (1995)*	*Spain (1999)*
A great deal	5.0	3.2	4.6	5.1	4.2	4.8	5.6	3.6	8.8
Quite a lot	38.1	49.4	49.3	24.9	26.3	28.3	35.4	31.1	34.5
Not very m.	45.1	38.9	40.1	43.0	46.6	47.7	43.5	40.9	39.1
None at all	8.7	7.6	5.1	26.9	22.5	16.4	13.4	19.2	10.8
DK	0.0	0.0	1.0	0.0	0.0	2.2	0.0	5.1	5.9
NA	3.1	0.9	0.0	0.0	0.3	0.5	2.0	0.0	0.9
Total	(100%)	(100%)	(100%)	(100%)	(100%)	(100%)	(100%)	(100%)	(100%)
	Pol (1989)	*Pol (1997)*	*Pol (1999)*	*Slov (1992)*	*Slov (1995)*	*Slov (1999)*	*USA (1982)*	*USA (1990)*	*USA (1999)*
A great deal	17.4	4.2	7.9	6.6	3.1	4.9	14.5	7.6	6.4
Quite a lot	43.9	26.9	23.1	29.0	20.5	19.4	37.0	34.1	30.7
Not very m.	26.9	42.2	40.5	48.0	49.6	50.8	40.1	39.3	47.9
None at all	4.0	16.8	19.8	15.9	22.1	21.0	7.0	12.0	12.7
DK	0.0	9.8	8.7	0.0	4.8	3.4	0.0	0.0	2.3
NA	7.8	0.0	0.1	0.5	0.0	0.6	1.4	7.0	0.0
Total	(100%)	(100%)	(100%)	(100%)	(100%)	(100%)	(100%)	(100%)	(100%)

Source: World Values Survey, 1981-1999

Appendix 2

Table 3.3 The relationship between Political Cynicism (PC) and Social Cohesion (SC) in Italy and Spain

		Italy		*Spain*	
Components	*Dependent variable Social Cohesion*	Correlation with Political Cynicism Spearman's rho	Correlation with Political Cynicism Somers' d Dep. SC (Dep. PC)	Correlation with Political Cynicism Spearman's rho	Correlation with Political Cynicism Somers' d Dep. SC (Dep. PC)
Voice/ Participation	*Membership organisations/Volunteer work*				
	Member of organisations	**-.072***	**-.042* (-.088*)**	-.043	-.026 (-.050)
	Participated in organisations	**-.060***	**-.032* (-.082*)**	-.016	-.009 (-.021)
	Donated money to organisations	-.013	-.005 (-.026)	-.001	-.001 (-.002)
	Did volunteer work in organisations	-.026	-.006 (-.084)	-.020	-.006 (-.050)
	Could take active role in pol. group	**-.181****	**-.131** (-.165**)**	**-.099****	**-.069** (-.097**)**
	Help others (not work/vol. org)	-.015	-.012 (-.013)	**-.058***	**-.043* (-.047*)**
	Member political party and voting				
	Member political party	**-.078****	**-.020* (-.229*)**	-.036	-.008 (-.115)
	Voted	**-.096****	**-.045** (-.150**)**	**-.068****	**-.040** (-.083**)**
	Political participation				
	Display campaign button/sticker	-.045	-.016 (-.098)	-.046	-.018 (-.086)
	Contacted politician/gov. official	**-.101****	**-.044** (-.174**)**	-.010	-.004 (-.017)
	Worked in political party or act. group	-.053	-.012 (-.180)	-.023	-.008 (-.055)
	Given money to party org. or group	**-.070***	**-.016* (-.235*)**	-.005	-.001 (-.012)
	Taken part in lawful demonstration	-	-	-.039	-.020 (-.058)
	Signed petition	-.055	-.028 (-.082)	-.043	-.024 (-.056)
	Boycotted certain products	-.011	-.004 (-.023)	**-.058***	**-.021* (-.121*)**
	Participated in illegal protest act.	-.025	-.004 (-.108)	-.049	-.009 (-.205)

Loyalty	*Patriotism/Xenophobia/Citizenship*				
	Allow few/many immigrants to live here	**-.104****	**-.075** (-.097**)**	-.009	-.007 (-.008)
	Immigrants take/don't take jobs away in country	**-.076***	**-.067* (-.067*)**	**-.061***	**-.046* (-.048*)**
	Cultural life is/is not undermined by immigrants	**-.073***	**-.057* (-.056*)**	**-.080****	**-.061** (-.062**)**
	Immigration is bad/good for the econ.	**-.101****	**-.078** (-.079**)**	**-.155****	**-.118** (-.122**)**
	To be good citizen: important vote	**-.163****	**-.127** (-.130**)**	**-.230****	**-.177** (-.174**)**
	To be good citizen: important act in pol.	**-.278****	**-.216** (-.208**)**	**-.279****	**-.217** (-.215**)**
	General Trust in people				
	You can't be too careful/People can be trusted	**-.248****	**-.193** (-.191**)**	**-.265****	**-.206** (-.204**)**
	People take advantage/are fair	**-.295****	**-.233** (-.226**)**	**-.229****	**-.176** (-.177**)**
	Most people selfish/helpful	**-.224****	**-.175** (-.172**)**	**-.242****	**-.188** (-.187**)**

Source: ESS 2002 data on Italy and Spain; * $p < 0.05$; ** $p < 0.01$ bold.

Appendix 3

Table 3.4 The relationship between Political Cynicism (PC) and Social Cohesion (SC) in Poland and Slovenia

		Poland		*Slovenia*	
Components	*Dependent variable Social Cohesion*	Correlation with Political Cynicism Spearman's rho	Correlation with Political Cynicism Somers' d Dep. SC (Dep. PC)	Correlation with Political Cynicism Spearman's rho	Correlation with Political Cynicism Somers' d Dep. Sc (Dep. PC)
Voice/ Participation	*Membership organisations/Volunteer work*				
	Member of organisations	**-.047***	**-.023* (-.073*)**	**-.073****	**-.049** (-.076**)**
	Participated in organisations	-.036	-.013 (-.075)	**-.099****	**-.054** (-.130**)**
	Donated money to organisations	-.030	-.011 (-.063)	**-.078****	**-.047** (-.093**)**
	Did volunteer work in organisations	-.043	-.011 (-.130)	-.043	-.021 (-.063)
	Could take active role in pol. group	**-.172****	**-.127**(-.154**)**	**-.169****	**-.125** (-.150*)**
	Help others (not work/vol. org)	-.038	-.029 (-.031)	-.020	-.019 (-.020)
	Member political party and voting				
	Member political party	-.041	-.007 (-.176)	**-.096****	**-.028** (-.246**)**
	Voted	**-.074****	**-.049** (-.082**)**	**-.133****	**-.076** (-.167**)**
	Display campaign button/sticker	**-.052***	**-.012* (-.171*)**	-.007	-.002 (-.032)
	Contacted politician/gov. official	**-.056***	**-.023* (-.107*)**	**-.063***	**-.028* (-.109*)**
	Worked in political party or act. group	**-.059****	**-.013** (-.195**)**	**-.065***	**-.016* (-.197*)**
	Given money to party org. or group	**-.080****	**-.031** (-.155**)**	**-.060***	**-.019* (-.138*)**
	Taken part in lawful demonstration	.006	.001 (.031)	-.015	-.003 (-.052)
	Signed petition	.011	.004 (.025)	-.008	-.004 (-.014)
	Boycotted certain products	.017	.005 (.052)	-.016	-.005 (-.042)
	Participated in illegal protest act.	-.019	-.001 (-.221)	-.038	-.005 (-.237)

Loyalty	*Patriotism/Xenophobia/Citizenship*				
	Allow few/many immigrants to live here	**-.099****	**-.071** (.094**)**	**-.141****	**-.100** (-.135**)**
	Immigrants take/don't take jobs away in country	**-.169****	**-.129** (-.131**)**	**-.191****	**-.145** (-.156**)**
	Cultural life is/is not undermined by immigrants	**-.097****	**-.074** (-.075**)**	**-.170****	**-.128** (-.136**)**
	Immigration is bad/good for the ec.	**-.129****	**-.098** (-.101**)**	**-.211****	**-.163** (-.168**)**
	To be good citizen: important vote	**-.143****	**-.110** (-.114**)**	**-.123****	**-.095** (-.095**)**
	To be good citizen: important act in pol.	**-.176****	**-.137** (-.132**)**	**-.181****	**-.139** (-.137**)**
	General Trust in people				
	You can't be too careful/People can be trusted	**-.221****	**-.174** (-.171**)**	**-.293****	**-.228** (-.226**)**
	People take advantage/are fair	**-.238****	**-.186** (-.182**)**	**-.287****	**-.225** (-.223**)**
	Most people selfish/helpful	**-.218****	**-.171** (-.168**)**	**-.278****	**-.216** (-.214**)**

Source: ESS 2002 data on Poland and Slovenia; * $p < 0.05$; ** $p < 0.01$ bold.

4. Quality of Governance in the European Union: old and new members in a comparative perspective

Matevž Tomšič and Urban Vehovar

Introduction

When we analyse governance in the sense of its 'quality' – especially if we seek to 'measure' this phenomenon and compare different units (in our case different countries) – we must be aware that we are dealing with one of the most complex and multilayered social phenomena. The term 'quality' itself is not 'value neutral', meaning it is related to the values of the researcher or to the wider cultural context of a particular society, which defines the desirability of a certain type of governance. Given that our analysis focuses on the situation in EU countries where democracy is accepted with a wide national consensus, it is natural that the political system with norms and principles characteristic of Western-type democracies is the referential framework for our analysis.

The main goal of our paper is to analyse different aspects of governance and democratic performance in the countries of 'old' Europe (EU-15) as well in those former communist countries from Central and Eastern Europe (ECE) that only recently became members of the Union, especially to detect differences between them and to compare EU members with other developed Western countries (USA, Canada, Australia, Switzerland...).

Our argument is that governance, which means affecting the frameworks within which people act and politics occurs (March and Olsen, 1995: 6), is a multidimensional entity that, nevertheless, can be conceptually apprehended and empirically evaluated. Different components of governance are interconnected and interrelated. The matching of 'quality' is significant especially for European (or, in wider terms, Western) countries. In this regard, different categories (clusters) of countries can be formed according to the performance of their governance as measured by different indicators.

Further, the relationship between the quality of governance and some other aspects of socio-economic development will be examined.[1] There,

[1] An important aspect of governance and democratic performance is economic efficiency. The

the focus will be on the level of social capital as one of the most important generators of the development of modern society (namely, a key topic of this book). We will seek to sustain the thesis that the quality of governance and social capital are mutually related, meaning that performance in the field of governance contributes to strengthening several aspects of social capital (trust, co-operation) as much as social capital serves as a factor for upgrading the performance of the institutions of governance.

Good governance as a property of developed democracy

The so-called third wave of democratisation (Huntington, 1993) that started in the 1970s in southern Europe continued in the 1980s in Latin America and which ended with the collapse of the communist regimes of Central and Eastern Europe in 1989 brought about the spread of democracy as a form of government that has been unprecedented in history. However, there are disagreements about the prospects of the development of democracy. While some analysts see some problematic elements in the situation after the fall of communism that may, instead of a worldwide democratic order, be bringing a new world disorder (see Jowitt, 1993), others claim that nowadays democracy has no equal contender on the global level (see Plattner, 1991). The fact is that the number of formally democratic countries has more than doubled since the early 1970s (Diamond, 1999: 25). However, evidence from different studies on democracy (like those conducted by Freedom House) show that many of these 'new democracies' only meet some minimal criteria of democracy (universal suffrage, periodical elections) while some other attributes of a free polity (independence of the judiciary, media freedom, autonomy of civil associations) are quite weak. This makes some analysts claim that what is actually spreading today is a certain type of 'hollow' and 'illiberal' democracy, which does not match established Western democracies (Diamond, 1999; Zakaria, 2003). However,

---

fact is that the quality of governance correlates strongly with economic performance: a higher level of the quality of governance provides for higher levels of income per capita, higher growth rates, and lower volatility of growth (IMF, World Economic Outlook, 2003: 111-112).

Moreover, some authors see economic performance as being closely related to the form of democracy. According to Persson (2005: 22), the form of democracy is 'critical for the design of trade and regulatory regimes', and 'the form of democracy has important consequences for the adoption of structural policies that promote long-run economic performance' (ibidem: 1).

Similarly, Rigobon and Rodrik (2004) claim that democracy and the rule of law are good for economic performance, a claim that directs us to the wide array of papers analysing the importance of institutional quality for economic performance that has been published in recent years.

the question remains of whether the singular development of democracy in advanced Western societies is an unquestionable given fact. Reversals of democratic processes are not prevented by a formal introduction of democratic order, and the same holds true for processes which could undermine the quality of the governance of advanced societies. Using the worldwide governance indicators set, i.e. a set of indicators of the quality of governance, Kaufmann shows that 'while on average macroeconomic stability is no longer a major binding constraint in emerging economies (with a few exceptions), the quality of governance has remained stagnant at a low level in many countries' (Kaufmann, 2004: 138). A worldwide deterioration is apparent in trends of judicial independence and control of bribery in the judiciary, which includes OECD countries (ibid.).

As a consequence, some questions are being raised about the very nature of democracy, especially in the light of its sustainability, i.e. the possibility of its future maintenance and development.

First of all, it should be pointed out that democracy is a complex phenomenon which could refer to some kind of ideal state of society, characterised by perfect freedom and equality where the real power is located in the hands of the people, as well as to the real or existing form of the socio-political order, usually referring to modern Western societies (often in connection with a market economy). Even with the notion of democracy as an existing system (which is nevertheless our research interest) we have different definitions of its 'scope' (in the sense of its constitutive elements). Many theorists advocate the minimalist approach, a kind of Schumpeterian definition of democracy as a system in which citizens can choose between different political actors/elites (Schumpeter, 1996). In that case, the most important issue is the existence of institutional mechanisms which enable free political competition (of course, with constitutionally determined exceptions) and the selection of a preferable alternative. The weakness of this approach is its 'shallowness'. Namely, because it focuses on the normative level of politics it often disregards back-stage happenings as well as factors that are not part of the political system but which still importantly influence its nature.

However, there is another, more 'qualitative' notion of democracy which takes into account the conditions needed for its 'healthy' functioning. Dahl's concept of polyarchy as 'real-existing democracy' contains the following institutional factors necessary for the persistence of democracy: elected officials, free, fair and relatively frequent elections, freedom of expression, alternative sources of information, autonomy of associations and inclusive citizenship (Dahl, 1971; 1989; 1998). Especially for the existence of alternative information sources it could be said that this is a 'non-political' factor, related to media pluralism, which is not formally an element of the political system but which is nevertheless necessary for its democratic performance. Some theorists stress the importance of institutional factors like a viable civil society, the rule of law, a competent and autonomous civil service etc., without which democratic political life is impossible. O'Donnell stresses the need for control over power-holders through mechanisms of so-called horizontal accountability, which refers to mutual control in the sense of a system of checks and balances – the principal condition for this is the existence of independent control institutions (judiciary, different agencies etc.) (O'Donnell, 1998; also see Schedler et al. 1999). There are also some other factors that are often mentioned as conditions of a fully developed democracy, for example the existence of welfare policies and other mechanisms for tackling social inequalities.

Despite the desirability of such a kind of qualitative completion it is necessary to warn against other kinds of bias where one seeks to include into the framework of democracy everything that is in their opinion necessary for the well-being of people. In this way, the characteristics of the concept could become blurred. Too idealised a notion of democracy is even more problematic in a comparative analysis. Considering the fact that every existing democracy has deficiencies and is thus imperfect, it soon becomes obvious that no real democracy fully matches the ideal and this could lead a researcher into disappointment and the belief that democratic order simply does not exist at all – in this way, they neglect the differences between different levels of democracy of existing political systems. As stated by Karl and Schmitter (1996: 59), democracy is even not necessarily more economically and administratively efficient and orderly run than other forms of government. Given this, we can agree with Samuel Huntington who said: 'Governments produced by election may be inefficient, corrupt, short-sighted, irresponsible, dominated by special interests, and incapable of adopting policies demanded by the public good. These qualities make such governments undesirable but they do not make them undemocratic' (Huntington 1991:10). Yet we could add to this that such characteristics make for lower quality democracies.

In our conceptualisation, we connect good governance to the notion of democracy as an 'extended polyarchy'. This means a supplementation of the original (Dahlean) concept that is primarily related to the electoral dimension of accountability (i.e. processes of political selection based on freedom of political action and political equality) with mechanisms of permanent control over power-holders through an institutional balance of power (a system of 'checks and balances') between different branches of government as well as through the mutual checking of civil and state actors on a different level of polity. The point is that a system of checks and balances and its upgrade, institutions of horizontal accountability, comprise a set of institutions that forms the institutional framework of good governance.

Our definition of good, i.e. democratic, governance is thus in accordance with the 'wider' notion of democracy, meaning not only formal rules and institutional norms but also the performance of democratic institutions and their agents. As stated by March and Olsen (1995: 44), 'democratic governance is more than the management of efficient political coalition building and exchange within prior constraints... It involves moulding social and political life – shaping history, an understanding of it, and an ability to learn form it.' In this sense, it is related to the state of political stability. Within this context, we understand political stability in a dynamic and flexible way, as the 'capacity of the political system to be selective (in the purpose of preserving its identity and self-referentiality) when including in its modus operandi relevant actors and topics, and the capability of developing the problem-solving capacities in order to fulfil the functions entrusted to it' (Adam, 1994: 37).

Components of good governance

Our concept of democratic governance refers to governance as politics (the expression of different interests, political competition and relations between political actors) as well to governance as policy (the creation and implementation of different policies, concerning different social spheres) or, in the language of systems theory, to the 'input' (impulses from the environment like political demand and support) and 'output' dimensions ('products' of a political system like legislation, the budget, different social arrangements) of a political system (Almond and Powell, 1966; Blondel, 1972). It refers to the institutional level as well as the level of political action and political values.[2]

The concept consists of the three following dimensions: system persistence, inclusiveness and effectiveness.

System persistence refers to the system's endurance and persistence of democratic principles. It consists of three main elements: absence of threats,

---

[2] In this sense, it matches to a considerable extent with the concept of governance as defined by World Bank analysts – it is an empirical model consisting of six clusters of indicators: voice and accountability, political stability, government effectiveness, regulatory burden, the rule of law and control of corruption (Kaufmann et al. 1999; 2003; 2005). More on this model follows in the empirical part of the article.

legitimacy, and stability of institutions and processes. The basic condition for the persistence of any polity is its 'physical security' as expressed in an absence of activities, whether by external or internal actors, directed towards a violent change of the political order. In practice, these activities are manifested in political violence and other forms of political destabilisation. Related to the problem of these threats is the issue of legitimacy which, as defined by Lipset (1959: 29), includes 'the capacity to produce and maintain a belief that political institutions, or forms, are the most appropriate for the society'. Legitimacy leads to the acceptance of both elites and ordinary citizens of the norms and principles of political order, as well as them practicing them (Beetham, 1991). As perceived by Olsen (2002: 593), 'the integrative power of democratic politics depends on the ability to rally broad public support for institutions and policies.' For democratic political process to function properly, a certain stability and continuity is necessary, meaning that political institutions need the time and resources to perform their tasks.[3]

Inclusiveness denotes the level of matching actual institutional arrangements and political process with the standards of a polyarchic type of democracy. It means the active involvement of the widest range of people in political processes on the basis of their individuality and thus diversity as well as autonomy regarding the choice of their political role. Its main elements are participation and competition – two that are also dimensions of the Dahlean model of poliarchy (Dahl, 1971). Citizens' engagement in the decision-making process through more or less formalised channels is meant by 'participation'. It consists of all activities that serve the affecting actions and results of a political system (Goel in Smith, 1980: 76). The elementary mechanism of political participation is (both passive and active) participation in national or local elections. The precondition for that is universal franchise which is nowadays a necessary condition for labelling a polity as democratic. Besides electoral participation, there are also other important forms of political participation (like engagement in political parties and civic associations) which are of a more complex nature and demand more commit-

[3] System persistence is related to political stability as defined in a more narrow sense, i.e. in the sense of the robustness of democratic institutions. However, the ambiguity of the concept should be stressed, especially if the frequency of government change is used for the detection of political stability – an indicator that is very common in comparative studies (Lane and Ersson, 1987). While it is undoubtedly true that a high amount of turbulence of politics in the sense of very frequent changes of government – a low level of stability – has a negative impact on the quality of political life and on social development in general, on the other hand an absence of change in power positions, i.e. a long-lasting entrenchment of one political group in ruling positions (and therefore a high level of 'stability'), is also not conductive to the development of democracy. What is important for political stability is a proper balance between the reproduction and circulation of power-holders.

ment from citizens. Participation has some meaning only in the context of political pluralism whose main characteristic is the competition of different actors for political support which leads to the existence of political alternatives. For real competition to take place institutional requisites are necessary that, first, enable the autonomous organisational of social groups and, second, assure their equal treatment in the political and public spheres. The level of freedom and protection of human rights and civil liberties undoubtedly belongs here, as do some factors of the political system's environment – media pluralism is especially important here.

In general, *effectiveness* refers to the ability of the state/political system to achieve consensually reached social goals and the maintenance of the sustained development of society. Its two key dimensions are efficiency and transparency. Efficiency[4] is the ability of state institutions to attain and implement optimal political decisions and includes the performance of government/political institutions, competence and autonomy of civil service on one hand, and the ability of the state to provide the optimal functioning of social (sub) systems in accordance with their own systemic logic. Especially in the economic field it refers to relative openness and the absence of discriminatory regulation. Transparency (which to a certain extent overlaps with efficiency) denotes the 'visibility' of the relationship between different institutional actors, the affirmation of social behaviour in accordance with consensually accepted social norms and the sanctioning of violations of these norms. The existence of the legal framework is connected with transparency and especially the efficient performance of the rule of law. Another important element of transparency is related to corruption. Corruption can be defined as the misuse of public resources for private gain (Friedrich, 1972; Thomas et al., 2000) and is one of the most evident indications of the weak rule of law and inefficiency of state institutions and, conversely, the ability to control it is an important element of good governance.[5]

Presented conceptualisation of democratic governance is, to be sure, ideal-typic to some extent, meaning there is some overlapping between components, which are also rather strongly interconnected and interrelated. Without some persistence of an institution system, democratic processes

---

[4] Here, we refer to Etzioni's distinction between 'effectiveness' which means the extent to which goals (of an organisation) have been fulfilled, and 'efficiency' which means the costs of certain results (Etzioni, 1964: 4). In our case, 'effectiveness' is perceived in wider terms (it refers to general developmental goals), while 'efficiency' is seen in a more narrow sense (for example, the competence of public administration and its ability to implement a certain policy).

[5] Research on corruption is abundant; we should mention the research efforts of a team of researchers of the World Bank, the IMF, Transparency International...

cannot evolve. Efficiency of state institutions and especially rule of law is necessary for system persistence as well as participation and competition. On the other hand, inclusiveness, in a sense of active role of citizens and competition of political actors for their support (which, at least to some extent, means control of the citizenry over political elite), has a consequence of a more institutional efficiency and transparency of political process.

It is obvious that inclusiveness and effectiveness are complementary and mutually reinforcing properties. The latter was often neglected in the analysis of democracy and disregarded in the evaluation of democratic performance. Some authors have also rejected inclusion of a system's stability as an indication of the level of democracy (see, for example, Bollen, 1991). The fact is that it nevertheless forms the framework for both of the abovementioned properties to take place. However, it should be stressed that sometimes there is a trade-off between effectiveness and inclusiveness. As Diamond (1990) stated in his thematisation of the paradoxes of democracy, three major tensions that are inherent in democratic order have to be resolved: between conflict and consensus; between the ability to govern and representation; and between efficacy and consent. For each of these, a proper balance should be established in order for the system to function in an optimal way. In this regard, we would especially like to warn against the idealisation of participation as some kind of panacea for all problems of modern democracy. (In a sense: 'Let the people decide on everything'.) Excessive participation could, in the absence of appropriate institutional mechanisms, cause problems to the functioning of the political system and even contribute to its destabilisation. As argued by Moravscik (2004: 346): 'If democratic decision-making is pushed too far, the result can be the collapse of democracy, if not violent conflict.' The key element of good governance, in the sense of generating socio-economic development, is the accountability of power-holders (compare Berg-Schlosser, 2003). This refers to the fact that decision-makers do not enjoy unlimited autonomy but have to justify their actions (Held and Koenig-Archibugi, 2004: 127). What is needed to achieve and maintain it are both 'internal' control in the form of mutual surveillance of autonomous government institutions and the effective rule of law, and 'external' control in the form of the dispersion of political power, the existence of counter-elites and societal pluralism.

Empirical analysis of the quality of governance

Any indication and evaluation of the different aspects of governance is a very difficult task because of the complexity of the research subject, especially since we are mostly dealing with factors based on human action and which are therefore hard to quantify. For this reason, the analysis of governance is usually based on so-called 'soft' data, mostly data from public opinion survey and expert assessments. This data is then used in the form of individual indicators or composed indexes (referring to some wider categories).

A problem of such data lies in its subjectivity that could produce a biased estimate. Inappropriately composed survey samples can themselves produce such a bias. The data might not be reliable as an objective indicator of the situation if the answers are only provided by selected focus group that expresses their self-interest through them. The second problem is excessive normativism which could bring about similarly biased results – in the case of a lack of in depth information. On the other hand, there are also problems with 'hard' data. There is a problem of the methodology used in collecting such data. Besides, in many fields of human and business activity it is completely impossible to obtain valuable information. Some fields are simply not accessible through hard data, while for others, e.g. in the field of corruption, the quality of the gathered data depends on the work of the judiciary and the police and therefore does not reflect social reality so much as the efficiency of the judiciary and police. It is interesting to note that Kaufmann states that so-called 'soft' data – in relation to the data needed to construct indicators of the quality of governance of the research team of the World Bank – are even more reliable than 'hard' data (Kaufmann et al., 2003).

These are some of the problems and reservations a researcher must keep in mind when analysing governance in a comparative way. The methodological part of the paper is interesting in this regard, in relation to methodological issues, as is the part on the quality of governance.

Indicators of the quality of governance

The research survey *Governance Research Indicators Country Snapshot* (GRICS) has been conducted biennially since 1996 and its latest results were presented on 9 May 2005.[6] Using the GRICS data we can arrange EU member states and OECD members in different clusters according to the

[6] For more information on the survey, its methodology and results, see Kaufmann et al., 2005, as well as other articles written by Kauffmann and other authors. Many of them are available via the website of the World Bank and are also used by the research team of the IMF (cf.: http://www.worldbank.org/wbi/governance/).

quality of their governance. The survey covers 209 countries and territories. Its estimates and indexes are constructed on the basis of a very wide spectrum of more than 300 indicators from 37 separate data sources.[7] The GRICS defines governance as the exercise of authority through formal and informal institutions for the common good. Governance encompasses the process of selecting, monitoring and replacing government; the capacity to formulate and implement sound policies; and the respect of citizens and the state for the institutions that govern the economic and social interactions among them (Kaufman et al., 1999).

The GRICS measures the following six dimensions of governance: voice and accountability (various aspects of the political process, civil liberties, and political rights), political stability (absence of the likelihood that the government in power will be destabilised or overthrown by possibly unconstitutional and/or violent means), government effectiveness (quality of the provision of public services, quality of the bureaucracy, the competence of public officials, and the credibility of the government's commitment to its policies), the quality of the regulatory ability of the government to provide conditions for free economic activities), the rule of law, the level of respect for social rules and the ability to enforce them), and the control of corruption (the presence of different forms of corruption, attitudes to corruption, and the ability to control it). This empirical model matches well the concept of governance we presented above. According to this concept, the first dimension is the indicator of *inclusiveness*, the second one of *system persistence*, while the other four are indicators of effectiveness. Moreover, effectiveness consists of two additional dimensions: government effectiveness and regulatory quality are indicators of *efficiency;* while the rule of law and corruption are indicators of *transparency*.

The analysis shows that the dimensions of the quality of governance are strongly related to each other since the correlations between them are very or even exceptionally high (see Table 4.1). Correlations between voice and accountability, control of corruption, the rule of law, and government effectiveness are very high. Government effectiveness correlates exceptionally strongly with the rule of law and the control of corruption. The correlation between the rule of law and the control of corruption is extremely high. In addition, the correlation between regulatory quality, the control of corruption and the rule of law is very strong. Only political stability shows weaker correlations, although these are also very strong.

[7] The countries are assessed with values on a scale from -2.5 to 2.5 (a lower value is worse).

Table 4.1: Matrix of Pearson's correlations of the dimensions of governance, 2004[8]

	V & A	POST	GEFF	REGQ	RLAW	CCOR
V & A	1					
POST	0.686**	1				
GEFF	0.830**	0.666**	1			
REGQ	0.780**	0.773**	0.796**	1		
RLAW	0.866**	0.719**	0.965**	0.802**	1	
CCOR	0.891**	0.691**	0.957**	0.812**	0.983**	1

** the correlation is significant at the 0.01 level

We assume that inclusiveness, as one of three components of democratic governance, besides system persistence and effectiveness, plays an important role in the functioning of democratic systems as established and realised in advanced societies. In addition, we assume that the efficient working of the government and state apparatus somehow encourages participation, and vice-versa. Of course, it would be interesting to know the direction of the influence, whether efficient governance encourages citizens to participate in decision-making processes, and whether citizens' participation contributes to higher levels of the rule of law, lower levels of corruption, and government effectiveness as such. We can assume that it is a mutually reinforcing process.

Let us now present the situation according to the GRICS. Regarding *voice and accountability* (data from 2004, published in 2005), the most favourably evaluated EU countries are Denmark, Sweden and Finland, while among the ECE countries there is Hungary, followed by Poland and Estonia. Among EU countries, Greece lags behind all ECE countries while Italy is behind some of them.

Regarding *political stability* (in the narrow sense), the best ranking 'old' EU countries are Finland, Sweden and Ireland, while Greece is the worst. Slovenia, followed by Estonia and Latvia are the best ranking of the ECE countries. These countries rank higher for this dimension than many Western democracies like Italy, France, Spain and the United Kingdom.

Among EU countries, *government effectiveness* is most favourably assessed in Denmark, followed by Luxembourg and Finland, while the least favourably assessed 'old' EU member is Italy which is ranked behind all

[8] The following abbreviations stand for: V & A for *voice and accountability*; POST for *political stability*, GEFF for *government effectiveness*, REGQ for *regulatory quality*, RLAW for *the rule of law*, and CCOR for *control of corruption*.

'new' members except Poland. Among the new EU members from the ECE, Slovenia is ranked highest, followed by Estonia and Hungary.

Regarding *regulatory quality*, Finland, Denmark and the Netherlands are at the top of EU countries. Estonia as the highest ranking 'new' member is better assessed than the vast majority of EU countries. Other 'new' members like Hungary, Lithuania and Slovenia also rank higher than some 'old' ones (Greece, Italy, France).

Luxembourg, Finland and Denmark rank highest among the EU countries regarding the *rule of law*. Slovenia is the most favourably assessed post-communist EU member, followed by Estonia and Hungary, yet all of them lag behind all 'old' EU countries except for Italy and Greece (both are behind the first three transition countries).

Slovenia, Estonia and Hungary are also the least *corrupt* ECE countries and they again lag behind all 'old' EU countries except Greece and Italy (behind the first two). The top three positions in the EU are occupied by Finland, Denmark and Sweden.

When arranging members of the EU and OECD into groups according to the dimensions of governance by using hierarchical cluster analysis, two groups emerge.

Members of the first group are Australia, Canada, the Netherlands, Austria, the United Kingdom, Sweden, Norway, Finland, New Zealand, Iceland, Denmark, Luxembourg Germany, Belgium and Ireland. Of these, Australia, Canada, New Zealand, Switzerland and Iceland are OECD members, while the rest are 'old' EU members. Not a single 'new' EU member belongs to this group.

Members of the second group are all 'new' EU members, some 'old' ones, and the USA. The group is divided into two subgroups. Members of the first subgroup as Portugal, Slovenia, Estonia, France, Spain, and the United States. Of these, Slovenia, Estonia and Malta are 'new' EU members; Portugal, Germany, France and Spain are 'old' ones, while the United States is an OECD member. Member states of the second subgroup are Italy, Greece, Czech Republic, Lithuania, Latvia, Slovak Republic, Hungary and Poland. Of these, Italy and Greece belong to 'old' EU member states, while the rest are 'new' members. No OECD member belongs to this group.[9]

[9] As a starting point, we analyse 'old' and 'new' EU member states, while the analysis of the OECD only adds to the analysis as a 'control' part of the sample. A strict delineation between members of the EU and the OECD is impossible since many members of the EU are also members of the OECD. Since the focus of our analysis is on EU member states, we define the OECD members as states which are members of the OECD but not simultaneously members of the EU.

Graph 4.1 Hierarchical cluster analysis of the EU and OECD countries, according to dimensions of governance (GRICS)

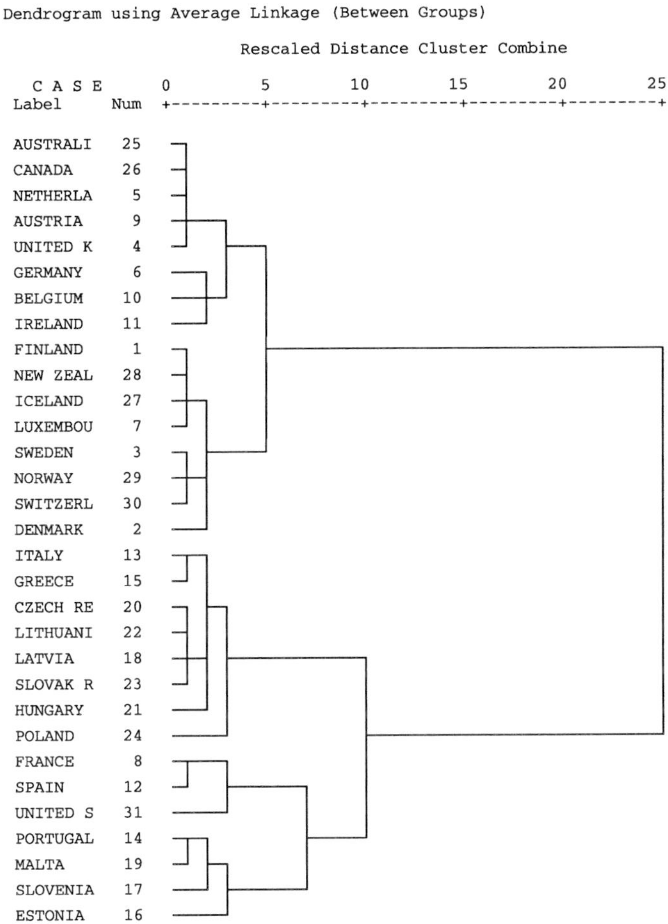

Therefore, as far as the quality of governance is concerned we can speak of three distinct groups, first, a group of excellence, composed of 'old' and OECD member states only, second, a group of relatively high levels of governance comprising 'old' EU member states, plus the United States from the OECD, plus Slovenia and Estonia of 'new' EU members and, third, a group of states in urgent need of revamping their governance, composed of 'new' EU member states, plus Italy and Greece of the 'old' EU members.

All in all, Italy and Greece are the two 'old' members of the EU that join the 'new' ones, i.e. a group of less advanced societies, according to the quality of their governance, while Slovenia and Estonia are the two 'new' ones that are joining the group of more advanced societies.

An assessment of the situation

Arranging member states of the EU into groups according to the quality of their governance using a hierarchical cluster analysis shows considerable differences between countries. We can discern three distinct groups, first, a group of excellence (the Netherlands, Austria, the United Kingdom, Sweden, Finland and Denmark) comprising 'old' member states only, second, a group with relatively high levels of governance composed of 'old' EU member states, plus Slovenia and Estonia of 'new' EU members and, third, a group of states in urgent need of revamping of their governance comprising 'new' EU member states, plus Italy and Greece of the 'old' EU members.

Comparing the EU-25 with other Western democracies (OECD countries), the latter reveal on average a better performance in terms democratic governance since all of them except the USA belong to the group of excellence. The latter is comparable to some large EU countries like Spain and France and, at least in some dimensions, not very far from the two most successful 'new' EU members.

Regarding the 'new' EU members from Central and Eastern Europe, we can say that they have successfully accomplished the democratic transition and the basic institutional requisites of democratic development have therefore been established. These are countries with a relatively consolidated democratic system, meaning that they have established the key institutional mechanisms necessary for the successful functioning of democracy (Adam et al., 2005: 102-103). However, regarding a substantial number of political indicators even these countries lag behind the majority of the world's most developed countries. It appears it will take quite a long time even for the most politically developed post-communist countries to achieve a level of democratic governance comparable to that seen in Western democracies.

It is interesting to note that differences in estimates between old and new EU members vary considerably from one dimension of governance to another.[10] The new EU countries from Central and Eastern Europe are the

[10] The range of estimates is smallest in the 'voice and accountability' index (from 0.91 to 1.59) and largest in the 'control of corruption' index (from 0.16 to 2.53).

closest to the EU core as regards their level of inclusiveness while, as regards transparency and efficiency, their lag is much wider. While they have managed to establish democratic standards close to those of old democracies, they still need to considerably improve the performance of their institutions, especially those in charge of the rule of law and control of corruption. This requires more effort and sophistication than the mere introduction of democratic order and is crucial for the successful development of modern society.

Quality of governance and attitudes to democracy and its institutions

Since democracy is the 'rule of the people' able to, in principle, impact on the selection of those who run the core political institutions, the attitudes of the citizenry can hardly be excluded from the analysis of the institutional performance of a democratic polity. In this regard, in addition to the data analysed above we present some 'subjective' data, i.e. data on public opinions on various democratic institutions, on democracy itself, and the question of whether individuals are satisfied with their livcs.[11] The results are quite interesting (see Table 4.2).[12]

Table 4.2: Pearson's correlations of attitudes to democracy and its institutions, and components of governance, 2004[13]

	LIFE[14]	PARLIA[15]	HEALTH[16]	JUSTIC[17]	EU[18]	SAT DE[19]	DE GOV[20]	DE BET[21]
IN	0.687**	0.569**	0.622**	0.706**	-0.057	0.635**	0.357	0.120
SP	0.540**	0.282	0.592**	0.680**	-0.109	0.423*	0.549**	-0.102
EF	0.532**	0.479**	0.590**	0.686**	-0.179	0.559**	0.509**	0.048
TR	0.603**	0.559**	0.634**	0.733**	-0.094	0.701**	0.503**	0.155

** the correlation is significant at the 0.01 level

* the correlation is significant at the 0.05 level

[11] Besides, these data stem from representative samples of citizens of respective countries. Data used for the assessment of various dimensions and/or components of governance are provided by various experts, business leaders, managers and analytical teams.

[12] We used the latest World Values Survey data available for a respective country. Most of them are from 1999. Not all countries used the same questionnaire, therefore the number of cases used in the analysis varies.

[13] The following abbreviations stand for: IN for *inclusiveness*; SP for *system persistence*; EF for *efficiency*; and TR for *transparency*.

[14] World Values Survey question (A170): All things considered, how satisfied are you with your life as a whole these days? (a scale from 1 'dissatisfied' to 10 'satisfied', 9 + 10 was used in the analysis).

As far as satisfaction with life in general is concerned, there is no doubt about the significant and strong correlations of satisfaction with life and all components of governance: the higher the satisfaction with life, the better the governance. Quite the same goes for confidence in various institutions, whether institutions are inseparable from a democratic establishment (parliament and the judicial system), or the general functioning of a system (health care system). The obvious 'outlier' in this case is the European Union. As far as opinions on the EU are concerned, they are scattered all over the place. It is interesting to note there is no relationship between confidence in parliament and system persistence, either.

We also analysed whether there is any relationship between the evaluation of the way democracy is developing in respective countries, the evaluation of whether the democracy is a proper system for governing a respective country, and the components of governance. Again, we encountered significant and high levels of correlations, with two exceptions, the absent correlation of the evaluation of the development of democracy and system persistence (still significant, albeit to a lower degree), and the evaluation of a democratic system and its inclusiveness.

In terms of Churchill's statement (democracy may be problematic, but it is better than other forms of government) it does not correlate at all, as in the case of confidence in the EU. We assume that both questions are quite theoretical, not based on experience, and therefore not related to the quality of governance in a respective country.

Therefore, we can say that opinions and evaluations of the general public in fact reflect the opinions and evaluation of experts, managers and analysts:

---

[15] WVS (E075): Could you tell me how much confidence you have in Parliament? (1 'a great deal' + 2' quite a lot').

[16] WVS (E084): Could you tell me how much confidence you have in the health care system (1 'a great deal' + 2 'quite a lot').

[17] WVS (E085): Could you tell me how much confidence you have in the justice system? (1 'a great deal' + 2 'quite a lot').

[18] WVS (E86): Could you tell me how much confidence you have in the European Union? (1 'a great deal' + 2 'quite a lot').

[19] WVS (E110): On the whole are you very satisfied, rather satisfied, not very satisfied or not at all satisfied with the way democracy is developing in our country? (1 'very satisfied' + 2 'rather satisfied').

[20] WVS (E111): People have different views about the system for governing this country. Here is a scale for rating how well things are going. (a scale from 1 'bad' to 10 'very good', 8 + 9 + 10 was used in the analysis).

[21] WVS (123): Democracy may have problems but it is better than any other form of government. (1 'agree strongly' + 2 'agree').

'ordinary' people can plausibly evaluate the quality of governance they encounter in respective societies based on the realities of everyday life.

Quality of governance at the EU level

Since the European Union has been developing in the direction of a more integrated form of political entity, the issue of governance at the Union is becoming increasingly relevant. In recent years the notion has gained in importance of the need to establish mechanisms and institutions of efficient and democratic governance on the supra-national level that are able to handle the problems brought about by globalisation processes, especially in the sense of the provision of global public goods (see, for example, Griffin, 2003) and enhancing the accountability of global actors (see Kahler, 2004; Held, 2004). In the case of the European Union, this is particularly important since it has stopped functioning as an inter-state association but instead become a political formation with institutions, activities and authorities on its own. What is often stressed here is the so-called 'democratic deficit' (see Norton, 1996), meaning the lack of many features we associate with democratic governance (Horeth, 1999: 249) like the involvement of citizens in the political processes at the Union's level and their influence on European affairs. One of the main targets of criticism of the process of European integration was its top-down nature that leads to it being perceived as an elite project or enterprise (see, for example, Dahl, 1999; Wood, 2002). The same elite-centeredness is also argued to be characteristic of the process of the accession of former communist countries from Central and Eastern Europe (see Raik, 2002).

In this regard, an important question is whether and to what extent the model of good governance described above is applicable to the level of the European Union. Aspects of democratic governance like system stability, inclusiveness and effectiveness are to some extent clearly important for political life at the EU level. However, it is impossible to simply transplant the principles of democracy that are in place at the level of member states into the EU institutions. There are certain limits to democracy at the EU level if one means by the term 'democracy' the majoritarian principle with the equal weight of each citizen's political preference (the rule 'one person, one vote'). The reason for this 'democratic deficiency' is the non-existence of a European constitutional *demos* (Weiler, 1995; 2002), i.e. a European-wide constituency sharing common values and identity that would replace – or at least complement – national ones. The European demos, European public and European civil society can only be established in an evolutionary way. In the current situation, the prevalence of unmediated political participation and corresponding decision-making on the basis of majoritarian rule would mean the domination of the biggest nations, thus causing frustration in many member states and potentially the disintegration of the Union.

This means that the model of indicators of good governance constructed by the World Bank team is only partly applicable to the EU level. This holds for the indicators of effectiveness, the rule of law and the control of corruption and, to a smaller degree, the indicators of political stability. As concerns political inclusion, especially its participatory aspect, the situation is different here, i.e. the status and role is not analogous to the level of the nation-state. In this regard, instruments for evaluating the quality of governance at the EU level should be modified taking into account the specific nature of this supra-state association.

According to the abovementioned, it can be argued that the establishment of mechanisms of vertical (electoral) accountability corresponding those in nation-states is, at the moment, not an option at the EU level. What is more feasible is the creation of institutions of horizontal accountability, i.e. highly professional, competent and autonomous bodies that would supervise the activities of the key executive institutions of the EU. In the first place, this means strengthening the European rule of law and policies so as to enhance the transparency of European policies.[22]

In the context of EU countries, the Union's institutional framework serves as a kind of 'external anchor' that guarantees the execution of democratic norms and principles. For the new EU members, integration in the EU, which was conditioned by the implementation of its core normative structure (including democratic standards), was an important factor in the consolidation of democracy. However, this type of external control is not unproblematic. It can neglect local specifics and be misused by external centres of power. Again, what is necessary is a proper balance of power or at least its dispersion to different political levels and actors that is achievable through proper institutional arrangements.

[22] Some analysts argue that the institutional setting of the EU already contains mechanisms to provide for the accountability of European policy-makers. As stated by Moravcsik (2002: 604): 'Constitutional checks and balances, indirect democratic control via national governments, and the increasing powers of the European Parliament are sufficient to ensure the EU policy-making is, in nearly all cases, clean, transparent, effective and politically responsive to the demands of European citizens.'

Quality of governance as a generator of social capital

The main factor that connects quality of governance with social capital is confidence. Elements of governance like government effectiveness, the rule of law and political inclusion influence the level of confidence in political institutions as well as the level of generalised trust. The influence also runs in reverse – institutional performance to a considerable degree depends on citizens' confidence in them. In this sense, two different courses of development are possible: a 'virtuous circle' where effective governmental and other political institutions strengthens citizens' confidence in this institution, which consequently increases their performance; and a 'vicious circle' where ineffective and dishonest institutions weaken the confidence of the citizens which then hinders their performance and reduces the possibility of improving their performance (in this case, because of mistrust in government and politics in general – in the sense of 'nothing matters', 'they are all the same' etc. – even well-intentioned and well-designed reforms are often unsuccessful). Besides, through the production of confidence and trust, successful governance also helps to produce and optimise social capital through its strategic action at the mezzo-level – in the form of intermediary negotiation systems where government in partner-like co-operation with relevant organisations and groups from different social systems participates in the design and implementation of developmental policies. To perform this role, government and political actors in general need a lot of knowledge and sensibility.

The concept of social capital can also be applied to the relations and functioning of the political system itself. It is a particular type of social capital that can be called institutional social capital[23] which refers to the ability for the co-operation and co-ordination of the actions of different institutional actors – as such it is an inherent characteristic of political system. Namely, government effectiveness depends strongly on the co-ordinated action of different functionally specialised government institutions based on their consensus about developmental orientations and goals.

Let us now present some indicators of social capital and the relations between them and the different dimensions of democratic governance.

Data on social capital – as measured by generalised trust as the most common indicator of it[24] – reveal exceptionally high levels of social capital

---

23 According to Collier (1998), there are two different types of social capital: 'government social capital' which appears as a consequence of the efficient working of the state apparatus and the government, and 'civil social capital' that emanates from civil society.

24 As a proxy for social capital we use the World Values Survey results, i.e. the percentage of respondents claiming »most people can be trusted«.

in Scandinavian countries, Norway, Denmark, Sweden, the Netherlands and Finland (68.4% – 56.2%), all of them 'old' members of the EU. The second group is made up of advanced industrial societies led by New Zealand (OECD), followed by Australia (OECD), Iceland (OECD), Canada (OECD), Spain (the 'old' EU), United States (OECD), Germany (the 'old' EU), Ireland (the 'old' EU), Switzerland (OECD), Italy, Austria, Belgium and the United Kingdom (all member states of the 'old' EU) (47.5% – 27.7%). The third group consists of 'new' members of the EU, yet it also includes three 'old' ones, namely France, Greece and Portugal (24.7% – 12.0%).

The analysis of generalised trust as a proxy for social capital and the components of governance also shows high levels of correlation (Table 4.3).

Table 4.3: Pearson's correlations of the level of social capital (generalised trust) and the components of governance, 2004[25]

INCLUSIVENESS:	0.684**
SYSTEM PERSISTENCE:	0.544**
EFFICIENCY:	0.612**
TRANSPARENCY:	0.596**

** the correlation is significant at the 0.01 level

It is evident that the level of social capital shows high levels of correlation with all dimensions of good governance to the highest level with *inclusiveness*, followed by *efficiency*, and *transparency*. Therefore, it seems plausible to assume that higher levels of good governance lead to, or are induced by, higher levels of social capital. Moreover, we have to note that the level of correlation between inclusiveness, i.e. the various factors that enable and encourage political participation (it is the *'Dahlean'* component), and generalised trust, is the highest.

In addition to generalised trust, we also used some other measures of social capital, namely those referring to citizens' civic involvement like the extent of belonging to various voluntary organisations,[26] and the global

[25] We proceed by analysing the components – as defined in our theoretical model – and not the dimensions of governance as defined in the GRICS project. We computed efficiency as a simple average of government effectiveness, and regulatory quality as a simple average of the rule of law and control of corruption, using the GRICS data.

[26] It measures the extent of belonging to various voluntary organisations, data extracted from the World Values Survey online database.

civil society index, measuring the inclusion of a particular 'national' civic sphere in global civil society[27] (Anheier and Stares, 2001) (for the results, see Table 4.4).

Table 4.4: Pearson's correlations of the global civil society index, the extent of belonging to various voluntary organisations, the extent of active involvement in various voluntary associations, and dimensions of governance, 2004

	Membership in voluntary organisations	Global CS Index
INCLUSIVENESS:	0.636**	0.797**
SYSTEM PERSISTENCE:	0.613**	0.574**
EFFICIENCY:	0.594**	0.786**
TRANSPARENCY:	0.591**	0.787**

** the correlation is significant at the 0.01 level
* the correlation is significant at the 0.05 level

In the case of the global civil society index and membership in voluntary organisations, all correlations are quite high and significant. Correlations with the global civil society index are even higher, although not in the case of system persistence. Again, it is plausible to assume that higher levels of good governance lead to, or are induced by, higher levels of civic involvement in voluntary activities, and a general 'global' orientation with values of tolerance and cosmopolitism.

Data on trust as well as other indicators of social capital show that the post-communist EU members in this field also lag behind the most developed Western countries (especially Scandinavian countries), while they are comparable with some other 'old' EU members (those from the Mediterranean region) (see Adam et al., 2005). The problem in these countries is the weakness of state institutions which impede the formation of good governance and, consequently, the strengthening of social capital. This is reflected by the low level of trust in key political institutions. A similar phenomenon, i.e. lowering the confidence in political institutions, is also present

[27] It consists of the measurement of political participation, the density of international non-governmental organisations, and tolerance, including the lack of xenophobia felt towards foreign workers, and the belief in encouraging tolerance.

in most established democracies (Putnam et al., 2002; Dalton, 2004), mostly due to certain malfunctions in governance (clientism, corruption, a lack of responsiveness). What is needed is effective institution-building, the establishment of optimal mechanisms for elite selection and selective engagement for political actors (a smaller but stronger state).

Discussion

The faith in building efficient governance, or the expectation that it will be built up spontaneously, is naive. Processes of reforms must be systematic and well-led: a conscious effort is also needed. Kaufmann and Kraay claim that only conscious efforts at good governance produce efficient institutions and that a high level of welfare does not produce good governance or efficient institutions by itself (Kaufmann and Kraay, 2002). Only efficient institutions enable economic reforms and developmental policies while, on the contrary, a poor institutional framework tends to reproduce itself and thus easily subvert any efforts at reforms (ibid.).

The quality of governance is a strong generator of different aspects of socio-economic development,[28] including social capital. According to our data, generalised trust as proxy for social capital is highly related to government effectiveness and other dimensions of governance. In further research, it would be interesting to establish the causal relation between social capital and the quality of governance. We assume that both are mutually reinforcing. Since the dimensions of governance in fact reflect the quality of the institutional environment, they reflect the 'government social capital'; therefore a detailed analysis of a wider range of indicators of civil social capital is needed.

What is especially worth stressing – and which has often been neglected in different evaluations of democracy – is the importance of the efficiency of state institutions. In this sense, we call for a more realistic, or in Schmitter's terms, 'postliberal' notion of democracy (Schmitter, 1996), meaning that some overwhelming participative involvement of citizens in the political processes is not feasible in today's complex society (where people perform so many different roles), thus control over the power-holders has to be per-

[28] Pearson's correlation of 2004 GDP per person, as measured by purchasing power parity, as one of the most frequently used indicators of the level of socio-economic development, and components of governance is also high. On this basis, we can assume that a higher level of economic performance and a higher quality of governance fit together well, with the sole exception of political stability.

formed by different specialised, highly professional and autonomous state institutions. However, there is the classical problem of 'who guards the guardians?' In this sense, control performed by the political opposition, the media and civil society is also necessary. What is needed is an institutional setting which provides a combination of mechanisms of vertical and horizontal accountability. It is interesting to note that efficient mechanisms of checks and balances also lead to better governance, including economic performance. Moreover, our results show that the dimension of participation remains important and that advanced societies with higher levels of GDP per person, higher levels of trust and better functioning governance show higher levels of participation and a more vibrant civil and political life. Therefore, participation is not something that is to be written off, rather it has to be complemented by the high quality of institutions.

It can be stated that governance 'matters even more' for small European countries, meaning their development and performance is more dependent on the quality of political institutions and processes than those of large and populous countries. Globalisation processes bring problems as well as opportunities for these countries. Small countries are usually endowed with fewer resources and are, due to their size, more exposed to influences and potential threats from their environment. Globalisation has been enhancing this exposure since many previously existing barriers are being dismantled and it is thus often perceived as a threat to the identity and sovereignty of small states. On the other hand, due to their small size they are more flexible and able to adapt to external influence. Further, they take adaptability as something necessary and do not pretend to be immune to outside (global) pressures. Globalisation of the economy brings evident advantages for small countries since it helps them overcome the problem of economies of scale (Griffin, 2004). For many years, some smaller European countries have been demonstrating they are able to make the most of a system in which they do not structure the rules of the game (Ingebritsen, 2004). They have been successfully adapting to the challenges of globalisation in a way that enables them to preserve their identity and high quality of life, and thus also a rather high level of political trust (Katzenstein, 2000). This ability to successfully function in the global environment not only applies to traditionally developed countries like Sweden, Denmark or Switzerland but also to some late-comers to modernisation like Ireland and even some post-communist countries like Estonia. These countries have managed to achieve a strong breakthrough in terms of enhanced competitiveness and efficiency and consequently a higher standard of economic and social welfare. In order to overcome their deficiencies and to make the most of their situation, small countries need an active approach in the sense of the skilful management of their potential and creation of their capacities. And this can be only achieved through efficient and inclusive institutions of governance.

Bibliography

Adam, Frane (1994) 'After Four Years of Democracy: Fragility and Stability', *Družboslovne razprave*, 15-16, 35-50.

Adam, Frane, Matej Makarovič, Borut Rončević and Matevž Tomšič (2005) *The Challenges of Sustained Development. The Role of Socio-Cultural Factors in East-Central Europe*. Budapest, New York: CEU Press.

Almond, Gabriel and G. Bigham Powell (1966) *Comparative Politics*. Boston, Toronto: Little, Brown and Company.

Ahheier, Helmut and Sally Stares (2001) *Introducing the Global Society Index*. London School of Economics.

Beetham, David (1991) *The Legitimation of Power*. Houndmills: Macmillan.

Berg-Schlosser, Dirk (2004) 'The Quality of Democracies in Europe as Measured by Current Indicators of Democratisation and Good Governance'. *Journal of Communist Studies and Transition Politics* 20, 1, 28-55.

Blondel, Jean (1972) *Comparing Political Systems*. New York: Praeger Publishers.

Bollen, Kenneth A. (1991) 'Political Democracy: Conceptual and Measurement Traps'. In: Alex Inkeles (ed.) *On Measuring Democracy*. New Brunswick, London: Transaction Publishing.

Collier, Paul (1998) Social Capital and Poverty. Social Capital Initiative Working Papers No. 4. World Bak,1-18.

Dahl, Robert A. (1971) *Polyarchy: Participation and Opposition*. New Haven & London: Yale University Press.

Dahl, Robert A. (1989) *Democracy and its Critics*. New Haven & London: Yale University Press.

Dahl, Robert A. (1998) *On Democracy*. New Haven & London: Yale University Press.

Dahl, Robert A. (1999) 'Can International Organisation be Democratic? A Sceptic's View'. In: Ian Shapiro and Casiano Hacker-Cordon (eds) *Democracy's Edges*. Cambridge: Cambridge University Press, 19-36.

Dalton, Russell (2004) *Democratic Challenges, Democratic Choices: The Erosion of Political Support in Advanced Industrial Democracies*. Oxford & New York: Oxford University Press.

Diamond, Larry (1990) 'Three Paradoxes of Democracy'. *Journal of Democracy* 1, 3, 48-60.

Etzioni, Amitai (1964) *Modern Organizations.* Englewood Cliffs: Prentice-Hall.

European Values Survey 1999-2000. WORC, Tilburg University. Tilburg.

Friedrich, Karl (1972) *The Pathology of Politics.* New York: Harper and Row.

Griffin, Keith (2003) 'Economic Globalization and Institutions of Global Governance'. *Development and Change* 34, 5, 789-807.

Held, David and Mathias Koenig-Archibugi (2004) 'Introduction'. *Government and Opposition* 39, 2 (Special Issue on Global Governance and Public Accountability), 125-131.

Held, David (2004) 'Democratic Accountability and Political Effectiveness from a Cosmopolitan Perspective'. *Government and Opposition* 39, 2 (Special Issue on Global Governance and Public Accountability), 364-391.

Horeth, Marcus (1999) 'No way out of the beast? The unresolved legitimacy problem of European governance'. *Journal of European Public Policy* 6, 2, 249-268.

Huntington, Samuel P. (1993) *The Third Wave: Democratization in the Late Twentieth Century.* London: University of Oklahoma Press.

Ingebritsen, Christine (2004) 'Learning from Lilliput. Small States and EU Expansion'. *Scandinavian Studies* 76, 3, 369-384.

Jowitt, Ken (1993) *New World Disorder: The Leninist Extinction.* Berkley: University of California Press.

Kahler, Miles (2004) 'Defining Accountability up: the Global Economic Multilaterals'. *Government and Opposition* 39, 2 (Special Issue on Global Governance and Public Accountability) 132-158.

Katzenstein, Peter (2000) 'Trust, International Relations, and Lessons from Smaller Democracies'. In Susan Pharr and Robert D. Putnam (eds), *Disaffected Democracies.* Princeton: Princeton University Press, 121-148.

Kaufmann, Daniel (2004) *Governance Redux: The Empirical Challenge, Global Competitiveness Report 2004-2005*, Geneva: World Economic Forum.

Kaufmann, Daniel, Kraay, Aart (2002) Growth without Governance, The World Bank, working paper, May 05.

Kaufmann, Daniel, Aart Kray and Pablo Zoido-Lobadon (1999) *Governance Matters*, World Bank. (http://www.worldbank.org/wbi/governance/working_papers.htm).

Kaufmann, Daniel, Aart Kraay and Massimo Mastruzzi (2003) Governance Matters III: Governance Indicators for 1996-2002, Working paper (draft for comment), The World Bank, May

Kaufmann, Daniel, Aart Kraay and Massimo Mastruzzi (2005) Governance Matters IV: Governance Indicators for 1996-2004, Working paper (draft for comment), The World Bank, May

Lane, Jan-Erik and Svante O. Ersson (1987) *Politics and Society in Western Europe.* London: SAGE Publications.

Lipset, Seymour M. (1959) *Political Man: The Social Bases of Politics.* Bombay: Vakils, Feffer and Simons.

March, James and Johan Olsen (1995) *Democratic Governance*. New York: The Free Press.

Moravscik, Andrew (2002) 'Reassessing Legitimacy in the European Union'. *Journal of Common Market Studies* 40, 4, 603-624.

Moravscik, Andrew (2004) 'Is the a 'Democratic Deficit' in the World Politics?' *Government and Opposition* 39, 2 (Special Issue on Global Governance and Public Accountability), 336-363.

Norton, Philip (1995) 'Conclusion: Addressing Democratic Deficit'. In Philip Norton (ed.), National Parliaments and the European Union. London: Frank Cass, 177-193.

O'Donnel, Guillermo, (1998) 'Horizontal Accountability in New Democracies'. *Journal of Democracy*, 1998, 9, 3, 112-126.

Olsen, Johan (2002) 'Reforming European Institutions of Governance'. *Journal of Common Market Studies* 40, 4, 581-602.

Persson, Torsten (2005) 'Forms of Democracy, Policy, and Economic Development'. National Bureau of Economic Research, Working Paper 11171, March.

Plattner, Marc (1991) 'The Democratic Moment'. *Journal of Democracy* 2, 4, 34-46.

Putnam, Robert, Susan Pharr and Russell Dalton (2000) 'Introduction: What's Troubling Trilateral Democracies'. In Susan Pharr and Robert Putnam (eds) Disaffected Democracies, Princeton University Press, Princeton, 3-27.

Raik, Kristi (2002) 'Bureaucratisation or Strengthening of the Political?: Estonian Institutions and Integration into the European Union'. *Cooperation & Conflict* 37, 2, 137-157.

Rigobon, Roberto and Dani Rodrik (2004) Rule of Law, Democracy, Openness, and Income: Estimating the Interrelationships, paper prepared for the Macro Seminar at the World Bank, accessible via the website of Dani Rodrik at Harvard University.

Schelder, Andreas, Larry Diamond and Marc F. Plattner, (1999) *The Self-Restraining State: Power and Accountability in New Democracies.* London: Lynne Rienner Publishers.

Schmitter, Phillipe (1996) 'More Liberal, Preliberal, Postliberal?' In Larry Diamond and Marc Plattner (eds) *The Global Resurgence of Democracy*. Baltimore, London: The Johns Hopkins University Press.

Schmitter, Philippe and Terry Lynn Karl (1991) 'What Democracy is … and Is Not'. *Journal of Democracy* 2, 3, 75-89.

Schumpeter, Joseph A. (1996) *Capitalism, socialism and democracy*. London, New York: Routledge.

Smith, David Horton et al. (1980) *Participation in Social and Political Activities*. San Francisco, Washington, London: Jossey-Bass Publishers.

Thomas, Vinod et al. (2000) *The Quality of Growth*. New York: Oxford University Press.

Zakaria, Fareed (2003) *The Future of Freedom*. New York & London: W.W. Norton & Company.

Weiler, Joseph H.H. (1995) 'European democracy and its critique', *West European Politics* 2, 4-40.

Weiler, Joseph H.H. (2002) 'A Constitution for Europe? Some Hard Choices.' *Journal of Common Market Studies* 40, 4, 563-580.

Wood, Stephen (2002) 'Germany and Eastern Enlargement of the EU: Political Elites, Public Opinion and Democratic Processes'. *Journal of European Integration* 24, 1, 23-38.

World Values Survey 1999. http://www.worldvaluessurvey.org.

5. Organised Civil Society in the Multilevel System of European Governance

Mateja Rek

Bridging the gap

The integrationist agenda pursued by European elites throughout the post-war period has amounted to a multifaceted constitutionalising project increasingly characterised by an overarching problem of political legitimacy. One can trace the impact of the emerging legitimacy discourse in a number of arenas. In recent years the debate on the involvement of civil society has largely been shaped by this debate. Civil society and its actors working at national and EU levels are often perceived and cited as crucial agents that will drastically contribute to the overcoming of many deficits and crises that the European Union is facing. These include a democratic deficit – a term that is becoming very well-established in both scientific and political debates. It is related to the realisation that EU institutions are increasingly, through a broadening of their policy scopes, and directly influencing the lives of EU citizens who, if we for instance consider the data from the Eurobarometer 2005, do not really care much for participation at the EU level, do not think that their voice is heard at the EU level and do not express high levels of trust in EU institutions[1] . Some argue that this might be

[1] According to the data from Eurobarometer 63 (May 2005) 53% of European citizens think that they cannot have an impact on processes at the EU level, while 38% claim the opposite. 53% of the respondents are satisfied with the democracy in their country. The percentage of respondents satisfied with democracy in the EU is lower – 49%. A decrease in the levels of trust in EU institutions is also evident. Trust in the European Commission decreased significantly in the first half of 2005 (from 52% in autumn 2004 to 46% in the spring 2005), similarly falling is trust in the European Parliament (from 57% in autumn 2004 to 52% in spring 2005). The dropping levels of the participation of EU citizens in the EU's political processes can be seen in the statistics about voter turnouts at elections to the European Parliament. Official data show that there has been a constant decrease of voter turnout since 1979, when 63% of citizens of member states voted at the elections. In 1984 this number fell to 61%, in 1989 to 58.5%, in 1994 to 56.8%, in 1999 to 49.8% while in 2004 just 45.4% citizens of the EU took part in elections to the European Parliament (source: Collaboration EP, Eos Gallup Europe, available at: http://www.elections2004.eu.int/ep-election/sites/en/results1306/turnout_ep/index.html).

related to the crisis of European identity (Shore, 2000), which again could be influenced by civil society actors since it is envisaged that they could foster the creation and development of European unification through its activities in what the European Economic and Social Committee calls the European public space (EESC, 1999, 2003; CEC, 2000: 5). On the other hand, many authors are worried about the crisis of politics which, among other things, presents itself in the tyranny of the short term looming, a high dependence on public opinion and a lack of long-term strategic thinking (see Delors in: EESC 1999: 44). There is also a crisis of the welfare state as to which civil society organisations could, both as service providers and as carriers of self-initiated action at the community level, help to overcome or at least help with finding and applying alternative approaches with win-win results for all included[2].

Let us not forget the positive contribution civil society organisations can bring to the multilevel character of the European construction. European decision-making depends not only on European institutions but also on the national, regional and local levels (Mazey and Richardson, 1999). Civil society organisations, which should by definition be in touch with the grassroots of society and on the other hand have (as part of their advocacy function) access to decision-making bodies, are often seen as ideal actors that can significantly contribute to fulfillment of the principle of subsidiarity.

But some recent research, albeit limited in scope, points to the conclusions that transnational civil society organisations in the EU are not necessarily bridges between the remote EU institutions and the everyday lives of citizens, which undermines one of the traditional roles cast for them in European integration – that of popularising the EU and encouraging a shift of perspectives among members from the national to European level. On the other hand, looking from the point of EU institutions it seems that they can only deal effectively with transnational and less so with national civic organisations and they seem too detached to deal with the multiplicity of local concerns. In that sense, it is important to ensure that local concerns

[2] Prompted in part by growing doubts about the capacity of the state to cope with its own welfare, developmental and environmental problems, analysts across the political spectrum have come to see NGOs as strategic components of a middle way between policies that put primacy on 'the market' and those that advocate greater reliance on the state. In fact, service provision was the fastest growing area of international NGOs' activities in the 1990s (Kaldor, 2003). With the rise of new public management, the emphasis on NGOs as service providers and instruments of privatisation casts them at the international level essentially in a subcontracting role. NGOs have become instruments of national and international welfare state reform guided by the simple equation of 'less government = less bureaucracy = more flexibility = greater efficiency'.

are sufficiently voiced by national and transnational civic organisations. The aim of this paper is to explore specific features of organised civil society at the EU level that seem crucial in determining its possibilities (or inabilities) to function as a bridge between the different levels of EU governance. The focus will be on the characteristics of relationships between EU associations and EU institutions on one hand and the relationships within EU associations on the other, while mainly considering the characteristics of relationships between the national and EU levels of organisations since it is assumed that strong links between those two levels are necessary in order to transfer local concerns to the EU level[3].

To do so, I will draw on some findings in the sphere of organised civil society at the EU level provided by authors such as Adam (1998), Greenwood (2002, 2003), Kohler-Koch (2005) and others. In addition, findings from a workshop entitled 'Social Capital, Civic Engagement and Quality of Governance in the European Union' will be used in the analysis. The workshop organised in December 2005 in Brussels by Frane Adam and Mateja Rek in the framework of the 6th framework CONNEX project was structured as a focus group. Focus groups are a form of group interview that capitalises on communication between research participants in order to generate data. Although group interviews are often used simply as a quick and convenient way to collect data from several people simultaneously, focus groups explicitly use group interaction as part of the method. This means that instead of the researcher asking each person to respond to a question in turn, people are encouraged to talk to one another: to ask questions, exchange anecdotes and comment on each others' experiences and points of view. The method is particularly useful for exploring people's knowledge and experiences and can be used to examine not only what people think but how they think and why they think that way (Barbour and Kitzinger, 1998)[4].

[3] At the same time, I would like to point out that analysing these linkages among the EU and national level provides only a very partial perspective on the issue of bridging the gap between citizens and the institutions of the EU. For a more holistic perspective analysis of the various circumstances of local civil society's development in particular national societies should be taken into account.

[4] The idea behind the focus group method is that group processes can help people to explore and clarify their views in ways that would be less easily accessible in a one-to-one interview. Group discussion is particularly appropriate when the interviewer has a series of open-ended questions and wishes to encourage research participants to explore the issues of importance to them, in their own vocabulary, generating their own questions and pursuing their own priorities. When group dynamics work well, the participants work alongside the researcher, taking the research in new and often unexpected directions. Group work also helps researchers tap into the many different forms of communication that people use in day-to-day interaction, including jokes, anecdotes, teasing, and

The aim of our focus group was to gain additional insights into current reflections on the role, functioning and characteristics of civil society organised at the EU level by bringing together practitioners (NGOs and interest group representatives, policy-makers etc.)[5] working in the field of civil society in the EU with scientists researching these issues. The focus group consisted of discussions and reflections on the following topics: 1) organisational aspects of civic engagement in the EU; 2) the role of civic associations in the EU's decision-making processes; and 3) the inclusion of civic associations from new member states in transnational European civil society.

As a result of the discussion in the focus group we can identify the following features of organised civil society at the EU level that seem crucial in determining its possibilities to function as a bridge between the different levels of EU governance:

- interest representation and influence orientation;
- balancing of private and public interests;
- fragmentation of the sphere; and
- internal organisational structural difficulties of EU associations.

In the following I will describe each of these features in more details, including the relevant literature. Against this background I will look for factors that either facilitate or hinder transnational co-operation and the coordination of organised European civil society in its attempts to function as a bridge between the different levels of EU governance.

The interest representation and influence orientation of organised civil society at the EU level

When defining the intermediary sphere Frane Adam (1998) does not only consider those associations and organisations which are usually added to

arguing. Gaining access to such a variety of communication is useful because people's knowledge and attitudes are not entirely encapsulated in reasoned responses to direct questions. Everyday forms of communication may tell us as much, if not more, about what people know or experience. In this sense, focus groups reach parts that other methods cannot reach, revealing dimensions of understanding that often remain untapped by more conventional data collection techniques (Barbour and Kitzinger, 1998).

[5] 14 individuals (4 scientists, 2 representatives of business EU associations, 1 representative of a think-tank dealing with EU policies, 2 representatives of civic EU associations, 4 representatives of liaison offices in the field of research and a representative of the European Commission) participated in our focus group. For further information on the participants and outcomes of the focus group, visit: http://www.connex-network.org/.

the civil society sphere, non-governmental organisations or the non-profit voluntary sector. This concept is enlarged to include mechanisms and networks which perform the function of inter-systemic co-ordination and communication and even various forms of co-operation and strategic links within a particular subsystem and its units. Adam points out that the intermediary sphere can be classified in relation to 'symbolic media', which form the referential or semantic framework that guides and structures the activities of the actors. He identifies five such media:

1. interests (to which professional associations, sport and cultural societies, co-operatives etc. belong);
2. influence (pressure groups, unions, ecological and environmental protection organisations, various discussion clubs, human rights activities etc.);
3. solidarity (self-help groups, voluntary activities etc.);
4. values (religious and spiritual groups, the local parish community, cultural activities of ethnic minorities etc.); and
5. community (citizens' initiatives at the local level, municipal and religious self-government, communitarian groups etc.) (Adam, 1998: 26)[6].

In the context of organised civil society at the EU level we can mainly establish the existence of the first two symbolic media, namely interests and influence or, to put it differently, interest representation and lobbying. On the other hand, the symbolic media of solidarity, values and the community remain bound especially to the local and national levels. The concept of participation within organised civil society at the level of the EU is limited to organised interests and groups (Magnette, 2001) and provides spaces of interest representation (Warleight, 2001, 2003) and not the active participation of citizens.

Interest groups can be defined and categorised in a variety of ways. They can be seen in terms of their organisational degree (peak associations vs. membership associations), their structure (traditional associations vs. spontaneous, unconventional initiatives and movements), their legal forms, or their motivational character. Much of the literature builds categories according to the kind of interests that groups pursue. Generally, public and private interests are distinguished. According to this classification, public

[6] As Adam (1998) points out, it is necessary to mention that this classification has a preliminary and heuristic value; the activities of specific associations do at times extend beyond their defining media. For example, at times professional associations function as pressure groups, while trade unions can also develop forms of mutual help.

interest groups seek benefits serving society as a whole, for example better consumer protection, improved environmental protection or lower taxes, while private interest groups seek to achieve goals for their immediate members only[7] (Lehmann, 2003).

The issue of balancing private and public interests came to the fore in discussions in our focus group and was obviously connected with the definition of civil society. Considering the numerous kinds of associations active in Brussels, we can see that behind these many forms there are very different values and very different interests which lead to the question of 'who is the real civil society?'

> … there are social affairs people, they call themselves the real civil society, and they would even define industrialists or lobbyists as not being part of civil society …
> — President, Society of European Affairs Professionals (SEAP)

We have seen that the definition which has been adopted was the definition of civil society actors organised at the EU level as defined by European institutions. In that sense, the participants of the focus group mainly referred to two major classifications of civil society actors that emerged in cooperation with civil society representatives working at the level of the EU in the framework of two European bodies – the European Commission and the European Economic and Social Committee – with the latter one being recognised as the institutionalisation of civil society at the EU level. In the documents of European Economic and Social Committee (EESC, 1999) we find the following definition. Civil society organisations include: (1) the so-called labour-market players, i.e. the social partners; (2) organisations representing social and economic players, which are not social partners in the strict sense of the term; (3) NGOs which bring people together in a common cause, such as environmental organisations, human rights organisations, consumer associations, charitable organisations, educational and training organisations etc.; and (4) CBOs (community-based organisations).

What is really disturbing is the unclear formulation under item two. This formulation might be taken as indicating that these economic actors are not

---

[7] Some authors challenge the common dichotomy between public and private interests (Young and Wallace, 2000). In their view, this assumption makes several false implicit assertions: that there is such thing as a single or predictable producer interest; that producers are in accord; and that producers by pursuing their own ends do not benefit the public good. An additional problem is that the asserted dichotomy between public and private interests also carries the implication that public interest groups always represent what is objectively best for society, while private interest groups are selfish.

seen just as potential but usual members of civil society. The reason for such a definition might be that representatives of economic associations form a major part of the EESC (as one side of the social partnership) and these actors want to be recognised as an integral part of the picture. Further, social dialogue is clearly well-established in the EESC and, although civil dialogue is seen as being separate from it, it may well be influenced by the older and better established structures of social dialogue. On a more general level, it can be easily pointed out that many EU interest groups are of an economic nature. Consequently, a strictly normative, non-inclusive definition would have excluded a large number of actors. Drawing a very strict boundary between the private and civil society sectors also downplays the interdependencies between them. However, it may be argued that this position of including economic actors into civil dialogue can only be accepted with a certain condition: economic actors are not *a priori* excluded from civil society if their actions are of a non-profit nature, are directed at the public interest and not only the fulfillment of private interest and are led by the principle of the 'free choice' and self-governance of those involved.

It is also relevant to mention the CONECCS definition of civil society actors organised at the EU level (CONECCS FAQ). It refers to the following organisations: (1) trade unions; (2) employers' federations; (3) professional federations; (4) NGOs; (5) service and production federations; (6) associations of public authorities; (7) political interests; (8) religious interests; and (9) other groups. By making a distinction between different kinds of business federations, the CONECCS definition is not only more detailed than that of the EESC, it surprisingly also includes political interests, defined as 'organizations, not themselves political parties, that represent a specifically party political perspective of Community polity or that have an interest in the party politic dimension of the European Union' (CONECCS FAQ). Thus, this definition is more inclusive with regard to actors from the political sphere.

Nevertheless, the participants of the focus group agreed that when assessing the state and role of civil society organised at the EU level, one must keep in mind the context and specific socio-historical development of the EU's construction. Certainly, much of EU politics is regulatory politics which, in distributing costs and benefits narrowly to selective constituencies, does make it suitable for interest group politics. There is little doubt that, as Greenwood (2003: 2) puts it interest groups are the 'natural constituency' of the European Commission in particular. Clearly, private and public interests contribute to the 'everyday policy-making' of the EU. As such, the activities of civil society organised at the EU level are linked to the decision power that has shifted to the European level. This brings us to the question: which interests are more represented than others?

As the European Union has an important role to play in the business world, it has a lot of decision power exactly in those areas connected to business. When it comes to the question of which interests are more represented than others, business interests, environmental, health and safety, consumer protection and other common market issues are set at the top of the list. But business interests are nowadays also faced with changing agendas such as Corporate Social Responsibility. They need to share the EU agenda with public interest NGOs. 'Back in the 1980s when the single market was being created, the agenda of the EU was dominated by concerns with wealth creation and competitiveness. Today, it is equally dominated by concerns to create a 'Europe of the Citizen' and to create a sense of legitimacy about the EU with the "average person on the street"' (Greenwood, 2003: 5). In addition, even though social policies mainly remain in the domain of national politics, the rise of social affairs and human rights civic organisations has been significant in recent years, even though when looking at organised civil society at the EU level as a whole they represent a smaller but ever louder part of interest representation and lobbying with EU institutions. In general, it can be argued that the large gap between this type of groups and the big corporatist actors in terms of their degree of integration and amount of resources is somewhat decreasing, albeit it is still significant. Looking from the technical point of view, whereby the specific know-how of lobbying is considered, it is clear that it will be easier for the business world to mobilise opinions and that an NGO will have a handicap simply because in most cases it does not know the technicalities as much. But as soon as we move towards politically sensitive issues, the picture is reversed.

> The NGOs have much easier access to parliamentarians who know that behind NGOs are voting people, and at the same time behind business people the voting people don't amount for very much in numbers. If one looks at the publicity one could argue that the balance between business interest and social affairs is being restored in that way. So, the power of lobbying of business life shouldn't be underestimate but, at the same time, as soon as you get to the political level, you see very clearly that NGOs these days have a very strong voice.
> — Secretary General, European Movement International

We could argue that the primarily symbolic or normative instruments that NGO networks employ to achieve their aims may compensate for the lack of material resources at their disposal that could place them at a natural disadvantage compared to self-interested business associations. As Ruzza

(2005) argues, public interest advocacy organisations can compete with powerful industry groups because their normative orientation bolsters their credibility and invites support from the media and public opinion. But if we consider only the numbers of organisations and what sort of decision-making bodies we can find on the EU level there is a huge imbalance and it does not favor social groups and organisations but strictly market-related issues. They argue that they are on the whole underrepresented.

> We often find that we are underrepresented in general. I mean, we have tried of course, if we also look at the capacity and how many people, just the number of people who are lobbying, the social groups are not in the majority. The amount of money that is being invested in lobbying and being represented at the EU level is certainly biased and we are being underrepresented.
> — Communication Manager, Climate Action Network Europe

In addition, the discussion in the focus group pointed out the diversity and complexity of European Union lobbying and representation, which makes any reliable generalisations very difficult. The relative ease of access and fragmentation of the fields and power partly explains the sheer number of 'lobbyists'. There are circumstances in which business interests can come to dominate particular dossiers with particular EU institutions. But not one type of player does, or can, routinely dominate a policy-making process with so many different levels of decision-making involving different institutions with quite different perspectives (Andersen and Eliasen, 2001). At the same time, the European lobbying landscape is extremely fragmented. According to Guéguen (in Lehmann, 2003) there are over 1,000 EU trade associations; around 750 NGOs (which represent consumers, ecologists, religions, families, Third World aid and so on), European representative bodies from around 500 major companies, about 150 regional offices, 130 specialist law firms working on European law (the large majority of which are of British or American origin) and an unspecified number of consultants, many of whom specialise in regulation and community finance programme monitoring. Although they are competing, the different types of organisations constitute an integrated ecology of associations (Warren, 2001). As Warren (in Ruzza, 2005) notes, in some circumstances they balance each other out and provide different democratic goods to governance structures. For instance, business associations might provide useful technical knowledge and information on the preferences of an important sector of society; they might effectively guarantee internal democracy as there are no exit barriers that stimulate an internal consensus and push out dissenters as identity-oriented groups might do. But their ability to represent society might be limited. This limitation could then be counterbalanced by the inclusion of public pressure groups. As Ruzza (2005) points out, it would be the task of decision-makers to ensure that a good mix of organisations is represented. Any such mix would, at a minimum, include a balance of vested interests and public pressure groups but also churches, trade unions, advocacy groups and social movements which is why EU institutions should continue to take an inclusive approach.

The relationship between EU-level civil society actors and EU institutions

Even if there is no clear agreement on how to balance out the private and public interests and who are the actors of civil society organised at the EU level, being a multi-form, multi-dimensional and multi-level phenomenon (which as it has been shown also has its up-sides), it is assumed that these civil society actors can play an important role in the processes of European integration in the form of representation (both quantitative and qualitative, on a national and EU level, at the level of special groupings regarding as well as functional representation), mediation, expertise, synergy between the market and politics etc. In order to express and utilise possible contributions, functional mechanisms of communication and co-operation among civil society actors and EU bodies are being sought and formed. But the existing mechanisms of co-operation and communication as possibilities for the intermediation of civil society actors with EU bodies are, as stated by a number of civil society representatives working at the EU level (EESC, 1999: 205; CEC, 2002), often left to the self-will and conditional openness of the EU's political bodies. A useful insight into the mechanisms and possibilities of civil society participation at the EU level is offered by George and Bache (2001: 291), who distinguish among three layers of civil society participation in EU policy-making according to the level of institutionalisation:

- fully institutionalised representation through the European Economic and Social Committee;
- semi-institutionalised social dialogue that gives the social partners the opportunity to participate in decision-making processes; and
- the lobbying of interests (the least institutionalised and at the same time the most common way of influencing decision-making processes).

The European Social and Economic Committee regards itself as being the institutionalised voice of civil society (EESC, 2001: 3). It is presented as a representation of various categories of economic and social activity, in particular of producers, farmers, carriers, workers, dealers, craftsman, professional occupations and representatives of the general public. This purely indicative list is deliberately left open as that best befits the evolving nature of civil society organisations. It is also important to note that the EESC was not created to represent national delegations, but European organisations, following common goals. Even if this is true, the members of the EESC are generally nominated by national organisations, although they are not bound to follow their instructions. In other words, they should be independent. The decision-making of the committee follows the consensus principle that is also perceived as the basic negotiating action in civil society (Machiavelli in: EESC, 1999: 24). As for the role of the EESC, it should be particularly visible in its possibility to guarantee the implementation of the participatory model of civil society. It should enable civil society to participate in the decision-making process and it should help to reduce a certain 'democratic deficit' and so underpin the legitimacy of the democratic decision-making process. However, the EESC is generally not regarded as a success since its opinions and actions are often evaluated as being 'of very variable quality' (George and Bache, 2001: 201).

Another form of civil society participation in EU policy-making is semi-institutionalised social dialogue that gives the social partners the opportunity to participate in decision-making processes. The Treaty of Maastricht established a regular consultation mechanism, the social dialogue, between the European Commission and what are termed the 'social partners', including the Union of Industrial and Employers Confederation of Europe commonly known as UNICE, the European Trade Union Confederation (ETUC) and the European Centre of Enterprises with Public Participation (CEEP). These organisations have played a decisive role in social and labour policies. Their functions include reaching autonomous agreements with the Commission, a development that has changed the social partners' role: they are no longer confined to a consultative function but have assumed 'decision-making' status. Social dialogue, nonetheless, is often paralysed by the members' diversity of interests. As the rights of civil society actors have grown within the social dialogue, and as the number of civil society representatives on the European stage has increased, there have been calls for an institutionalised dialogue with a true legal basis. It has been argued that such a civic dialogue is the best way to close the democratic deficit by expanding civil society's participation in the preparation of decisions. This is widely regarded as a contribution to subsidiarity and a means of fostering Europeans' awareness of the political processes in Brussels, thereby aiding the development of a European public space and a European identity. The idea is broadly supported by the Commission and the European Parliament (Crawley, 2004).

Regarding lobbying, the third layer of civil society participation in the EU's policy-making as identified by George and Bache (2001), the possibilities to represent civil society interests differ from one EU institution to other. Traditionally, the European Commission is regarded as being most open to lobbying by non-profit civil society interests (Mazey and Richardosn, 1999: 113). The European Parliament has less influence on the policy-making process than the European Commission or the Council of Ministries, although it has gained importance through the expanded application of the co-decision legislative procedure. However, as already acknowledged, the European Parliament is very interested in communication with civic actors as it is a good opportunity to interact with the electorate and to become a 'spokesman' for the voters' concerns, although this applies more to NGOs than to business interests. The European Court of Justice is also subject to intense Brussels lobbying. The Council, by contrast, is generally regarded as being the least open to lobbying – here an indirect route, through member states, is often more successful (see Mazey and Richardson, 1999: 118-199). In that sense, lobbying at the national level remains an important route for influencing the EU's decision-making processes.

The actors lobbying on the level of the EU need to take into account that the fundamental relationship between them and European institutions is one of exchange: EU institutions seek information, interest groups seek influence. If they want to have an influence, they have to provide information (Bouwen, 2002; Michalowitz, 2002). The Commission is the type of political institution where influence from an outside source can have an impact. The openness of the Commission to all comers is fundamental to its core needs to engage with civil society: Further, its role in initiating and drafting legislation makes it a place where its ideas and information injected into the early stages of preparing measures can be influential. But the Commission itself is divided into sections, committees and there is usually no united response to the problem, a systemic response. It is a complex institution in itself, '*but you can't avoid complexity because we have a great diversity and we have to respect that*' (representative of DG Research, European Commission). Accordingly, the politics of co-operation with civil society actors also vary within the Commission.

Similarly complex are the communication channels used to represent interests by civic organisations. According to the participants in our focus group their use is highly influenced by the procedures and structure of the

Commissions' body involved in the process. Usually a mixture of both formal and informal channels is used, but the combination of it depends on the process of decision-making itself, the possibilities that this process and the institutional structure offer. So lobbying requires good skills for analysing the situation and the process and then good skills for communicating with the right people at the right stage. In general, we could say, judging by the responses of the representatives of civic organisations participating in our focus group, that the use of informal channels of communication is much more established compared to the formal ones. Regardless of whether a person comes from industry or civil society, one has to analyse the process in which the decision is taken, then define the key elements and channel the right information through the right channels. The extent of knowledge and understanding of the EU machinery frequently makes a big difference between successful and inefficient participants in the lobbying theatre. The desired outcome being set as the dependent variable, stakeholders' expertise in the decision-making process can be taken as one of the most important independent ones. In that sense, it was outlined that building relationships with political institutions presumes certain skills and expectations from the civic actors at both national and EU levels: negotiation skills[8], a negotiation mandate, expertise, vision over a time span (long-term orientation) and skills to shape the (long-term) perspective[9].

If we take into account the abovementioned different layers of civil society participation in EU policy-making and the complexity of the communication channels used also incorporating the multilevel approach, we can assume that the transnational European civil society is developing into an 'hardly manageable' sphere of very different, heterogeneous and sometimes competing groups. In order to gain an influence in this diversified field strong coalitions among civic networks as well as formal access to the EU institutions can play a significant role. The larger the extent and the

[8] *'We are in a process of negotiations, so if each of us has negotiation skills, this is excellent because that means there is mandate, because everybody knows the position of each other and we can all progress together towards a common position. This is really important'.*

— Representative of DG Research, European Commission

[9] From the point of civic associations in the EU, there is especially a lack of a long-term perspective. There are very few civil society organisations which are aware of the importance of long-term engagement. In the decision-making processes a voice should be given to people who are really innovative in long-term issues they are concerned about. And that should be one of the main priorities of civil society. They are the only actors in the policy-making field who can carry the capacity to be long-term thinkers. The other three constituencies – consisting of business, politics and media – are short-term decision-makers. There are several issues concerned with that and this element is needed in political discussions.

more diversified the structures of organised civil society at the EU level are, the more important seems the question of the internal and inter-organisational structuring as well as access to EU institutions.

Up till now we have clearly emphasised the relationship between EU-level civil society actors and EU institutions. Similarly, the White Paper on European Governance (2001) clearly emphasises the role of EU-level civil society actors. It is the relationship between these transnational organisations and the EU institutions (particularly the Commission) that the White Paper envisages as improving through structured processes of consultation. Moreover, the focus of the White Paper is not just on structuring relationships within transnational civil society; it is more about managing the existing relationship of dialogue than about building new mechanisms. As Armstrong (2001) points out, civil society's engagement with governance cannot be reduced to this assertion and the lack of concern with a more multi-level and multi-dimensional European civil society is regrettable. Nevertheless, arrangements that prompt civil society organisations to tighten up their internal structures, furnishing guarantees of openness and representatively, and prove their capacity to transfer information or lead debates in the member states were stressed in the White Paper and perceived as an important part of attempts to bridge the perceived gap between the EU and national levels of organising.

The relationships within the EU associations – the importance of a feedback-loop between the EU and national levels

European consent is consent between member states and the structuring of EU associations mainly follows these guidelines. EU associations are mostly confederate structures, i.e. associations of national associations, that were set up by their members for the purpose of representing their political interests in EU policy-making (Greenwood, 2003); even though other forms are also present (individual-based organisations, virtual organisations etc.). Some recent research, albeit limited in scope, confirms the Commission's fears about public interest NGOs suggesting that they display little interest in educating their members back in the member states about EU issues but instead get caught up within an ivory tower world of Brussels institutional politics (Warleigh, 2001; 2003). The news that they are not necessarily bridges between the remote EU institutions and the everyday citizen undermines one of the traditional roles cast for interest groups in the European integration – that of popularising the EU and encouraging a shift of perspectives among members from the national to the European level. As Beate Kohler-Koch (2005) points out, overall the empirical evidence is sobering yet it does not come as a surprise. Just like in the national realm, public interest groups are a minority at the European level and are dependent on the support of EU institutions. EU associations have structural difficulties to act as 'schools of democracy'. Their performance is low, even when sharing the skeptical view that also at the national level associations have limited capacities to effectively fulfill this function (Offe, 1995). The reason is obvious: the majority of these EU associations are composed of national groups and not of EU citizens. When they are built on private membership or support they mostly act as political entrepreneurs in the market of public opinion. Their democratic effects are thus highly contingent. They depend on the particular relations with national associations and the structural conditions in which they operate. Kohler-Koch further (2005) outlines three conditions for successful member participation that can be derived from existing case studies, namely that vertical communication and co-operation within the multi-level structure of interest group associations will be stronger: (1) when the Euro group is dependent on its members' expertise; (2) when successful interest representation demands co-ordinated action at both the member state and European levels; and (3) when the choice of instruments includes the simultaneous use of an insider and an outsider strategy. As long as Euro associations can take recourse predominantly to independent sources of expertise and pursue their interest dominantly with insider strategies at the European level their linkages to their national members will remain weak.

The participants in our focus group painted a similar picture of co-operation and communication across different levels of the internal organisation of EU associations, even though they pointed out that, what Kohler-Koch (2005) refers to as an ideal model, is rarely achieved in concrete organisational settings.

Talking about European associations, ideally there is a European representation and membership – national members, regional members. In order to be effective in interest representation and in influencing policy decisions, all members should be well prepared to be engaged in the agenda of the discussion and to make compromises and good decision-making possible. It is highly important that everybody is prepared to find a common position and that this common position is accepted across different levels of the confederal composition. This is a question of culture, both the national characteristics that individual players 'bring to the table' as well as the organisational culture of a particular association. Once the composition has been agreed on, it is lobbied during the European decision-making process, preferably with one voice, at the national level vis-à-vis the national institutions and at the same time vis-à-vis the Commission and the parliamentarians in the EU. If everybody is well briefed then there are much greater chances of a successful lobbying outcome. Yet, as argued by the participants in the focus groups, this is an ideal model but in practice there are usually issues of communication and problems of co-ordination among the different layers. On one hand a specialised body of expertise is centered in Brussels and they are the only ones who have contacts, knowledge and up-to date information about the current state of affairs at the EU level. But at the same time it was argued that regional and national organisations, even though they are affiliated with the Brussels level, often do not recognise the importance of lobbying at the EU level or taking advantage of these affiliations for co-ordinated actions among different levels. In that sense, the vertical communication and co-operation within the multi-level structure of interest group associations seems to be very weak.

> In Brussels everything makes sense to everyone in Brussels. It makes perfect sense, all the policies, and the processes. But this needs to be translated down to the national level to regional levels and so on. And visa-versa, when it comes to this 'bottom-level' the information has to come back up.
> — Research Advisor, Slovenian Business and Research Association

Why is a feedback loop important for the lobbyists? The members give them support for lobbying and a negotiation mandate for lobbying at the EU level and often act as lobbyers at the national level. National members or, better said, national organisation and experts are usually correspondents for the EU level, feeding them with information from the national and local levels. Members provide resources for the lobbying activities at the EU level, which is crucial especially for the pressure groups of private interests[10] which are usually more dependent on the resources of their members compared to NGOs dealing with social issues, as the latter have easier access to funding by an EU institution. There is a need for a positive, well-informed communication loop between the Brussels level and the national level.

---

[10] *Of course it is our interest and our need to inform the membership on what is going on and to keep them interested, for the simple reason, as in the other case, they won't continue to pay my subscription any more .*

— President, SEAP & CERAME-UNIE

> Everybody is trying to get this loop up and running, but there seems to be a filter - the information gets stuck on the way down and there is rarely a feedback loop.
> — Secretary General, European Movement International

In that sense we could argue that civil society organised at the level of the EU and the national levels represents introverted circles that have in most cases only weak (face-to-face) links to the other level. The (horizontal) links between national representations are even weaker – which is an obstacle to building a stronger common position and identification with the organisation as a whole as federal strategies are especially effective when members can participate in more than one national group, thus weaving personal ties among these groups and reinforcing a sense of identity with the larger whole (Putnam, 2004: 278) – but as it seems building horizontal ties among national or local groups remains the future task of EU associations. What is the reason for this state of affairs?

Lobbying in Brussels is a very technocratic job. It is a profession on its own grasping specialised knowledge of EU affairs and contacts in a specific sector of policy-making in the EU. The national members are not interested in having the skills of an EU lobbyer and to be able to actively participate in lobbying, but they need representation. Another reason for 'communication filters' between national and EU levels was seen in the predominantly virtual form of communication among different levels. Members are geographically distanced from each other and in many cases they do not know each other or even the Brussels office does not know them personally. If there is no personal contact it is even harder to engage them in the process. If somebody is disinterested to begin with, if they only hear from 'Brussels' in a virtual setting, it is really hard for them to become actually get physically involved in the process. When there is just interest from one side in this quasi-virtual space; this creates problems and gaps in communication.

How can the communication between the layers be improved?

- Personalisation of experience: by trying to find ways to increase the human touch because this is ultimately the best way of communication. Examples of good practices are small-scale workshops and 'field trips'[11], which make the experience of the EU level tangible, applicable and more personal.

[11] *Well for example, for use, one thing that we do practically that we found very successful, well this is for our needs, are study trips. Just last week, we had one of our members here with us for two weeks. So he came here, he got to know Brussels, he got to know better what we do, we took him around to all the different stakeholders. So it is showing the people what is happening in Brussels*

- Leadership – leadership of the EU associations is an under-researched area but what can be detected is a lack of 'big' or, better put, European leaders. Leadership as perceived in the modern world is really an American concept. In Europe we have to redefine the concept of leadership in terms of the capacity to lead in a multi-national, multicultural and multi-lingual environment. Strong leadership figures who are present over a long period of time could have a stronger capacity to mobilise people for participation and to facilitate communication across the filters of different layers[12].
- Legitimacy – in the sense of having trust and confidence in certain organisations as opposed to others. There is a certain boldness on the part of European institutions and the civic organisations at the EU level to fulfill their goals and to present their implementation. Even the Commission and all the civic associations should have to legitimise themselves; by fulfilling their obligations to the members. This is broader than just communicating the ideas or being transparent. Incorporating legitimacy into the organisation's strategy could have positive effects for both communication and transparency.
- The issue of transparency – all of the stakeholders are calling for transparency – at the EU level and at the level of member states. A more transparent structure of communication could facilitate communication within the organisational structure. In this context, a problem of virtual or semi-virtual organisations was presented – in the majority of cases it is hard to identify their actual membership and the role of the members in the organisation.

Conclusion

The devolution of state power to non-state actors including civil society organisations raises questions about the role of these actors and, more spe-

that is important, not just telling them about it second hand. And they can also take the information down. It is our role to give them this information but also to apply it to their experience, to make it tangible, make it personal, so they can more easily understand what is the importance of Brussels. In reality, we are doing the same type of work as they are doing at their level; we are just not communicating it well across both levels. It is about making this communication tangible

— Research Advisor, Slovenian Business and Research Association.

[12] *It is much easier for people to follow somebody, with the face and everything, than to follow a concept and/or idea. People need to have ideas embodied in somebody. Otherwise, it is hard to catch the attention and energy.*

— Representative of DG Research, European Commission

cifically, about their democratic legitimacy. The democratic challenge is one of the reasons the EU is, for instance, producing a new constitution and fostering the development of organised civil society at the EU level that is designed to make the union easier to understand, more open and more efficient. It hopes this will help it connect with the citizens, to help to 'bridge the gap'. One cannot avoid tagging these processes with the label 'top down approach'.

When it comes to civil society in Europe, the Commission primarily takes into account the so-called EU associations which are predominantly federal (umbrella) organisations of nationally bound associations, and refers specifically to the Brussels-based governance arrangements that encompass civil society organisations. Moreover, the Commission perceives the Euro associations as transmitters of expertise and forums for discussion and dialogue. To a certain extent the lobbying function of these umbrella organisations in Brussels is also acknowledged. As pointed out in this paper we can mainly establish the existence of interests and influence or, to put it differently, interest representation and lobbying in the context of an organised civil society at the EU level. As such, the activities of civil society organised at the EU level are linked to the decision power that has shifted to the European level. Since the European Union has an important role to play in the business world, it has a lot of decision power exactly in those areas connected to business which explains the high share of lobbyists in these areas, even though as it has been pointed out that nowadays business interests are also faced with changing agendas such as Corporate Social Responsibility and concerns to create a 'Europe of the Citizen' etc. One of the features that we have not really touched on in this paper but which is definitely worthy of further attention is the question of the top down and bottom up approaches in forming EU associations, aloing with the assumption that a majority of the civil society organisations that address social responsibility and especially the 'Europe of citizens' agenda' are 'top-down projects' (predominantly facilitated by the European Commission) and therefore experience a number of problems with responses from the grassroots of the societies that they are addressing (European citizens). For business interest groups it is, in that sense, much easier to justify the legitimacy of their activities and to contain the representativnes' criteria as it is assumed that their formation is driven more from the bottom up.

In a predominantly pluralist system it is assumed that, although they are competing, different types of organisations constitute an integrated ecology of associations while it is noted in some circumstances that they balance each other out and provide different democratic goods to governance structures. The openness of the Commission to all comers is positive, while assuming that due to the high levels of fragmentation of the lobbying landscape in Brussels can assure that no one type of player does or can routinely dominate a policy-making process with so many different levels of decision-making involving different institutions with quite different perspectives.

However, the lack of reference to the social capital dimension and the vertical dimension of the multi-level governance of these Brussels-based governance arrangements is evident. It was argued in this paper that the symbolic media of solidarity, values and the community, that also presume active participation and not solely representation, remain bound especially to the local level and national levels. We have seen that organisations of both private and public interests are faced with a similar problem (while the issue applies more strongly to the former) of how to organise the flow of communication between the Brussels-based EU associations and their nationally bound membership organisations. We have pointed out some practical solutions of these intra-organisational arrangements aimed at strengthening co-operation and establishing a feedback-loop among different levels of governance, such as the need for the personalisation of experience (as opposed to merely virtual or semi-virtual forms of communication among geographically distant members), reassessing the role of leadership, and strengthening the legitimacy and transparency, among others. Further attention in research and applying of policies should seek to 'prompt civil society organisations to tighten up their internal structures, furnish guarantees of openness and representatively, and prove their capacity to relay information or lead debates in the Member States issues' (CEC, 2001: 15) and would ideally also include not just their intra-organisational capability to 'bridge the gap beteen the national and EU levels' but also their capacity to bridge the gap between two groups of, as it seems a fairly distant concept of civil society arrangements, interests and influence on one hand and solidarity, values and the community that also presume active participation and not solely representation, which remain bound especially to the local level.

The irony of all this focus on the transnational structures of organised civil society is that EU policies do open up spaces for civic engagement that hold potential to connect societal actors with transnational systems of governance. Though they may not directly bring about democracy-enhancing effects they nevertheless can function as agenda-setters and provide a counterbalance to state and economic actors. By providing an intermediary infrastructure they support the articulation and bundling of societal interests and are able to give their own impetus to the definition of these interests. But by placing so much emphasis on the need for a transnationalised and Europeanised civil society, the EU institutions seem to undermine the very claims for the inclusion of civil society which prompted the search for a means of bridging the gap between society and transnational governance. As Armstrong points out (2001), while the explicit objective is to further transnational co-operation EU policies focusing predominantly on the EU-level of organised civil society may in practice create additional obstacles and domestic civil society actors may further lose influence as transnational governance and transnational civil society take on greater roles – with a stress on representing interests and lobbying, while having only weak links among the different levels of EU governance, which does not really offer fertile grounds for voicing local concerns at the level of the EU.

Bibliography

Adam, Frane (1998) 'The Relevance of Social Capital and Intermediary Structures for the Creation of Systemic Competitiveness: Some Lessons from Southern and Eastern-Central Europe'. In: Srubar, Ilja and Adam, Frane (eds), Problems of European Integration: The Case of the Southern and East Central European Countries, *Družboslovne razprave*, vol. 14, no. 26, pp. 48-58.

Andersen, S. Svein and Eliassen, A. Kjell (2001), *Making Policy in Europe*. 2nd edition, London: Sage.

Armstrong, A. Kenneth (2001) 'Civil Society and the White Paper – Bridging or Jumping the Gaps?'. *The Jean Monnet Working Paper,* no. 6/01, Symposium: Mountain or Molehill?, A Critical Appraisal of the Commission White Paper on Governance. Available at: http://www.jeanmonnetprogram.org/papers/01/011601.rtf

Barbour, S. Rosaline and Kitzinher, Jenny (1998) *Developing Focus Group Research: Politics, Theory and Practice.* Thousand Oaks, London, New Delhi: Sage Publications.

Bouwen, Pieter (2002) 'Corporate Lobbying in the European Union: the Logic of Access'. *Journal of European Public Policy*, vol. 9, no. 3, pp. 365-390.

George, Stephen and Bache, Ian (2001) *Politics in the European Union.* Oxford: OUP.

Greenwood, Justin (2002) *Inside the EU Business Associations.* Basingstoke: Palgave.

Greenwood, Justin (2003) 'Demos Rules OK?'. ARENA Research Seminar, University of Oslo, 8 April.

Kaldor, Mary, Anheier, Helmut and Glasius, Marlies (2003) 'Global Civil Society in an Era of Regressive Globalisation'. In: *Global Civil Society Yearbook 2003.* Oxford: Oxford University Press.

Kohler-Koch, Beate (2005) 'The Organisation of Interests and Democracy in the European Union'. Workshop 'The Institutional Shapping of EU-Society Relations'. Research Group 4, Connex, MZES, University of Mannheim, October 14-15, 2005. Available at: http://www.mzes.uni-mannheim.de/projekte/typo3/site/index.php?id=478 .

Lehmann, Wilhelm (2003) 'Lobbying in the European Union: Current Rules and Practices'. Working Paper, Constitutional Affairs Series. Luxembourg: European Parliament. Available at: http://europa.eu.int/comm/secretariat_general/sgc/lobbies/docs/Workingdocparl.pdf.

Magnette, Paul (2001) 'European Governance and Civic Participation: Can the European Union be Politicised?'. *Jean Monnet Working Paper,* 6/01. Available at: http:/ /www.jeanmonnetprogram.org/papers/01/010901.html.

Mazey, Sonja and Richardson, Jeremy (1999) 'Interests'. In: Cram, Laura, Dinan, Desmond and Nugent Neil (eds), *Development in the European Union.* New York: St. Martins' Press, pp. 105-129.

Michalowitz, Irina (2002) 'Beyond Corporatism and Pluralism: Towards a New Theoretical Framework'. In: Warkeigh, Alex and Fairbrass, Jenny (eds): *Influence and Interests in the European Union: The New Politics of Persuasion and Advocacy*, London: Europa Publications, pp. 35-53.

Offe, Claus (1995) 'Some Skeptical Considerations on the Malleability of Representative Institutions'. In: Cohen, Joshua and Rogers, Joel (eds), *Associations and Democracy*, London: Verso, pp. 114-132.

Putnam, D. Robert and Feldstein, Lewis (2004), *Better Together: Restoring the American Community.* New York: Simon & Schuster.

Ruzza, Carlo (2002) 'Frame Bridging and the New Politics of Persuasion, Advocacy and Influence'. In: Warleigh, Alex and Fairbrass, Jenny (2002): *Influence and Interests in the European Union: The New Politics of Persuasion and Advocacy.* London: Europa, pp. 93-118.

Ruzza (2005) 'Organized Civil Society and the EU level'. Paper presented at the European Consortium for Political Research (ECPR) General Conference Budapest, 8-11 September 2005.

Shore, Cris (2000) *Building Europe: The Cultural Politics of European Integration.* London, New York: Routledge.

Warleigh, Alex (2001) 'Europeanizing Civil Society: NGOs as Agents of Political Socialization'. *Journal of Common Market Studies*, vol. 39, no. 4, pp. 619-39.

Warleigh, Alex (2003) Informal Governance: 'What Contributions to the Legitimacy of the EU?'. In: Christansen, Thomas and Piattoni, Simona (eds), *Informal Governance in the European Union.* Aldershot: Edward Elgar Publications, pp. 22-35.

Warren, E. Mark (2001) *Democracy and Association.* Princeton, Oxford: Princeton University Press.

Young, Alasdait and Wallace, Helen (2000) *Regulatory Politics in the Enlarging European Union: Weighing Civic and Producer Interests.* Manchester: Manchester University Press.

Sources

Commission of the European Communities (2000) 'The Commission on Non-Governmental Organizations: Building a Strong Partnership'. Available at: http://europa.eu.int/infonet/library/f/20001 l/en.pdf.

Commission of the European Communities (2001) 'European Governance. A White Paper'.Available at: http://europa.eu.int/comm/governance/governance_eu/index_en.htm.

Crowley, Andrew (2004) 'Establishing Consultation Mechanisms with Civil Society in Integration and Trade Initiatives: A Dialogue Between the Andean Community and the European Union'. Semenar Report, Inter-Americal Developement Bank and European Commission. Available at: http://www.iadb.org/europe/PDFs/SOE_PAPER_SERIES/Lima%20Conference%20Report_final.pdf.

Eurobarometer 63 (2005) Standard Eurobarometer (Spring 2005). Available at: http://europa.eu.int/comm/public_opinion/archives/eb/eb63/eb63_en.htm.

European Economic and Social Committe (1999) 'The Civil Society Organized at European Level'. Proceedings of the first Convention, Brussels, 15 and 16 October 1999.

European Economic and Social Committe (2003) 'Social Dialogie, Civil Dialogie and Social Economy'. Working Seminar Organized by the Socio-Economic Category of the European Economic and Social Committee, 28 October 2003. Available at: http://www.esc.eu.int/pages/en/acs/events/28_10_03_social_dialogue/index_en.htm.

Transcript of the Workshop on Social Capital, Civic Engagement and Quality of Governance in the European union (CONNEX RG5), Organised by Prof. Dr. Frane Adam and M. A. Mateja Rek from the Centre for Theoretical Sociology, Faculty of Social Sciences, University of Ljubljana, 1. December 2005, Brussels. Further information about the workshop is available at: http://www.mzes.uni-mannheim.de/projekte/typo3/site/fileadmin/research%20groups/5/RG5-minutes-users-workshop-Brussels-1-dec-2005.pdf.

6. Religion and Social Capital: the Diversity of European Regions

Igor Bahovec, Vinko Potočnik and Siniša Zrinščak

Introduction

In contemporary Western society religion is one of those subjects about which specialists hold very different opinions. Due to secularisation processes, some scholars are convinced that religion does not play an important social role in Western civilisation. Similar opinions can be found when certain authors write about social capital, for they pay little attention to religion as a source of social capital or simply do not mention it at all. On the other hand, research undertaken in the last few decades reveals different expressions of the revival and revitalisation of social religion (Beckford and Luckmann, 1989). In her influential writings Davie shows different religious images of various parts of Europe, very often the unexpected ways in which religion matters (i.e. controversies about religion as public/private matters or still controversial ideological debates on religious influence today) and important differences between Europe and other parts of the world (Davie, 2000; 2002). In a similarly but sharper way, Berger (1999) is even developing a desecularisation thesis; according to him the world today is massively religious with two exceptions: (Western) Europe and an international subculture composed of people with Western-type higher education, especially in the humanities and social sciences. Others (like Norris and Inglehart, 2004) have used the secularisation thesis with certain limitations, while many others are trying to understand religious influence in contemporary societies beyond the secularisation/revitalisation division.

When speaking about the impact of religion on social capital it is meaningful to start with the observation that some key authors in the area of social capital, such as James Coleman and Robert Putnam, consider religion to be an important and/or indispensable source of certain segments of social capital. Many authors analyse a direct link between the indicators of religion and the indicators of social capital: trust, voluntary work, voluntary associations as well as informal gatherings and close bonds in primordial groups. In the majority of these cases, religion is treated more or less in the same way as other sources of social capital in the domain of private life and civil society, i.e. as a source of civic norms and associations.

On the other hand, the impact of (the type of) religion as a whole on society should be taken into account, i.e. religion as a carrier of cultural and ethnic orientations, meanings and symbols that make up a constituent part of social and cultural identity. Religions have not only bound together people and cultures, individuals and community/society, but placed everyday events within the context of the eternal, they have placed individual and communal life within the framework of the entirety of natural, socio-cultural and otherworldly reality.

As a result, our thesis is that we cannot exclusively look for an answer to the question of the social capital of religion in the social dimensions of religion without showing how they are included in the whole of religion. Thus, it can be expected that religion's impact on social capital depends on one hand on the variations between religiously different parts of Europe.

We presume that religion influences – albeit in different ways, according to various religious-cultural traditions – at least some aspects of social capital. We presume there are important differences based on various religious-cultural traditions concerning trust and other indicators of social capital. The question in this regard is which division of Europe is the most appropriate here: into two parts (Western and Eastern (ex-communist) Europe), four parts (denominational traditions: Protestant, Catholic, Orthodox and religious mixed religions), five parts (Scandinavian Protestant countries, Roman-Mediterranean Catholic countries, non-Roman (Germanic) Western countries, Central European (ex-communist) countries, Orthodox (mostly Slavic) Eastern European)? We also presume there are differences in terms of individual religiosity, attendance at religious rituals and belonging to volunteer religious organisations.

This chapter first presents the results of some studies about religion and social capital. In the second part we will analyse the European Value Survey 1999/2000 data (and partly also the European Social Survey data) to try to answer the question of how cultural-religious differences are reflected in the indicators of social capital. In the conclusion we shall link the results of the analysis with the question of social development.

Some findings on the relationship between religion and social capital in the literature

One of the first chapters in the development of social capital theory is linked to religion. James Coleman was led to the concept of social capital by a study of education in the USA, first of all regarding the greater successfulness of private Catholic schools than other private schools and public schools. According to Coleman, the underlying reasons involve several interlinked reasons but one that strongly prevails is the fact that these schools had better developed active co-operation with parents and bonds with civil communities of the environment, especially religious and local ones. The social capital emerging from these relations together with other conditions of good schooling (for example high standards, better discipline, successful integration of economically and culturally deprived students[1]) significantly contributed to the more successful education in private Catholic schools. In other words, religious social (and cultural) capital together with other socio-cultural resources leads to better education.

While Coleman underlines the importance of primordial groups (family, neighbourhood, religious community, people of the same age; most of them can be called 'small life-worlds' ('*kleine Lebenswelten*', Luckmann), Putnam draws attention to religion as a generator of secondary association linkages, that is the bonding and bridging dimensions of social capital. In a study of social capital in the USA Putnam (2000) shows that Churches, synagogues and mosques as well as various associate forms connected to religion (ranging from church choirs, various volunteer associations to youth work etc.) – in spite of their obvious diminishment in the past few decades – still remain an important milieu of civil life, a school of civil culture, trust and civic norms.[2] Putnam (2000: 66) states that 'faith communities in which people worship together are arguably the single most important repository of social capital in America'. However, this does not mean that religious practices and communities and associations connected to religions usually contribute to 'positive' civic social capital, that is, to the common good of society. Putnam (1993: 107-109) also showed that in Southern Italy an organised Catholic community is 'an alternative to the civic community'. The civic community in (Southern) Italy is a secular community. Yet, since two other parts of Italy showed a different picture – the EVS data from

[1] When comparing children of similar backgrounds, the authors discovered that students performed about one grade level higher in Catholic schools. Low-income and minority students in particular did better in Catholic schools than in public schools. Coleman and Hoffer (*Public and Private High Schools: The Impact of Communities*, 1987) show that Catholic schools were functioning better to diminish the effect of family culture and income.

[2] Moreover, in *Bowling Alone* Putnam argues that, as churches have traditionally played a vital role in American civic life, the process of secularisation has significantly contributed to the erosion of community activism. Putnam regards religious organisations, particularly Protestant churches, as uniquely important for American civic society.

1981 and 1990 also show a modest positive link between religiosity and social capital (Halman and Pettersson, 2003: 181-182) – it seems that more relevant reasons for the 'non-civility' of Catholic Southern Italy are connected with cultural and historical development, and with the prevailing hierarchical structure of the Church in that part of Italy. All in all, Putnam's study of the development of democracy in three parts of Italy showed that, beside the associate factor, other factors also need to be considered, above all the cultural and historical circumstances and the level of norms of civility.

Social capital debates frequently highlight questions linked with democracy and capitalism. According to contemporary authors, democracy needs sources which cannot be produced by the democratic state itself. Some have stressed the importance of intermediary institutions and a mediating structure (Durkheim, 1933 [1893]; Berger and Neuhaus, 1996 [1977]; Berger and Luckmann, 1995) or communitarian elements (Selznick, 1992; Etzioni, 1994; Bellah, 1995/96), others like Dahrendorf and Wuthnow (2003) place the importance of rebuilding the institutional aspect of our human life in the centre of development. Common to all these approaches is that the core problem of contemporary Western civilisation is its too individualistic understanding of our human life. This is not surprising since both central institutions of Western societies – that is democracy and the free market – are according to Bellah (1995/1996) individualistic by their very nature. Yet, the positive development of both needs communitarian resources and social capital. Although the state and free market cannot by themselves produce enough social capital elements, the state and the free market are very important in view of the fact that they have the resources to enable structural frameworks (economic and political mechanisms) for the positive development of these elements.

Conceptualising social capital

Thorough and systematic research into the influence of religion on social capital is a complex task due to the variety of factors regarding religion as well as the potential influence on religion that must be taken into account. The fact that there is no unified conceptualisation of social capital, nor for its operationalisation, makes this task even more difficult.[3]

[3] For example, Smidt (2003) argues that in some cases differences in the conceptualisation and choices of indicators (religion and/or social capital) are so great that they influence interpretation, leading to different interpretations, or even to different conclusions.

According to Coleman (1994: 302), social capital is 'defined by its function. It is not one whole entity, but it represents differences of resources, which have two groups of characteristics: all are made of some social structure's points of view and they make an easy individual's activity in this structure'. The basic ingredients of social capital are trust, networks, participation and norms of reciprocity (trustworthiness).

We subscribe to the thesis that social capital is – as with any other capital – a quantity which can be used either to benefit or to damage individuals and society. It is reasonable to distinguish among different social capitals as well as different contexts of social capital. Social capital is, according to Putnam (2001: 41-42), much like physical capital, anything but homogeneous: 'Some forms of social capital are good for certain things and not for others'.

To understand the complexity of religious influence on social capital, it is useful to impose certain distinctions. First, it is necessary to distinguish among the three subtypes of social capital: bonding, bridging and linking social capital. The term *bonding* applies to links inside (close) groups/communities; *bridging* applies to relationships outside close-knit groups (for example, relationships with other groups and individuals) and between different social status (Wuthnow, 2002) – while *linking* refers to relationships with the wider institutional environment (state institutions, the economy etc.) (Woolcock, 2001; Field, 2003).

Social capital includes a structural dimension (links, networks, organisations) and a cultural dimension (norms of reciprocity, trust etc.). Some authors distinguish between the structural, relational and cognitive aspects or dimensions of social capital (Naphiet and Ghosal, 1998; Norris and Inglehart, 2004). This conception emphasises the role of a wider environmental cultural mentality, i.e. the system of meanings, interpretations, habits, values etc. We believe that the role of the interrelated influence of cultural mentality, cognition and (interpersonal and intergroup) relations are essential for understanding the religious impact on the social capital since they lie within the very essence of religion.

Authors in the area of the social capital concept argue it is necessary to view social capital as a linked whole, which is why we cannot treat any of its parts (or indicators) in isolation from the others. Different kinds of social capital are suitable for different purposes. Coleman associated successful education with the complementary effects of primordial groups interpreted in mutual interrelationships. Primordial groups contain entire sets of lifestyle differences which make them different from 'constructed' groups (their relative durability and transfer from generation to generation and which leads towards permanent and more solid forms of social capital).[4] This kind of social capital does not necessarily also lead to a better economy, better democratic development and a more healthy society (also see Nemeth and Luidens, 2003; Woolcock, 2001).

Religion and social capital

As an integral interpretation of life, religion includes several dimensions, some of which we consider are worth mentioning at this point. The word 'religion' stems from Latin, *re-ligare,* which means 'to connect' or 'to re-connect'. Specifically, we refer to the following kinds of connections: (1) the relation of a person to man's transcendent reality, God; (2) relationships and links with other people; (3) an individual's attitude to created nature as a whole and the human socio-cultural reality; and (4) an integral relationship with (attitude to) one's own self. Although it is possible to analytically distinguish between different dimensions of religion, in all religious systems they are always interconnected and mutually conditioned.

An important link between religion and social capital can be understood through the ethical teaching of religions. All world religions require that you have to do others the same as you would want them to do to you. Through this requirement religion expands the range of human obligations from self, family and friends to neighbours, visitors and unknown strangers; religion expands responsibility beyond family, village or ethnical group boundaries. Realisations of these ethic principles stimulate the development of civic norms and virtues, community integration and responsibility for other individuals and communities.

That is why religious bonding, bridging and linking (all of them in principle and as a tendency) are unable to remain – in comparison with some other forms of civic associations – solely at the instrumental level of reaching certain/particular aims. Religious linking inseparably comprises the question of profound identity, the dimension of one's relationship with superhuman reality, nature and history, past and future. In this sense, reli-

[4] Similar findings concerning religious influence on the moral education of youth are reported by Ebstyne King and Furrow (2004: for example 710). Religiously more active young people are more likely to interact with, trust and to share similar perspectives with a non/familiar adult than those who are less or not at all involved in religious activities. However, general religiousness can be interpreted as a necessary but insufficient condition for such an outcome. Social capital associated with religion is the most effective determining factor of moral development among young people, however in connection with religion three social resources – family, friends and non-familiar adults – are the most important for establishing a durable network of relationships.

gious social capital not only limits itself to achieving specific aims about living in this world but also locates these aims within the context of the whole human existence on Earth.

The relevant analyses of how both instrumental and substantial religion impact on social capital should include three levels: 'the level of individual religiousness; the level of religious organisations; and the level of the society in which that action takes place' (Ammerman, 1997: 203). In practice, this means that beside the individual religiosity and religious community aspects the cultural-historical and structural aspects should also be included in the analysis.

A great part of vital civic sociability is done in a good way by small vital communities (from family to small groups) and broader civil society associations. In this sense, religion plays an important role because it is strong source of civility. For America, the authors of 'Bettertogether' (2000) stressed that nearly half of the stock of social capital is religious or connected with religions regardless of whether it is concern associational membership, philanthropy or volunteering. For Europe, this share is smaller and differs according to different regions – but it is still important (Norris and Inglehart, 2004; de Hart, 2001; also see the different authors in Arts, Hagenaars, and Halman, 2003). In this regard the classification of societies used in Norris and Inglehart (2004: 44 ss.) analysis of religion's impact on politics worldwide is significant. Their classification includes two categories: historically predominant major religions (Christian: Catholic, Protestant and Orthodox, Muslim and Eastern religions) and economic development (agrarian, industrial and post-industrial). We also expect political history (especially a Communist past) can play an important role and should be taken into consideration.

Some aspects of religion as a source of social capital

Charities

Charity is the basic form of a solidarity relationship with others. Charity can be understood as part of (informal) social capital – although some social capital authors do not pay any attention to it.

Certain degrees of charity exist in all human societies regardless of the differences in the religious or unreligious orientations of individuals and cultures.[5] Some contemporary research studies show that religious people

[5] In this regard, Ammerman (1997) stressed the importance of religious practices for charity:

contribute more to charity than non-religious individuals (Nemeth and Luiders, 2003; Greeley, 1997). But is this limited to intra-community charity (as an expression of an exclusively bonding dimension) or not? So far, research has shown that religious individuals are more likely to contribute to non-religious charities than those who are not members of religious organisations, and tend to spend greater sums of money on charity. The decisive religious factor seems to be attendance at religious services. It could be interpreted that community experience is a necessary condition for an increased engagement in charity work. Similar findings are found in the USA and Canada (Greeley, 1997; Nemeth and Luidens, 2003; Smidt et al., 2003), in the Netherlands (Dekker et al., 1999), and Finland (Yeung, 2004).

Belonging to voluntary associations and active voluntary involvement

Material philanthropic contributions to charity are an important indicator of human interconnectedness and solidarity. However, greater impacts on social capital have more permanent and durable forms of social networks and active volunteering. Most researchers agree on an interpretation that membership in volunteer associations and active participation in such organisations (or volunteering for them) is a good indicator (or predictor) in this regard.

Some researchers doubt the adequacy of these data to provide solid grounds for establishing the level of social capital. We feel, however, that the analysis of these data does offer some important insights regarding the state of social capital.

As a reference point within the quantitative interpretation of the associative aspect of religion we propose the findings of Norris and Inglehart (2004). It is worth mentioning that their interpretation is based on secularisation theory, but with certain limitations – in other words, they are not secularisation maximalists nor do they advocate an end to the secularisation theory.

Here are some of their conclusions based on data from the two waves of the World Value Survey (in the early 1990s and in 1999/2000).

1. There is a statistically significant correlation between membership in religious volunteer associations and/or organisations and religion. On a global level, they show that different faiths have different levels of support

'Organized collective religious practice involves situations in which rituals and other religious activities introduce transcendent perspective into social life. This involves social structures that make charitable activity possible and likely.'

and/or encouragement of membership in religious associations. The results of a logistic regression – even after a battery of controls (level of human development, level of political development, age, gender, education, and income) was applied – show that regular attendance at religious services has a significant impact on membership in volunteer religious organisations. The highest positive correlation was found within Protestant, Hindu and Jewish communities. A negative correlation was only found among Orthodox communities (Norris and Inglehart, 2004: 186).

2. Studies also show that religious participation is positively associated with a higher level of belonging to different non-religious volunteer organisations and community associations. 'Regular church-attendance was most strongly associated with membership in associations concerned with traditional philanthropic functions of religious institutions, including those for social welfare such as for the elderly or handicapped [...] the only negative relationship was membership in trade unions' (Norris and Inglehart, 2004: 188). Jewish, Hindu, Buddhist and Protestants belong to more groups than average, while Catholics, Orthodox, Muslims and atheists belong to fewer groups than average.

3. Regarding the influence of religion on civil society and on active participation in democratic processes within society, Norris and Inglehart (2004: 192) found that: '*[B]elonging to religious organisations does indeed go together with community engagement and democratic participation,* as social capital theory suggests.' They found that *membership* in religiously affiliated organisations is positively linked with civil activity (measured through indicators of civic engagement including social attitudes and political behaviour). The findings regarding church attendance are contrasting: high rates of church attendance are '*negatively* linked with civic activity'.

Yet, it is unclear whether this correlation can be expressed in terms of causality. The authors suspect there is no uni-linear causal relation, but a reciprocal causal process.[6]

Their findings are corroborated by other studies (Greeley, 1997 and Smidt, 2003 for the USA and Canada; Beugelsdijk and van Schaik, 2003 and de Hart, 2001 for the Netherlands). Especially interesting is a comparative study

[6] 'The available database is inadequate to determine the causality in these associations, which requires panel surveys. But a process of mutually reinforcing reciprocal causation is probably underlying these relationships, whereby 'joiners' who are active in local sports clubs, arts associations, and youth work, as well as having a positive sense of political and social trust, also belong to religious organisations' (Norris and Inglehart, 2004: 194).

about social capital in three European countries (Sweden, West Germany and Spain) and the USA because these countries differ greatly in their religious traditions and welfare systems, and covers a broad variation in terms of value orientation and social capital (Halman and Pettersson, 2003). These studies bring about a deeper understanding of qualitative differences which explain relationships between religion and social capital:

1. The Halman and Pettersson (2003: 173 ss.) study confirms that, at the individual level, social capital is positively related to religiosity. Among the components of social capital the norms of reciprocity seem to be most strongly related to religiosity. Religious people appear somewhat more trustworthy than less religious people. Interpersonal trust is positively related with religiosity in West Germany, while in the USA and Sweden engagement in social networks is higher among religious people than among less religious people. The regression analysis with social capital as the compound variable reveals positive associations with religiosity, particularly in the USA and in West Germany and, to a lesser extent, in Spain, with hardly any in Sweden.

2. Americans are more religious and civically engaged than Canadians. But, 'while the aggregate level of such involvement and engagement differ across the two countries, the nature of the relationship between religious involvement and civic engagement tends to be identical in both countries' (Smidt et al., 2003: 169). Such findings are not limited to North America. For example, the results of a national 'God in the Netherlands' survey (data from 1996) show that religion supports civic engagement in all three religious communities. De Hart (2001: 96, 98-99) prove that 'church members are more likely to do voluntary work than non-church members, and regular churchgoers are the most likely to volunteer. This applies even to volunteer work that is not associated with the church'. Yet, Calvinists are the most likely to do voluntary work and to be a member. Catholics are less likely to do voluntary work than Calvinists and members of the reformed Church, 'but they do spend more time on their voluntary work'. Churchgoing is a more important factor of volunteering among Catholics than among Protestants. Research also shows that Calvinists are more likely to be members of an organisation with an ideological aim, and of youth clubs; Protestants are more likely to join political groups and Catholics leisure organisations. These results fit well into a broader religious-cultural tradition and history of the Netherlands.

3. One of the key reasons for the difference between Protestants and Catholics may lie in the level of development of horizontal authority and horizontal connections in Church organisations / associations. Horizontal connections are more likely to be found within religious groups that en-

courage active participation instead of submissiveness and passivity. According to their studies, congregational forms of religion encourage horizontal authority – which according to theory is essential for social capital – rather than hierarchical authority (Halman and Pettersson, 2003; also see Nemeth and Luidens, 2003).

John Coleman (2003) points out a great difference among Protestants in the USA in this regard: this particular aspect (horizontal authority) is more developed within mainstream churches than within charismatic and Evangelical groups. (It is worth noting that, in the USA, the former are rapidly declining while the expansion rate of the latter is the highest among all types of religious groups.) Similarly, within the Catholic Church there is a great difference between traditionalist groups with strongly developed vertical links and those groups that have been organised in the spirit of the renewal following Vatican II and are characterised by stronger and more active lay participation with more horizontal links and less hierarchical links. This difference within the Catholic Church is also reported in Europe (de Hart, 2003; Halman and Pettersson, 2003). On the other hand, strong horizontal links/connections may have a negative impact on social capital – they could foster an 'implosion', i.e. a movement of concentration inwards, towards group seclusion (comp. Coleman, 2003). This inward movement could be compound by a fear of the harsh realities in broader society (reflected by the motto 'heaven in a heartless world').

These findings echo the opinion of certain authors who have warned that the international surveys (WVS, EVS, ESS...) should be interpreted with certain reservations, claiming that these indicators only offer an approximate assessment of social capital indicators. The sheer number of volunteer organisations does not provide a complete picture of the social capital involved. It does not tell us whether it serves society at large or just the narrow interests of a small circle. More importantly, the number does not tell us anything about their impact on a particular society. The quality of the impact is more connected with the historical and cultural properties of a specific society, type of welfare state etc.[7] Numerical data, for example, do not reflect variations among qualitatively different organisations: they might include clientelistic networks, rent-seeking groups, narrow-scope special interest groups, amoral familism etc. Therefore, other aspects should also be considered such as qualitative data, the value orientation of groups etc.

[7] For example, there are 28,000 registered NGOs in Croatia but their impact on society is relatively weak and invisible (comp. Bežovan 2004).

In this regard Knack and Keefer (see Beugelsdijk and Schaik, 2003) proposed a distinction between different types of volunteer associations. They differentiate between Putnam groups and Olson groups. According to these authors, each of them has an opposite effect on social capital. Membership in Putnam groups (voluntary religious organisation; education, arts, music or cultural activities; and youth work) appear to contribute more to social capital that benefits society at large, while members of Olson groups (trade unions; political parties or group; professional associations) tend to benefit narrower segments of society.

This contradicts the usual interpretations that emphasise the power of the structural aspect: strong connections within a group are supposed to have a positive impact on bonding and a negative impact on bridging social capital. This would tend to confirm that the feeling of responsibility towards other people, as an ethical/spiritual component, plays a major role regarding the influence of religion on social capital. Some create bonding, others bridging social capital. According to some studies (Smidt, 2003), the type/kind of social capital that a religious group chooses to develop is determined by its view of the world, or ideology, i.e. by ethical and cultural aspects.

Trust

For many authors trust and/or trustworthiness is the central indicator of social capital.

Regarding the influence of religion on the level of trust, there are two points of particular interest:

1. Research studies have shown that, within Europe, the level of trust in traditionally Protestant countries is generally higher than in Catholic countries. Especially significant is the difference between northern Scandinavian countries and the traditionally Catholic countries of Western Europe (France, Spain, Portugal). Comparative research of European regions does show, however, a high level of trust in some Catholic environments, notably the North of Italy, the South of the Netherlands, Flanders, and Madrid (Beugelsdijk and Schaik, 2003). These regions have the highest scores for trust (0.447 – 0.646), far above both the average and some Protestant areas. This indicates that trust does depend on several interconnected factors, with religion being one of them.

2. Studies show that religious (confessional) affiliation has little or no effect (either positive or negative) on the level of trust. For the Netherlands, Dekker et al. (1999) have shown that 'attending church proves to have no influence on social trust.' On the global level, Norris and Inglehart (2004) reached the same conclusion.

Religious impact on trust and voluntarism according to the European Value Survey data

Europe is a diverse continent consisting of very different historical, religious, cultural and political traditions and history. The East-West divide is mainly based on political history (democracy – communism) and economic development. The North-South-East divide is mainly based on religious matters: the Northern Protestant culture differs from the Southern Catholic and Eastern Orthodox culture. On the other hand, important differences are based on groups of languages and/or nations, especially between the three main linguistic groups (Romanic, Germanic and Slavic).

Our hypothesis is that these differences can also be seen in social capital. But which one of the divisions mentioned above is more appropriate for social capital aspects? Religious culture is one of the relevant factors for differences in social capital, for example, the Catholic-Protestant divide is accepted in all studies about social capital. In accordance with this we may analytically divide Europe into four religious confessional traditions: mainly Protestant, mainly Catholic, mainly Orthodox, and mixed. On the other hand, a multidimensional division which includes religious traditions as a primary factor and socio-cultural and historical-political differences as a secondary one show there are at least five European regions: Protestant democratic Scandinavian North, Catholic democratic South (mostly Romanic speaking), Orthodox ex-communist East, mainly Catholic ex-communist Central (or Central and Eastern) and religiously mixed non-Romanic speaking democratic West (and Central and Western) Europe.[8]

We will test our hypothesis with the European Values Survey (EVS; 1999/2000) and partly the European Social Survey (ESS; 2002). The classification of countries included in the EVS into two, four and five European regions is given in a footnote[9] and is also evident in Table 6.1. Given the limitations

---

[8] These classifications have echoes in two existing studies about social capital. Halman and Pettersson (2003) speak about three very different Western European countries (Germany, Spain and Sweden). Norris and Inglehart (2004: 46) divide Europe into four regions, two of them are post-industrial (Catholic and Protestant countries of Western Europe – without Portugal), two industrial (Catholic ex-communist Central Europe and the Orthodox East).

[9] European regions by countries (EVS 1999/2000 countries):

- Europe divided into 2 regions (Western/Eastern Europe): (1) Western Europe: France, Great Britain, Germany, Austria, Italy, Spain, Portugal, the Netherlands, Belgium, Denmark, Sweden, Finland, Iceland, N. Ireland, Ireland, Malta, Luxembourg, and Greece; (2) Eastern Europe (mostly ex-communist): Estonia, Latvia, Lithuania, Poland, Czech Rep., Slovakia, Hungary, Romania, Bulgaria, Croatia, Russia, Slovenia, Ukraine, and Belarus.

- Europe divided into 4 regions (European Confessional Traditions): (1) Catholic: France, Austria,

of space we will analyse the two aspects of social capital which are central for many authors: interpersonal generalised trust and voluntarism (belonging to voluntary organisations and unpaid work).

Trust, religion and European regions

Research studies have shown that, within European states, the levels of interpersonal generalised trust are very different; in traditionally Protestant countries the level of trust is generally higher than in Catholic countries, in the West higher than in the East, in countries with a democratic tradition higher than in ex-communist countries. Table 6.1 indicates that most Western European countries have a higher level of trust than Eastern European ex-communist countries. However, there are some exceptions and differences within the countries of Western/Eastern Europe. These differences need an additional explanation. Some differences can be interpreted through the religious confessional tradition of the countries involved. On the other hand, countries with the same religious confessional traditions have very different values.

A division into five European regions gives more homogenous groups of countries. Especially homogenous are the groups of Scandinavian countries and Central European ex-communist countries (also see Table 6.2). The low level of trust in ex-communist countries shows how a specific legacy and specific transitional circumstances influence both the general level of social capital and the possibility of religion to create social capital (Črpić, Zrinščak, 2005). In two other regions just one or two countries have levels very different from the other countries. In the Orthodox East these two countries are Romania (10.1%) and Belarus (41.9%), in the non-Romanic speaking West there is the Netherlands (60.1%).[10] Only within the group of

---

Italy, Spain, Portugal, Belgium, Ireland, Lithuania, Poland, Czech Republic, Slovakia, Croatia, Malta, Luxembourg, and Slovenia; (2) Protestant: Great Britain, Denmark, Sweden, Finland, and Iceland; (3) Orthodox: Romania, Bulgaria, Greece, Russia, Ukraine, and Belarus; (4) Mixed: Germany, Netherlands, Northern Ireland, Estonia, Latvia, Hungary.

- Europe divided into 5 regions (Religious Cultural European regions): (1) Scandinavia (Protestant): Denmark, Sweden, Finland, and Iceland; (2) West Europe, non-Romanic-speaking (different religion): Great Britain, Germany, Austria, the Netherlands, Belgium, Northern Ireland, Ireland, and Luxembourg; (3) Western Europe, Romanic-speaking and Malta (mostly Catholic): France, Italy, Spain, Portugal, and Malta; (4) Central (/ex-communist) European region (mostly Catholic) : Estonia, Latvia, Lithuania, Poland, Czech Republic, Slovakia, Hungary, Croatia, and Slovenia; (5) Eastern Europe (Orthodox, mostly Slavic): Bulgaria, Russia, Ukraine, Belarus, Romania, and Greece.

[10] We think the main reason why the Netherlands differs so much from other countries within the region is that the Netherlands is much more influenced by (a specific form of) Protestantism than any other countries in 'non-Romanic-speaking' Western Europe.

the Catholic Romanic speaking West are levels of trust in countries very diverse, being very low in Portugal (12.3%) and France (21.3%), while relatively high in Spain (38.5%) and Italy (32.6%). All in all, it may be concluded that the classification into religious cultural regions forms much more homogenous results regarding trust than the two other divisions examined.

Table 6.1 Trust in Europe (EVS 1999/2000), in percentages
(Q: Generally speaking, would you say that most people can be trusted or that you can't be too careful in dealing with people? A: Most people can be trusted.)

	Europe	Two European regions		Main Religious confessional traditions				Five Religious Cultural European regions				
		West, Democratic	East, Ex-communist	Catholic	Protestant	Orthodox	Mixed	Scandinavian, Protestant	West, non-Romanic speaking, religious mixed	West, mostly Romanic speaking, Catholic	Ex-communist Central Europe, mostly Catholic	East, mostly Slavic, Orthodox
Romania	10.1		10.1			10.1						10.1
Portugal	12.3	12.3		12.3						12.3		
Slovakia	15.9		15.9	15.9							15.9	
Latvia	17.1		17.1				17.1				17.1	
Poland	18.4		18.4	18.4							18.4	
Croatia	20.5		20.5	20.5							20.5	
Malta	20.7	20.7		20.7						20.7		
France	21.3	21.3		21.3						21.3		
Slovenia	21.7		21.7	21.7							21.7	
Hungary	22.3		22.3				22.3				22.3	
Estonia	23.5		23.5				23.5				23.5	
Greece	23.7		23.7			23.7						23.7
Russia	24.0		24.0			24.0						24.0
Czech R.	24.5		24.5	24.5							24.5	
Luxembourg	24.8	24.8		24.8					24.8			
Lithuania	25.9		25.9	25.9							25.9	
Bulgaria	26.8		26.8			26.8						26.8
Ukraine	26.9		26.9			26.9						26.9
Great Britain	28.9	28.9			28.9				28.9			
Belgium	29.2	29.2		29.2					29.2			
Italy	32.6	32.6		32.6						32.6		
Austria	33.4	33.4		33.4					33.4			
Ireland	36.0	36.0		36.0					36.0			
Germany	37.5	37.5					37.5		37.5			
Spain	38.5	38.5		38.5						38.5		
N. Ireland	39.5	39.5					39.5		39.5			
Iceland	41.1	41.1			41.1			41.1				
Belarus	41.9		41.9			41.9						41.9
Finland	57.4	57.4			57.4			57.4				
Netherlands	60.1	60.1					60.1		60.1			
Sweden	66.3	66.3			66.3			66.3				
Denmark	66.5	66.5			66.5			66.5				
Average (region)	**30.3**	**36.2**	**22.7**	**25.6**	**52.3**	**24.9**	**34.0**	**58.1**	**35.5**	**26.2**	**21.2**	**24.9**
Average *	30.9	37.8	22.9	25.3	52.0	28.7	33.3	57.8	36.2	25.1	21.1	25.6
St. Dev.*	14.4	16.5	7.0	7.8	16.6	7.6	15.8	11.9	10.8	10.4	3.4	10.2
Minimum *	10.1	12.3	10.1	12.3	28.9	23.7	17.1	41.1	24.8	12.3	15.9	10.1
Maximum *	66.5	66.5	41.9	38.5	66.5	41.9	60.1	66.5	60.1	38.5	25.9	41.9

* The average, standard deviation, minimum and maximum is calculated from country aggregate values.

Table 6.2 Trust in European regions (EVS 1999/2000), in percentages

Number of regions	Regions	Trust in region	Min /max (country within the region)	Country with min /max level of trust	Second min /max value
1	Europe	30.3	12.3 / 66.5		
2	West, Democratic	36.2	12.3 / 66.5	Portugal / Denmark	20.7 / 66.3
	East. Ex-communist	22.7	10.1 / 41.9	Romania / Belarus	15.9 / 26.9
4	Catholic	25.6	12.3 / 38.5	Portugal / Spain	15.9 / 36.0
	Protestant	52.3	28.9 / 66.5	Great Britain / Denmark	41.1 / 66.3
	Orthodox	24.9	10.1 / 41.9	Romania / Belarus	23.7 / 26.9
	Mixed	34.0	17.1 / 60.1	Latvia / Netherlands	22.3 / 39.5
5	Scandinavian, Protestant	58.1	41.1 / 66.5	Iceland / Denmark	57.4 / 66.3
	West, non Romanic speak., religious mixed	35.5	24.8 / 60.1	Luxembourg / Netherlands	28.9 / 39.5
	West, Romanic speak. + Malta, Catholic	26.2	12.3 / 38.5	Portugal / Spain	20.7 / 32.6
	Ex-communist Central Europe, mostly Catholic	21.2	15.9 / 25.9	Slovakia / Lithuania	17.1 / 24.5
	East, mostly Slavic, Orthodox	24.9	10.1 / 41.9	Romania / Belarus	23.7 / 26.9

What about the relationship between (individual) religiousness and generalised trust? According to our analysis of the EVS there are significant differences in regions regarding personal religiousness.[11] A regression analysis shows that religious persons are less trusting than non/religious persons and convinced atheists in the Orthodox East (biggest differences); the same relationship is found in both Western regions – but not in Central Europe, where there are very few differences in trust between religious persons and atheists while in the Scandinavian region there is no difference at all. Attendance at Church services and Church membership have very low or no influence on trust at the level of regions. However, there are

[11] We undertook a regression analysis for Europe and in each of the five European regions. Due to the limited space we only present the most important results without tables.

countries where these relationships are positive and others where they are negative. Religious membership and trust are positively correlated in Austria, Sweden, Belarus, Croatia, Ireland, Malta, Northern Ireland; negatively in Czech Republic, Denmark, Estonia, Germany, Iceland, Italy and Romania.

We can conclude that religious tradition does matter – but not by itself and not all aspects of religion in the same way. Differences are caused by many interrelated reasons: different histories, a different socio-cultural development, a different political past (and present). In this regard, the analysis of secularisation processes by D. Martin (2005) clearly showed that the contemporary influence of religion on society strongly depends on the relationship of Catholic political power with the process of national affirmation – being unfriendly (as in France or the Czech Republic) or supporting (Poland, Croatia...).

Two factors seem very relevant: State-Church relations and the civil society situation. Countries and regions with a strong 'cultural war' (*Kulturkampf*) in the past seem to have lower levels of trust than countries where these conflicts did not exist. Low levels of trust in Central European countries and the Orthodox East could be connected with their communist past. It is also important to keep in mind that the Scandinavian form of State Church, or Free Folk Church as was recently more appropriately described (Bäckström, Beckman, Pettersson, 2004), has a different practical implication than other Protestant countries: Scandinavia is the most secularised part of Europe if we look at personal religiousness and attendance at religious services but (!) it has the highest level of 'associational' religiousness in the form of belonging and participation in religious (para-Church) voluntary associations and voluntary work for religious associations. That also indicates the difficulties of the secularisation thesis in grasping different aspects of religious processes in Scandinavian countries, which combines the low level of practice, even low visibility of churches in public with remarkable continuity in the high nominal membership together with the fairly high and stable participation in church rituals (Repstad, 2005). Many of these differences are in line with the classification into five European religious cultures.

Belonging to voluntary associations and active voluntary involvement

In the previous part of the article, we broached the question of whether the high level of religious social capital in the USA is an exception, or whether religious social capital is also important in Europe. It is clear that Europe is much more secularised than America, but the EVS data show that religion in Europe is still a very important factor of voluntarism. In comparing data about belonging to volunteer associations in Europe it is clear that the four types of associations with the highest levels of involvement are: trade unions (16.6%), sports/recreation organisations (16.5%), religious organisations (14.5%), and cultural activities (10.4%) (see Table 6.3). A very similar pattern can be seen within the regions. A similar pattern appears regarding unpaid work (Table 6.4). The only difference is that labour unions do not play such an important role.

Table 6.3 Belonging to volunteer organisations (EVS 1999/2000), in percentages

	Europe	Two European regions		Five Religious Cultural European regions				
Do you belong to:		West, Democratic	East, Ex-communist	Scandinavian, Protestant	West, non-Romanic speaking, religious mixed	West, mostly Romanic speaking, Catholic	Ex-communist Central Europe, mostly Catholic	East, mostly Slavic, Orthodox
welfare organisation	6.3	8.5	3.2	14.4	9.1	4.7	3.9	2.7
religious organisation	14.5	19.9	6.9	52.7	16.9	8.3	8.8	4.1
cultural activities	10.4	14.0	5.3	19.5	15.6	7.4	6.6	5.8
trade unions	16.6	17.5	15.3	55.6	12.7	5.1	10.3	21.6
political parties/groups	4.7	6.0	2.8	11.0	5.9	3.1	3.2	3.1
local community action	3.2	3.7	2.5	5.5	3.9	2.3	3.3	1.7
3w-development/human rights	3.3	5.4	0.5	8.8	6.5	1.8	0.5	1.2
environment	5.3	7.5	2.2	9.1	9.6	2.5	2.8	2.7
professional associations	5.8	7.6	3.3	13.3	7.0	4.0	4.1	3.9
youth work	4.0	4.9	2.7	7.4	5.3	2.8	3.7	1.7
sports/recreation	16.1	21.2	8.9	34.0	23.4	11.5	12.1	5.3
women's groups	2.7	3.5	1.6	3.9	5.1	0.8	2.2	1.3
peace movement	1.0	1.4	0.5	1.3	1.5	0.9	0.6	0.9
voluntary health organisations	3.7	4.7	2.3	5.9	5.4	3.0	3.0	1.7
other groups	6.1	7.3	4.4	14.3	7.0	4.1	5.9	2.6
do you belong to: none	51.2	42.8	62.1	11.8	41.8	62.6	57.7	65.3

It can also be concluded that 'associational culture' differs between regions. First, levels range from very low levels of belonging (and unpaid work) in the Christian Orthodox; a lower than average level is found in Central Europe and in the Romanic speaking Western Europe (both mostly Catholic); an almost average level is seen in the non-Romanic West and it is much higher in Scandinavia.[12] Second, there is a relatively high level of

[12] Again, it should be kept in mind that in some countries questions about membership reflect partly the different administrative practice and, because of that, authors in a recent article about social

Table 6.4 Unpaid work (EVS 1999/2000), in percentages

	Europe	Two European regions		Five Religious Cultural European regions				
Do you work unpaid for:		West, Democratic	East, Ex-communist	Scandinavian, Protestant	West, non-Romanic speaking, religious mixed	West, mostly Romanic speaking, Catholic	Ex-communist Central Europe, mostly Catholic	East, mostly Slavic, Orthodox
welfare organisation	4.5	6.0	2.5	10.4	6.0	3.9	3.1	2.4
religious organisation	6.3	7.8	4.3	13.5	7.7	5.9	5.2	3.2
cultural activities	5.7	7.2	3.7	9.8	7.4	4.5	4.7	3.9
trade unions	3.1	2.7	3.7	6.7	1.9	1.5	2.8	5.2
political parties/groups	2.3	2.7	1.9	4.7	2.4	1.9	2.0	2.2
local community action	2.4	2.6	2.0	4.0	2.2	2.0	2.6	1.9
3w-develop./human rights	1.7	2.7	0.3	3.9	3.0	1.3	0.3	1.3
environment	2.3	2.8	1.6	3.5	3.0	1.3	1.8	2.5
professional associations	2.3	2.9	1.6	4.7	2.7	1.8	1.9	1.8
youth work	3.3	4.2	2.2	6.8	4.9	2.2	2.9	1.5
sports/recreation	7.6	9.5	5.1	18.3	9.0	6.2	6.9	3.1
women's groups	1.5	1.8	1.1	2.6	2.4	0.6	1.4	1.0
peace movement	0.8	1.2	0.3	0.7	1.2	0.6	0.3	1.1
voluntary health org.	2.6	3.4	1.5	3.5	4.2	1.9	1.9	1.7
other groups	4.0	4.8	3.1	8.5	5.0	3.0	4.1	1.9
None	73.2	68.8	79.0	59.0	68.6	76.2	73.8	83.0

similarity between regions. However, some specifics of regions are evident. With the exception of Scandinavia and the Orthodox East, sports/ recreation ranks are higher than any other kind of volunteering and belonging. In the Orthodox region, where belonging to a Church organisation is very low relative to the pattern seen in other regions, the relative level of unpaid work for those organisations is much higher.

We have already stressed that the very high levels of membership in religious organisations and in trade unions in some Scandinavian countries (especially in Sweden) are partly due to differences in how the question is understood. Therefore, we have tried to test the conclusions concerning the participational and voluntaristic aspects of (religious) social capital on other sets of data. We realised that the European Social Survey data (2002) could be helpful here. On one hand, the formulation of questions in the ESS is

capital excluded from the scale of passive participation organisations called 'trade unions' and 'religious organisations': 'For instance, in Sweden and Denmark union membership is a requirement for eligibility for most social-security benefits. And Swedes score extremely high on membership of 'religious organisations' because they are for the most part automatically administered as members of the Lutheran Church' (van Oorschot and Arts, 2005:11).

slightly different from that of the EVS and the result could be a clearer understanding of the questions. On the other hand, the formulation of participation (membership and unpaid work) in the ESS is similar enough to the EVS survey so that it is possible to make an approximate comparison of data from both surveys (with the exception of the Orthodox region – in the ESS the only Orthodox country included is Greece).[13] The ESS data show that the level of membership in religious (para-church) organisations (and in volunteer work) is essentially lower compared to the EVS data, especially in the Scandinavian region (see Tables 6.5 and 6.6)[14]. Nevertheless, religious organisations in Scandinavia still have high levels of membership and unpaid work. Although it is possible to doubt the exact levels of empirical measurement (differences exist not only in religious organisations and trade unions but also in other organisations; they are not limited to Scandinavia either), we cannot doubt the nature of the role of religion. The ESS survey data corroborate our conclusion from the EVS data that religion is one of the most important resources of the associational aspect of social capital in every region and in Europe as a whole, measured by active participation as well as membership.

Table 6.5 Members of volunteer organisations (six types of organisations with the highest levels of membership; ESS 2002), in percentages

	Europe	Two European regions		Five Religious Cultural European regions (Orthodox region not included)			
Member in last 12 months:		West, Democratic	East, Ex-communist	Scandinavian, Protestant	West, no-Romanic speaking, religious mixed	West, mostly Romanic speaking, Catholic	Ex-com. Central Europe, mostly Catholic
sports/outdoor activity club	22.3	25.5	8.1	31.8	30.6	9.7	8.1
cultural /hobby activity organisation	14.4	16.3	5.1	21.2	18.3	7.4	5.1
trade union	21.8	24.7	9.9	52.6	19.5	6.2	9.9
consumer/automobile organisation	17.7	20.0	3.6	23.6	26.3	3.6	3.6
religious/church organisation	13.2	15.3	5.4	19.5	18.5	5.3	5.4
social club etc.	11.7	13.4	2.5	16.9	15.6	5.5	2.5

[13] European countries included in the ESS are Denmark, Finland, Norway, Sweden (the Scandinavian group), Austria, Belgium, Switzerland, Germany, the United Kingdom, Ireland, Luxembourg, the Netherlands (Western non-Romanic group), France, Spain, Italy, Portugal (Western-Romanic group), Czech Republic, Hungary, Poland, Slovenia (Central European ex-communist group) and Greece (the only country in the Orthodox group).

[14] The ESS includes four questions about participation: membership, unpaid work, participation and donations. Due to the different approach it is impossible to make a strict comparison between the ESS and EVS data.

Table 6.6 Voluntary work (six types of organisations with highest levels in membership; ESS 2002), in percentages

	Europe	Two European reg.s		Five Religious Cultural European regions (Orthodox region not included)			
Voluntary work in last 12 months:		West, Democratic	East, Ex-communist	Scandinavian, Protestant	West, no-Romanic speaking, religious mixed	West, mostly Romanic speaking, Catholic	Ex-com. Central Europe, mostly Catholic
sports/outdoor activity club	6.3	7.4	3.2	13.0	7.5	1.1	3.2
cultural /hobby activity organisation	4.4	4.9	2.8	7.6	5.2	1.4	2.8
trade union	1.0	1.1	0.9	2.2	0.8	0.3	0.9
consumer/automobile organisation	0.2	0.3	0.2	0.4	0.3	0.0	0.2
religious/church organisation	3.0	3.4	1.8	3.7	4.3	1.3	1.8
social club etc.	3.2	3.6	1.5	4.9	4.3	0.7	1.5

Our regression analysis of the EVS data[15] shows that indicators of individual religiousness are not as important as the indicators of 'community participation' religiosity – that is, attendance at religious services (in rituals, community elements are very important) and belonging to (para-Church) religious associations seem to be of more importance than individual religious feelings/ attitudes. However, the influence of religious community participation does not influence all kinds of voluntarism in the same way. According to our analysis, in Europe as a whole and in each of the five religious cultural regions attendance at religious services (a dependent variable) is significantly and positively correlated to belonging to religious voluntary organisations and doing unpaid work for religious organisations. A weak negative correlation is, however, found between attendance at religious service and belonging to sports/recreation groups in four European regions (but not in the Orthodox East European region) as well as between attendance at religious services and belonging to trade unions (with the exception of Catholic Western and Central Europe). For other types of voluntarism, we found there are significant differences among regions. For example, in protestant regions a weak positive correlation was found between attendance at religious services and youth work – much less is true for the other regions. A weak negative correlation between attendance at religious services and belonging to environmental groups was found only in the non-Romanic speaking Western and in ex-communist Central Europe, but not in the other three regions. It is interesting that in the Orthodox

[15] Due to the limited space here, we only present the most important results without tables. Comp. footnote 11.

East attendance at religious services is negatively related to only one type of voluntarism: belonging to trade unions and unpaid work for trade unions – and positively related (or without any relationship) to all other types of volunteer associations and unpaid work. However, due to a certain lack of clarity there is a need for additional analyses in this respect.

Conclusions

This paper raises many aspects of the impact of organised religion on social capital (indicators). Overall, we can say that religion does matter – not only in the world at large, but also in the secularised Europe. In fact, it is still a very important generator of associational life and voluntary activities. We can say that our hypotheses were supported in most cases – we do offer some interpretation but we expect additional work to deepen our knowledge and the interpretation of the data. However, it is important to note that the impact of religion is inter-connected with different historical social and cultural factors which shape the influence of religion. That complexity does not exclude religion but calls for a more detailed analysis. Of particular interest is the general level of religiosity and/or general social role of religion in society as it was shown that in more secularised societies religion can have more visible links with the individual behaviour of (truly) religious people while, on the other hand, in more religious societies the impact of religion can be less visible on the individual level but more spread in a diffused way across different aspects of social life.

Our analyses of the European (EVS and ESS) data confirm many of the claims present in the literature. A lower level of religious participation and denominational belonging seems not to lead to a change in the 'inner nature' of religion. It is true that attendance at religious services influences the associational aspect of social capital much more than individual religiousness does. Religious (sometimes called para-Church) voluntary organisations appear to have an even stronger influence on associational aspects. This supports the thesis that the communitarian aspect of religion should be taken as the key factor of religious based social capital.

Still, there are two additional aspects of the research question of religion and social capital that should be further researched. In Europe, engaged ways of social behaviour less rely on individual/associational efforts within communities/societies than in the USA, but the same social responsibility is usually achieved in the context of collectivistic social action, churches included. Therefore it is reasonable to expect that some forms of trust or other civil society values are highly constructed by the social role of dominant churches, particularly in the fields of welfare, educational or health activities.

The second one comes from the current ideological divisions observable in different European societies, very often highly connected with religions. The links between religions and ideological cleavages show that religion can be very powerful in bonding inside particular groups and in not bridging links between different groups. It can be said that the strong religious associational aspects of fundamentalist religious groups do not support the appropriate social capital for the whole of society. That is why further research should not be restricted for example to the links between religion and general trust but should more closely examine different aspects of trust in different social/cultural/linguistic/ethnic groups.

Literature

Ammerman, Nancy T. (1997) 'Organized Religion in a Voluntaristic Society: 1996 Presidential Address.' *Sociology of Religion* 1997, 58, pp. 203-215.

Arts, Wil, Jacques Hagenaars and Loek Halman (eds) (2003) *The Cultural Diversity of European Unity*. Leiden, Boston: Brill.

Arts, Wil, Loek Halman (eds) (2004) *European Values at the Turn of the Millennium*. Leiden, Boston: Brill.

Bäckström, Anders, Ninna E. Beckman and P. Pettersson, (2004) *Religious Change in Northern Europe. The Case of Sweden*, Stockholm: Verbum Förlag AB.

Ballin, Ernst H. (2003) 'European Identity and Interreligious Dialogue,' in: Arts, Hagenaars and Halman 2003, pp. 421-432.

Beckford, James A. and Thomas Luckmann (eds) (1989) *The Changing Face of Religion*, SAGE Studies in International Sociology, vol. 37, London: Sage.

Bellah, Robert N. (1995/96) 'Community Properly Understood: A Defense of 'Democratic Communitarianism'.' *The Responsive Community*. Vol. 6, 1 (Winter1995/96), pp. 49–50.

Berger, Peter L. and Richard J. Neuhaus (1996 [1977]) 'To Empower People: from State to Civil Society' (text of orig. edit.), in: Berger et al. (eds) (1996) *To Empower People: from State to Civil Society*. Washington: American Enterprise Institute, pp. 155–208.

Berger, Peter L. and Thomas Luckmann (1995) *Modernity, Pluralism and the Crisis of Meaning: The Orientation of Modern Man*. Gütersloh: Bertelsmann Foundation.

Berger, Peter L. (1999) 'The Desecularisation of the World: a Global Overview,' in: P. L. Berger (ed.). *The Desecularisation of the World. Resurgent Religion and World Politics*. Grand Rapids: Eerdsmans, pp. 1–18.

Beugelsdijk, S., S. Smulders (2003) 'Bridging and Boding Social Capital: which type is good for economic growth?', in: Arts, Hagenaars and Halman 2003, pp. 147-184.

Beugelsdijk, S. and T. van Schaik (2003) 'Participation in Civil Society and European Regional Growth', in: Arts, Hagenaars and Halman 2003, pp. 119-143.

'Bettertogether: Religion and Social Capital.' (2000) Seguaro Seminar Civic Engagement in America: http://www.ksg.harvard.edu/saguaro/ (June 2006).

Bežovan, Gojko (2004) *Civilno društvo.* Zagreb: Nakladni zavod Globus.

Candland, Christopher (2000) 'Faith as Social Capital: Religion and Community Development in Southern Asia.' *Policy Sciences* 33, pp. 355-374.

Coleman, James S. (1994) *Foundations of Social Theory.* Harvard Univ. Press.

Coleman, John A. (2003) 'Religious Social Capital: Its Nature, Social Location, and Limits', in Smidt 2003, pp. 33-47.

Črpić, Goran and Siniša Zrinščak (2005) 'An Emerging Civil Society', in: J. Baloban (ed.) *In Search of Identity: A Comparative Study of Values: Croatia and Europe.* Zagreb: Golden marketing – Tehnička knjiga, pp. 19-44.

Davie, Grace (2000) *Religion in Modern Europe. Memory Mutates.* Oxford: Oxford University Press.

Davie, Grace (2002) *Europe: The Exceptional Case. Parameters of Faith in the Modern World.* London: Darton, Longman and Todd Ltd.

de Hart, Joep (2001) 'Religion and Volunteering in the Netherlands', in: *Social Capital and Participation in Everyday Life,* edited by P. Dekker and E. M. Uslaner. London / New York: Routledge.

Dekker, P., J. de Hart, M. Leijenaar, Kees Niemöller and Eric M. Uslaner (1999) *Voluntary Work: a comparative study; Civil society and voluntary work III.* (Summary: http://www.scp.nl/english/publications/summaries/9057491214.html)

Dekker, P., P. Ester, H. Vinken (2003) 'Civil Society, Social Trust and Democratic Involvement,' in: Arts, Hagenaars and Halman 2003, pp. 217-247.

Durkheim, Emile (1933 [1893]) *The Division of Labor in Society.* (trans. G. Simpson) New York: The Free Press.

Ebstyne King, Pamela and James L. Furrow (2004) 'Religion as a Resource for Positive Youth Development: Religion, Social Capital, and Moral Outcomes.' *Developmental Psychology* Vol. 40, No 5, pp. 703-713.

Etzioni, Amitai (1994) *The Spirit of Community: The Reinvention of American Society.* New York: Simon & Schuster.

Field, John (2003) *Social Capital.* London /New York: Routledge.

Fukuyama, Francis (2000) *The Great Disruption: Human Nature and the Reconstruction of Social Order.* New York: Touchstone.

Greeley, Andrew M. (2004) *Religion in Europe at the End of the Second Millennium.* London / New Brunswick (USA): Transaction Publishers.

Greeley, Andrew (1997) 'Coleman Revised: Religious Structures as a Source of Social Capital.' *The American Behavioral Scientist*; Vol. 40, No. 5 (Mar/Apr), pp. 587-594.

Halman, Loek and Thorleif Pettersson (2003) 'Religion and Social Capital Revisited', in: L. Halman, O. Riis (eds) *Religion in secularizing society. The European's religion at the End of the 20th century*. Leiden / Boston: Brill, pp. 162-184.

Martin, D. (2005) *On Secularization. Towards a Revised General Theory*. Aldershot: Ashgate.

Nahapiet, Janine and Sumantra Ghoshal (1998) 'Social Capital, Intellectual Capital, and the Organizational Advantage.' *The Academy of Management Review*. Mississippi State: Apr. 1998: vol. 23, 2, pp. 242–266.

Nemeth, Roger J., Donald A. Luidens (2003) 'The Religious Basis of Charitable Giving in America: A Social Capital Perspective', in Smidt 2003, pp. 107-120.

Norris, Pippa and Ronald Inglehart (2004) *Sacred and Secular: Religion and Politics Worldwide*. Cambridge University Press.

Putnam, Robert D. (2000) *Bowling Alone: The Collapse and Revival of American Community* New York: Simon&Schuster.

Putnam, Robert D. (2001) 'Social Capital Measurement and Consequences.' *Canadian Journal of Policy Research*. Vol. 2, 1. (Spring), pp. 41–51.

Putnam, Robert D., Robert Leonardi and Raffaella Y. Nanetti (1993) Making Democracy Work: Civic Traditions in Modern Italy. *Princeton: Princeton University Press.*

Repstad, Pål (2005) 'Churches, Religion and Civil Society: A Nordic Perspective. A Response to Nancy T. Ammerman', in: Bäckström, Anders (ed.) *Welfare and Religion. A Publication to Mark the Fifth Anniversary of the Uppsala Institute for Diaconal and Social Studies*. Uppsala: Uppsala Institute for Diaconal and Social Studies, pp. 35-46.

Schuller, Tom, John Preston, Cathie Hammond, Angela Brassett-Grundy and John Bynner (2004) *The Benefit of Learning. The impact of education on health, family life and social capital*. London / New York: RoutledgeFalmer.

Schuller, Tom (2001) 'Complementary Roles of Human and Social Capital.' *Canadian Journal of Policy Research*. Vol. 2, 1. (Spring 2001), pp. 18–24.

Selznick, Philip (1992) *The Moral Commonwealth: Social Theory and The Promise of Community*. Los Angeles: University of California Press.

Smidt, Corwin (ed.) (2003) *Religion as Social Capital : Producing the Common Good*. Waco: Baylor University.

Smidt, C. et al. (2003) 'Religious Involvement, Social Capital and Political Engagement: A Comparison of United States and Canada', in Smidt 2003, pp. 153-169.

Uslaner, Eric (2001) 'Volunteering and Social Capital: How trust and religion shape civic participation in the US', in Dekker, Paul and Eric Uslaner. *Social Capital and Participation in Everyday Life*, London: Routledge, pp. 104-117.

van Oorschot, Wim and Will Arts (2005) 'The social capital of European welfare states: the crowding out hypothesis revisited.' *Journal of European Social Policy*, 15(1), pp. 5-26.

Woolcock, Michael (2001) 'The Place of Social Capital in Understanding Social and Economic Outcomes.' *Canadian Journal of Policy Research.* Vol. 2, 1 (Spring 2001), pp. 11–17.

Wuthnow, Robert (1996 [1994]) *Sharing the Journey. Support Groups and America's New Quest for Community.* New York / London: Free Press.

Wuthnow, Robert (2002) 'Religious Involvement and Status-Bridging Social Capital.' *Journal for the Scientific Study of Religion* 41, 4, pp. 669-684.

Wuthnow, Robert (2003) 'Can Religion Revitalize Civil Society? An Institutional Perspective', in Smidt 2003, pp. 191-209.

Yeung, Anne Brigitta (2004) 'Religiosity, Volunteering, and Social Capital: The European Perspective, the Case of Finland.' *Nonprofit and Volunteering Sector Quarterly*, 33, 3 (Sept.), pp. 401-422.

Part II
National Case Studies

7. Study Circles in Sweden and Slovenia - Learning for Civic Participation

Petros Gougoulakis and Nevenka Bogataj

Introduction

The study circle is the dominant educational form applied in both popular education in Sweden and in adult education in Slovenia. While study circles in Sweden have been organised since the end of the 19th century, in Slovenia study circles were introduced one hundred years later based on the Swedish tradition. Despite outward resemblances, it is presumed to be certain dissimilarities and similarities concerning the role of study circles on the issue of social capital in the compared countries.

In this article, study circle activities in Slovenia and Sweden are compared from a socio-cultural perspective with regard to their significance for the creation and maintenance of social capital in each one country. Different kinds of data sources are used and presented in a comparative table.

The presentation consists of: 1) a short historical background where the study circles are illustrated within the country's context; 2) an account of the current state of the art of the study circle phenomenon based on both statistical data and qualitative research outcomes from at least three points of view (*the state's, the civil society's* and *'the participants'* point of view); and 3) a reading of conceivable links between participation in study circles and the state of social capital in society.

Popular Education and the Study Circle

Work in study circles is characterised by a specific philosophy of education. Underlying this philosophy one can find a distinct view of the human, knowledge and society. The popular education programme is oriented towards enlightenment. Its interest in knowledge and action is both libertarian and emancipatory. It is libertarian according to the effects on a societal and organisational level. It is emancipatory in terms of its interest in the citizens involved and the opportunities for their self-fulfilment. The least popular education programme seems to be control-oriented. This is explained by the fact that 'teaching' in study circles is free from the paralysing grasp of grade-setting. Studies in a circle environment therefore have a different meaning to studies in more traditionalised educational contexts. While education in the latter case is focused on the aspect of contents, namely the curriculum, learning in study circles focuses on the process and the outcome, namely a democratic dialogue. While learning in formal education is instrumental in character surrounded by fixed regulations, learning in the study circles' free and voluntary framework is authentic – a basically educative learning process occurring together with others. The significance of popular education's authentic learning derives from the idea (with roots going back to Plato's philosophy) that 'bildning' (*paedeia*) can never be taught but can only arise by allowing a free and creative learning situation where different arguments and perspectives diverge in a democratic dialogue. It is certainly the same philosophy that underpins the humanistic branch of enlightenment and modernity. As a project, modernity relies on man's expectations for a better world, in which man's reason and scientific progress are capable of creating a new societal order governed by equality, freedom and democracy (Kondylis, 1981; Liedman, 1997).

Enlightenment as a time of awakening and belief in every man's reason was nicely formulated by Kant in 1784 in the following words:

'Enlightenment is man's leasing his self-caused immaturity. Immaturity is the incapacity to use one's intelligence without the guidance of another. Such immaturity is self-caused if it is not caused by lack of intelligence, but by lack of determination and courage to use one's intelligence without being guided by another. Sapere aude! Have the courage to use your own intelligence! is therefore the motto of the enlightenment' (Kant 1784, in Friedrich, 1993).

The concept of 'folkbildning'

The concept of *popular education* (*folkbildning*)[1] in this article refers to the 'educational project' developed in the 19th century as a result of urbanisation and industrialisation by the emerging social movements of that time. In its broadest sense, the concept includes everything that contributes to raising society's education level. It may include everything from newspapers and radio to public cultural institutions such as theatres and museums. Viewed

[1] The term '*folkbildning*' is difficult to translate into English. It is sometimes translated as liberal or popular adult education. However, the specific conceptual foundation of '*folkbildning*' extends beyond the term 'adult education'. Here, the term '*folkbildning*' is used in this wide sense.

in a narrower traditional perspective, popular education in Sweden – 'free, voluntary popular education' – is supported and carried on via four large institutions with historical roots: public libraries, folk high schools (*folkhögskolor*), lecture societies/workers' institutes and study associations.

The word popular (*folk*) as a term is being introduced into the political vocabulary in conjunction with establishment of the modern project. It denotes a new force – a new historical subject – which constitutes and legitimises the modern democratic form of government. The term has simultaneously been used to acknowledge the large number of people who normally are associated with weak political, economic and cultural resources. In this sense and from a power-perspective the people (*folket*) make up a lower class with a marginal influence on the political process. When the people's political rights were presented at the beginnings of modernity this reasoning was connected to political liberalism's idea of the social contract, according to which the citizens' responsibilities to the social body was brought face to face with the social body's responsibilities to the contractors.

Behind the notion of 'people' one can glimpse not only a description of society as a whole or how civil society in particular is, but also a representation of how society should be, i.e. democratic, equal and just. Popular movements should also be interpreted in contrast to the state or market. Popular movements arise on a civil initiative and often stand in clear opposition to the authority of the state and the power of the market. It is based on free will, it has or should have a large membership and an idealistic state of mind. It puts people into motion mentally and physically. A common characteristic of the significant Swedish popular movements seen at the end of the 19th century is asserted to be the protest and struggle for change of the prevailing yet somewhat unpleasant social, cultural and economic conditions for the majority of people. Thus, the revivalist movement was formed as a protest against the church's approach as regards questions of faith, the temperance movement as a protest against alcoholic beverages' damaging consequences for society, and the workers' movement as a protest against industrialisation and the negative sides of the political system (see Arvidson, 1985; Eyerman and Jamison, 1991; Micheletti, 1994).

Popular education in Sweden: a short historical outline

The need to educate the broad masses arose at the end of the 19th century in a different way than earlier epochs due to industrialisation and democratisation processes which demanded a well-educated and well-disciplined workforce. Popular education was strongly influenced by the Enlightenment's utilitarianism and empirical rationalism. The dissemination of useful knowledge (booklets) to the people was considered a guarantee for a stable social order and an effective means to counteract the 'harmful' impact of 'libertarian teachings'. At that time, on one hand popular educators from the ruling class strove to foster and cultivate people from the working class in order for them to become used to new habits, to a more rational way of thinking and to adapt to the new morality of the capitalistic production paradigm.

On the other hand, social movements of which the workers, the Free-Churchism and the Temperance movements were the most large-scale and well-organised unfolded their visionary reform programmes for a better and more equal society.

In these circumstances, the philanthropic features of popular educational activities faded and became an affair *for* the people *by* the people. Progressive liberals were also engaged in the struggle for an extension of the democratic rights and better educational conditions of the broad masses. Such intentions may be interpreted as manipulative. Through popular education the working class was to be 'educated away' from socialistic thinking and ideology. The truth, in fact, is located somewhere between an authentic self-organised and self-directed popular education derived from the real needs of ordinary people and an intentional indoctrination into the bourgeoisie's ideology and world view. The appearance of new radical social movements on the country's socio-political scene gave rise to a tremendous educational movement and has marked Sweden's political culture since then (see for example Andersson, 1980; Arvidson, 1985; Johansson, 1985; Vestlund, 1996; Gougoulakis, 2001).

At the same time, popular education was used by civil society organisations as an instrument for the dissemination of their political ideas and realisation of their power aspirations. From another point of view, the relation between popular education and civil society is quite dialectic. At the very beginning – more than one hundred years ago – the former could hardly be imagined without the latter as one was conditioned by the other. Indisputably, both popular education and the new social movement of that time was turned to and intended for those who had few social, cultural and political resources.

As time went on, the study circles became an autonomous movement and a symbol of the democratic breakthrough. The study circle was a public sphere for recurrent meetings of citizens with common interests who formed a unique pattern of communication. The study circle's free, open and permissive milieu of dialogue between equals, who exchanged ideas and experiences with respect to each other and without limits, was well suited to the efforts aimed at achieving fundamental human rights in society. Human rights were exercised in study circles since, at the same time, they were demanded in society as a whole. In a sense, the pedagogical context seemed to work to ennoble/refine the social capital and common values necessary for a well-functioning modern society.

The history of study circles in Sweden reminds us, *mutatis mutandis*, what Alexis de Tocqueville observed in his nine-month tour of the United States in 1831-32; a staggering number of groups that were spontaneously organised for mainly learning purposes (comp. Hardin, 2005). For more than a hundred years people in Sweden have come together to study different subjects, to listen to lectures, to take part in cultural projects, to organise social and political activities etc. People meet to learn together, to strengthen their opportunities, to influence their own life situation and try to impact on changes in society.

The official view considers popular adult education as free and voluntary, that is to say free from state governance, and voluntary for the participants. The government's 1998 draft law submitted to the Swedish parliament maintains, among other things:

> '(p)opular education is and should be free and voluntary. This free and voluntary popular educational work enables all to seek knowledge on the basis of their own experience, preferences and learning style, without limitation from demands for results, and without mechanisms of exclusion. The approach permits dialogue, involvement and questioning, without a preconceived framework. By reason of this, popular education fulfils a role not covered by any other educational institution, a role which also contributes to maintaining the vitality of democracy' (Government Bill, 1997/98:115, p. 5).

Even in the most recent governmental bill (2005/06:192), the Parliament reconfirmed its support in the conviction that popular education contributes to strengthening democracy and promoting lifelong learning opportunities for all citizens.

Study circle associations and study circles

The movements along with their branches supported over time the establishment of nationwide study organisations – study circle associations (*studieförbund*). Today, there are nine study associations that receive government grants. Each study association has a more or less marked profile depending on which popular movements/organisations are members of the association.

Altogether the nine study associations have over 250 member organisations. The study associations also have central co-operation agreements with 80-plus other organisations and co-operate locally with a number of different associations.

The study circle (‘*studiecirkel*’) is the most common form of activity characterising the study associations. Study circles offer different subjects according to the wishes of the participants. Every year about 300.000 circles are organised across the country involving a total of 2.5 million participants. Since many people participate in more than one circle per year the actual number of participants is estimated at between 1.5 million to 2 million.[2]

Slovenian study circles

Model and development in the context of adult education

The Scandinavian model of study circles was introduced in 1991 in order to contribute to the democratisation of society and to develop adult education. This model has remained unchanged, consisting of three key actors: the main financing body, the Ministry for Education and Sport, the main development agent, the Slovenian Institute for Adult Education (hereinafter: the SIAE) and a network of study circles organisers. The SIAE serves as the »node« of the network and is responsible for mentor training, documentation and its evaluation, for promotion at different levels, for research and development and – particularly in the last three-year period – for finding new financial sources. There were around ten study circles organisers in 1993. They were primarily educational institutions. In ten years a broad network of diverse institutions was established consisting of NGOs, public and private institutions all over the country. A weak point of interpretation of study circle development in Slovenia might be lack of knowledge about historical roots of group learning (e.g. common readings in rural areas). However, it is important to underline that Slovenian study circles might be understood as intentional (community-based) learning and an important contribution to the emerging field of ‘*folkbildning*’ in Slovenia (in the same broad sense as in Sweden).

[2] Facts about *folkbildning* from the Swedish Council of Adult Education: http://www.folkbildning.se/download/543/x/FBR_fickfakta2006.pdf.

The main components of Slovenian study circles

The main components of Slovenian study circles are: a non-hierarchical, action-oriented setup, trained leadership of a locally rooted mentor (who is regularly offered further training) and a sense of togetherness among the participants with a common shared goal set in the communicative process. Every study circle has to set two obligatory goals:

a. an educational goal (participants have to establish the goal of their learning at the very beginning, in the planning phase); and
b. an action goal (the way every study circle has to publicly disseminate the results of its learning process); this aspect is specific to Slovenia.

The leadership staff are called 'mentors' and are mostly recruited from the local environment. Their role is indispensable. They take care of the primary principles, they motivate participants, apply for additional funds and write reports. They have several own motives (education, voluntarism, curiosity) and a strong idealistic and enthusiastic character. The combination of these motives and idealism is considered as a key element of the project's success.[3].

Participants themselves find additional funds for their action goals (e.g. for publishing brochures, organising local events e.g. reading evenings, round tables, learning paths, excursions etc.). Their sources are mainly local, sometimes European. However, only one-fifth of the total Slovenian local authorities financially support study circles.

Features of Slovenian study circles

An important feature of Slovenian study circles is their detailed documentation. It is certainly not meant as some kind of control but as an act supporting the responsible use of public finances and enabling their evaluation. The latter is done annually by the SIAE on the basis of forms, copies of media occurrences and material results (if available, e.g. local guides, postcards, historical or literate collections, small handicrafts or other products of an ethnological or aesthetic value). On this basis quality indicators are identified which serve for their yearly ranking. The »best ones« are promoted each year in the *Novičke* bulletin (a national adult educational publication of the informational-promotional nature). Study circles are usually nominated for the Lifelong Learning Week Award (by local authorities,

[3] http://www.surrey.ac.uk/politics/ETGACE/Final-Report-Screen-version.pdf, page 81.

by institutions or individuals), which is understood as indicating their publicly recognised quality. In the 1997-2004 period individuals from study circles were awarded for outstanding achievements in learning and the enriching of their own knowledge, making up 8% of all awards in this category (n=25). Study circles won 46% of awards in the category of groups for outstanding own achievements (n=26), while awards for achievements in knowledge enrichment of 'others' were given to study circles in 24% of the cases (n=49).

Comparative presentation of 'the state of art'

Table 7.1: Comparison of study circles in Sweden and Slovenia

	Sweden	Slovenia
Participation in 2004 (share of the population)	27.47 %	0.15 %
Participation trend in the 1993-2005 period	Stagnation, decrease	Increase
Attending study circles is a regular part of life	10% of the population	<0.01%
Attending a study circle is a lifestyle	Approx. 5%	Presumably 0%
Average number of participants in 2003	8.1	12.5
Average duration	41.6 study hours	35 study hours in the period of over 3.6 months
Topics*	*Aesthetic subjects,* include music, drama and handicraft (51.6%); *social-oriented subjects* (about 17%), *behavioural science & arts* (about 9%) and *languages* (about 6%), mainly Swedish as a second language, and English.	handicraft, ethnological subjects, learning – (altogether 53%)*
Structure of participants	60% women	75% women

*The categorisation of topics is not directly comparable – as can be seen in the table.

The table illustrates the large contextual differences between the two countries. Slovenia is far away from the »mass phenomenon« that applies to Sweden. The establishment of the Slovenian Institute for Adult Education – with its mission research, development and counselling in the AE field – stands behind the development of study circles and illustrates the wave of special energy that was unleashed after Slovenia became an independent state for the first time in 1991.

Study circles today: a quick view of public definitions and regulations

The state point of view

Sweden

Popular education is largely financed by grants from the government, regional governments and local councils. Although, formally speaking the popular study organisations are autonomous in comparison to other tax financed institutions, it the Parliament that lays down the aims and conditions for granting government support to popular education.

The modern reason for ensuring public support to popular education is to contribute to democratic development in society. The following excerpt originates from the 'Decree on the Government Subsidy for Popular Education':

2 § The government's subsidies of liberal adult education shall aim at:

1. furthering activities that empower women and men to shape their lives and create a commitment for taking part in developing society,
2. strengthening and developing democracy,
3. broadening a cultural interest in society, increasing participation in cultural life and furthering the enjoyment of cultural events and people's own creativity.

Activities that aim at filling educational gaps and raising the educational level in society should be given priority, as well as activities that are geared for educationally, socially and culturally disadvantaged people. Particularly important target groups for government subsidies are people of foreign descent, physically or mentally dysfunctional participants and the unemployed.[4]

In a 1998 governmental draft law submitted to the Swedish Parliament it was written, among other things:

---

[4] The Swedish National Council of Adult Education:
http://www.folkbildning.se/download/271/x/FBR_fickfakta2003_engelsk.pdf

'The role of liberal adult education today is also a matter of defending, vitalizing, and developing democracy. The instability of democracy is obvious, when seen in an international perspective. There is the risk of weak popular support and alienation between the elected and the electors; there is a feeling of impotence in the face of social development that we don't seem able to influence. Through our membership in the EU, the Swedish decision making process has extended beyond the national boarders. A series of new rights and obligations has also taken effect for the individual. This situation demands new knowledge.

The survival and vitality of democracy must build on a culture of democracy with dialogue, discussions, and participation as important elements. It must also comprise knowledge about values, conditions, and institutions necessary to democracy.

Giving liberal adult education the opportunity to grow is - in its essence - just this: strengthening democratic culture, and filling gaps of knowledge and information in society. Liberal adult education has a key role in this process. It can help create meeting-places for change and bridge the gaps between groups of people and between humans and technology.'

Through active state involvement, popular education has gained an educational-political legitimacy that has contributed greatly to today's institutionalised structure, not least in the study associations. The survey (Gougoulakis, 2001) does not focus on the specific forms a study circle may take but, rather, on the functions and purposes it has had during the period studied.

However, popular education and the state in Sweden, it can be said with hindsight, achieved a successful symbiosis where each is dependent on the other for its continued existence.

Slovenia

Economic and political pressures on Slovenian population in the last century resulted in either leaving the country or an adjustment to the circumstances: in terms of languages (more than 60% of the population speaks at least one foreign language) and the development of non-formal rules alongside the formal ones (comp. Hake 2000; Bron, 2004).

As educational investments were low – particularly for adults – and are of a long-term nature, Slovenia faces a low share of formally educated people (in 2002 56% of the population aged over 15 did not finish secondary school) and a critical level of literacy according to the IALS (77% of adults aged between 16 and 65 are below the third level of literacy (Možina, 2000))[5]. In

[5] Comparing the Slovenian results from the IALS survey to the Swedish ones, we note that 75%

the 1990s – after the state's independence in particular – the educational offer for adults flourished. Today the crucial regulative document for adult education is the Resolution of the National Programme for Adult Education (the 'ReNPIO') adopted by the Government of the Republic of Slovenia and its Parliament. It defines three priority areas for the period up until 2010: an increase in the general education of adults; an increase in the level of educational attainment of adults; and an improvement of the qualifications of adults to meet the needs of the labour market. Since, along with suitable legislation, Slovenians have 76% of the average GDP of the EU-25 today[6] one could expect high levels of investment in non-formal adult education and the establishing of '*folkbildning*' in Slovenia. This share is still more than ten times less than that in Sweden (Adam et al., 2005: 74). However, the participation level has risen (Mohorčič, 2005) and the trend of study circles is positive. Their normative dimension is fixed in the Act on Standards and Normatives in Adult Education (Odredba, 2000), which is in the process of being refined. The growing trend certainly expresses the enhanced interest of the state and the participants and, last but not least, some correspondence with the related European priorities (Memorandum, 2000; Future Objectives, 2004). Of course, there is the question of the density and time period needed to foster democracy through participation in adult education but it seems that Slovenia has only taken the first step in this direction.

The civil-society perspective

Sweden

The entrance of popular movements into the nation's political and social life gave rise to an immense educational movement which put its mark on the nation's political culture, in turn influencing societal development. The modern study circle movement symbolised the Swedish democratic breakthrough and was established as a way of managing civil rights, i.e. the freedom of assembly (freedom to establish civic organisations) and the right to education (see e.g. Arvidson, 1985; Andersson, 1980).

The history of social movements and popular education during the twentieth century is largely the history of modern Sweden. Their historical development is divided into four phases using distinct signs that mark shifts in the value basis of civil society.

---

of adults in Sweden demonstrate a high level of reading competence, i.e. levels 3 and 4 (Lindén & Kvarnström 1999, pp. 18-19). It seems to be well grounded to claim that there is a connection between a high level of reading skills and adults' participation in study circles.

[6] (http://evropa.gov.si/evropomocnik/question/43-9/)

In the struggle for social and political rights in the late part of the 19th century, the popular movements – civil society – used education as an important instrument. This educational work found its organisational expression in, among other things, study associations. The study associations, as the educational organisations of the popular movements, are the 'organisations of organisations'.

With the breakthrough of industrial society, popular education appeared as an educational instrument in the working class' struggle to wrest political power through the intensive and yet popular work of enlightenment and education.

Following a radical phase of formation the new social movements became established as legitimate actors in the country's political life. This was made possible through state recognition and public economic support. Civil society was gradually incorporated within the dominant political culture marked by a social-democratic, reformist orientation towards co-operation, pragmatism, compromise and equality among social groups. The new movements toned down their protest profiles and supported the new *folkhem* – the 'people's home' – project. The extension of the modern Swedish 'people's home' is just as much the creation of civil society.

Its co-option into the public administration is, however, subtle since popular education was nevertheless guaranteed a large degree of pedagogical autonomy, enshrined in Parliament's stipulated principles of liberty and voluntariness.

The post-war spirit of consensus was followed in the 1960s and 1970s by a new phase of civil-social development. During this time of reappraisal, radical new social forces entered the political arena as impelled by the agenda of post-material values. The individual's need for personal integrity and self-realisation was the value focused upon, infusing cultural debate and challenging the predominant collectivistic thinking of the period. This phase of awakening and criticism of civilisation that the new actors of civil society brought targeted the social model of production and its ramble up an ecological dead end. The popular education organisations became more independent vis-à-vis their 'original' principals and were rejuvenated with their new members, the new social movements.

A number of tendencies during the last three decades of the twentieth century are assumed to underlie great changes in society, the economy and cultural life.

However, a new 'social morphology' is being established in the last three decades, of networks that in turn use *information* as a basis for productivity and power. In the swell of globalisation the role of the state in public life is decreasing at the same time as individualisation spreads. The redrawing of the power map involved in globalisation is generating both new winners and losers and new areas of resistance. New movements are emerging, organised on a network basis and not dependent on national borders. In some ways, these movements express civic commitment with global awareness and responsibility. They are composed of new identities constructed chiefly out of *meaning* and *spirituality*. The roles of established movements are being questioned as more and more people abandon them. Yet this cannot be seen as a waning interest in politics, but an expression of an individual-centred search outside given collective structures (comp. Larsson, 2001). The purpose is largely the same as it always is, to reduce susceptibility to various risks; but the means seem to consist to a greater extent of individualised strategies for eliminating the effects of these risks. Popular education and its teaching theory are compelled to take a stance regarding the social changes and mental adjustments that are demanding a redefinition of the relationship between the individual and the collective. The individual is clearly becoming the actor of the new era, but a focus on the individual must not be allowed to imply a denial of the significance a well-functioning collective has for the individual's opportunities to develop and be well.

The movements' input to the established social order may be approached as a changing process during the abovementioned four phases. Initially, the movement's purpose is to accelerate the deconstruction of the old order so as to gain sufficient legitimacy and influence in the next phase. The achieved position of power partly entails an adaptation to the new changes, partly a continual endeavour to achieve additional changes which hopefully result in a more satisfactory, cultural system. Like all living organisms, however, even social movements have their own lifecycles. A few of these succeed in developing an ability to constantly renew themselves while others degenerate into something unrecognisable. In the latter cases, the organisations either die out or vegetate on preceding generations' cultural inheritance or alternatively the subsidies of society.

As a field, civil society is not homogenous but rather an arena full of conflict where the various agents compete for preferential right of interpretation, the creation of world images, and ideological hegemony. In addition, every agent undertakes a certain position in the societal structure characterised by defined relations toward other agents within civil society and toward the state and the economy (see Granovetter, 1985).

The degree of success depends on the adaptive ability which is demonstrated by strategies that effectively capture the demands for change in the present. This is more easily achieved by democratic (dialogic) forms of communication and through openness which includes, recognises and respects individual expression.

A vital civil society is a prerequisite for a healthy society. If the developmental tendencies of that time can be described in terms such as democratisation, industrialisation, internationalisation and individualisation (see Micheletti, 1994; Lundkvist, 1979), then they may get their specific Swedish meaning and configuration through the active impact of civil society. There are many signs indicating that today we find ourselves in a similar phase of transformation, which is described in similar terms. The difference is that the terms used one hundred years ago are used today to describe new tendencies such as globalisation, decentralisation, privatisation, marketisation, post-industrialisation etc. Civil society is being challenged. Old popular associations which played an important part in the establishment of the 20th century's society are forced to reconsider their goals and methods. Meanwhile, new social movements rise as both a reaction to established movements and as an attempt to demonstrate the right of the individual to influence their own situation. At the same time, today more than ever before, the individual experiences tangible uncertainty as he/she is exposed to an unprecedented vulnerability strengthened by the emergence of new threats and risks (see e.g.: Beck, 1998; Castells, 1996; Giddens, 1994).

The various movements are differentiated by their choice of tactics and strategies as they strive to get power and influence. Despite different opinions on which strategy was the most appropriate – collective or individual action – there is something that all movements share; *popular education* and *study circles*. In other words, they created public spaces for dialogue where they could practice their civil freedoms. We dare claim that this development contributed to the rise of a specific Swedish political culture which, in turn, has shaped the mentality of Swedish people.

Through study circles and popular education a gradual impression is being made on the cultural level with the purpose of changing the prevailing patterns of thinking, behaviour and communicating. A revolution is taking place on a reformative path. The popular educational work run by popular movements contributes to its members' learning and provides them with democratic virtues enabling them to function and live up to the expectations posed by political participation in a modern society.

Slovenia

The strengthening of cultural competencies, cognitive mobilisation, social cohesion and openness of individuals and local environments (Adam et al., 2005) are clearly important prerequisites for the activation of a passive public with a low level of functional literacy. As Slovenian civil society shares its developmental paths with the societies of the former communist countries the low density of study circles and their annual difficulties in gaining state and sponsors' money cannot create any serious impact – despite their growing trends and positive experience in line with their recognition among participants. However, long-term results of study circles are particularly important among those who are 'educationally passive'. In most European countries this means more than 50% of the population.

The role study circles play in the creation and/or maintenance of social capital is important. All three theoretical implications of social capital (network, culture, civic engagement) have been found in Slovenian study circles during the monitoring of their long-term results (Report, 2003; Bogataj, 2005; 2006). Long-term results were reported in 46% of the reports in 2003. They were structured over at least two levels – individual and community level. Individual level results prevail in urban lifestyle and is represented by overcoming the model of learning as an obligatory, unpleasant and indoctrinating process. Community level results prevail in the rural lifestyle. Mentors explained long-term results on the collective/group level as:

- knowledge and skills exchange/flow/transfer, as a model contrasting with the external powers of 'teaching' and 'control' present in the past experience of ideologically-driven education; and
- establishment of the »common« in terms of a 'common history, common goals etc.', including personal responsibility.

A small group is a safe environment to build and/or strengthen ties among participants who share a common goal (Bahovec, 2005; Wuthnow, 1996). Participants as individuals are activated in terms of their socialisation, involvement in learning activity and innovation (comp. Slee, 2003).

As study circle integrates individual and group initiatives by establishment of the »common«, including personal responsibility, we see its particular role in overcoming the lack of intermediary bodies in post-modern society. This is the arena for building social capital.

Another role – building the ties of the community with the local natural environment – is more common in rural environments, in distant rural ones in particular (comp. Elands, Wiersum, 2003). One reason for this is the lack of both an educational offer for adults and socialisation opportunities there. As the 'local environment' is not precisely defined here, a question remains about the density of study circles in time and space. How many study circles are needed to change attitudes e.g. from passive to active learners? How long should a tradition last for such an effect to emerge? Where is the meeting point – if at all – between the Swedish and Slovenian experiences with study circles in this respect?

The abovementioned yearly report on Slovenian study circles (2003) structured results of study circles into the 'social integration and higher motivation of participants' (43% respondents, n=196), 31% in terms of 'our relationships, thinking has changed' and 24% in terms of 'they bring new knowledge'. These results, confirmed by some later unpublished research (Bogataj, 2006), clearly show that a free reciprocal interaction in active learning (in general) makes people: 1) active; 2) tied; and 3) (more) critically-minded (than before undertaking learning in the study circle). One-fifth of participants helped themselves with skills from study circles in their entrance to the labour market. All these impacts might be strong or weak, short- or long-lasting. During our field visits we met people who did not look at all active, yet their presence (according to the arguments of mentors and participants) proved their strong interest, even their breaking off from their previous social exclusion, distrust in common settings and stimulation of an innovative mood. Even the ties might be strong and other weak, short- or long-lasting. As a low share of study circles in Slovenia connect with each other on their own initiative, structural holes (weak ties among the groups) are seldom. To strengthen these ties the SIAE annually organises at least two educational meetings for study circle mentors. They are not only for the provision of new information and knowledge but offer an opportunity for networking (building bridges) and information cycling among representatives of different topics and local environments.

Participants' viewpoints

Sweden

In many respects the study circle fulfils the conditions for a *learning community*. The participants' world of life and systems is in many respects the ground in which the learning process is rooted. Participants' reasons for studying testify to an experiential need arising from the existing conditions of the family, the community and working life. People make their way to the study circle's non-formal but structured meeting culture to learn things they cannot, or do not, understand and together with a few others to acquire a grasp of what appears to be happening and what is influencing their circumstances.

Studying in circles is associated with specifical characteristics probably due to their free and voluntary character. The freedom aspect is fundamental, be it the independence in the work vis-à-vis external power factors or the participants' autonomous choice of what to study and their influence on the pedagogical process. Study circle work is a social opportunity structure and tallies with people's deliberate action when they decide to transcend themselves – to become another person and to leave the state with which they happen to be dissatisfied. The transcendent action, however, presupposes genuine opportunities to exercise one's liberty to choose a life project, including an educational project, and the ability to exercise this liberty. The community's view of adult learning during the period covered by this thesis indicates that popular education represents a 'creative environment' for people's free growth and self-determination. The study circle's freedom and voluntariness appear closely linked to cherished adult-pedagogical ideals such as:

• Self-education

Self-education as a notion denotes from where the educational initiative is derived, who controls the content of education as well as the forms and responsibilities of learning. The prefix 'self' is therefore essential in the notion.

• Collaborative learning

Even if the study circle is primarily an environment for learning together with others, it is distinguished for the multifarious meanings it holds for every participant. In the study circle's social interaction a collaborative learning occurs that encompasses the acquisition of meta-cognitive insights into one's own ability to learn and function in various social situations.

• Open and flexible learning

Against the backdrop of the study circle's weak framework, characterised by:

- independence of time and space;
- a lack of outward dictated knowledge controls and centrally established curricula; and
- regulated prescriptions with regard to previous knowledge, entrance requirements and qualifications

there is reason to claim that the pedagogy of study circles fulfils the requirements allowing it to be characterised as the 'pedagogy of open and flexible learning'.

• Experience-based/individualised learning

In the adult educational *ethos,* the 'curriculum' is understood to be open and flexible and adapted partly to the individual's understanding of their personal educational needs, and partly to the developing opportunities in the life cycle.

• Contextuality

Learning within the non-formal education sector is contextual, i.e. it depends on the situation in which learning occurs and the individuals who learn. Study circles are formed in various contexts, most often in an association or by a group of people starting a study circle based on a common interest and/or values.

• Meaning and context

Knowledge and information characterises our era. More people today study more and longer and in a variety of educational environments. The production of information and knowledge is immense and rapidly spread to ever more people by means of new information technologies. The specialist has been the hallmark of our time: one who knows a lot about less. Certainly, this specialisation is a precondition for the development of science but scarcely consistent with a wide and open mind in the public sphere of life. The informational paradigm of our society today is impaired by a paradox. On one hand, humanity's collected knowledge is being boosted enormously. On the other hand, it seems as we possess less knowledge about more subjects. Consequently, we are becoming increasingly dependent on others' knowledge. The learning design in study circles therefore has an important role to play considering the pedagogical philosophy (and the tradition) of popular education.

• Influence

Participants' influence is assumed to be an essential factor which explains the study circle's concept of success. Each participant in the study circle is in the centre of attention. He or she participates in a learning process to which they are invited to have an active influence on. In consequence, they control the own learning process. They are the owner of the learning process in the same way a free artist possesses the intentions and means for their own creation. The study circle participant's relation to his/her own learning is seldom instrumental. Learning is not alienated with respect to the learner's existing situation and learning needs.

The view of knowledge underlying the study circles is in agreement with a particular view of the learning human being, i.e. someone is learning best when he/she.

- get the opportunity to put the acquired information in its proper context; and
- meet and communicate with others who share common interests and curiosity, believing that others' knowledge is an important value (Gougoulakis, 2001: 300-303; Gougoulakis, 2006: 116-118).

Basically, the knowledge view of popular education is non-hierarchical. It is democratic for the reason that is the learning needs of the study group, and every individual participant's, which form the necessary grounds for learning to take place.

Historically, popular education has signified a shift of power in the relation between the content of learning and those having access to it (Bergstedt and Larsson, 1995). Popular education was not only a matter of spreading the knowledge of the elite, but above all a medium to introduce new types of knowledge. For the most part, the new knowledge was linked to new groups' endeavours for power and influence in society as well as to individuals' personal development and fulfilment. Popular education is growing to be the infrastructure of public places for meetings for democratic dialogue, disciplined social interaction and co-operative learning that are also self-directed.

Slovenia

As we can only agree with the characteristics described above, we here merely add some minor comments:

1. The described features are (mostly) rooted in 'eye to eye' meetings. Traditionally, Slovenian study circles consist of local participants. No virtual study circles have been recorded up to now.
2. Indirect contribution of study circles to decision-making through development of competencies for active participation seems very important in Slovenia even after more than a decade of democratic state. We assume that vertical social capital emerges more or less unintentionally and only occasionally, along with plenty of horizontal one.
3. Our field experience confirms the constraints on participation found in the literature (Preston, 2004). The semi-voluntary leading of a study circle is a demanding task – only those with special energy and (self-) motivation are engaged for longer time periods (compare the motives found in the ETGACE research).[7]
4. Slovenia will focus on the participants' point of view in the future. At the moment we only know that the motivation for continuation among study circle participants is above 90% (Černoša, 1997), while most Slovenians still do not even know what a study circle is. The reason is, in our point of view, the decision-makers' weak understanding of their positive role in Slovenian society and, consequently, their lack of support for their development.

[7] (http://www.surrey.ac.uk/politics/ETGACE/).

Similarities and differences in the roles of study circles in both countries

The context of the study circle phenomenon in the two countries is hardly comparable. Not only are the countries of a different size, population and religion. They are particularly different in their historical and political backgrounds, last but not least in the political weight of adult education (at least in the last decade), resulting in different financial and infrastructural levels of support for study circles in the two countries. On account of the different socio-cultural contexts for learning, e.g. ordinary (adult) people do not share the same experience such as of WW II or neighbouring foreign languages, the civil society of the developed Swedish democracy is hardly comparable with that of the post-communist country where the component of 'fear' still has impacts on social capital and non-formal education (comp. Fuwa, 2004; Bron, 2004).

If study circles in Sweden have been a socially acceptable form of gathering for decades, we can hardly say that for Slovenia where the foreign model was taken to overcome the lack of an educational offer for rural communities (Krajnc, 2005) and to improve democracy (Klemenčič, 1995). If the Swedish tradition of popular education is analysed in detail, Slovenia is celebrating the success of study circles in overcoming individual passivity e.g. in educational terms. However, if the generation of adults over 50 needs an impulse of encouragement, it is the younger generations that are more educated and less life-experienced, have a lack of social cohesion, a lack of 'a common' (non-material) experience and – particularly in rural areas – a lack of cognitive mobilisation (comp. Adam et al., 2005).

What both states have in common is that participation in study circles is a socio-cultural behavioural pattern – one amongst other collective symbolic actions (meaningful) – through which people practice their culture, confirm their group affiliations, enhance their social capital and renew their social contract. In study circles citizens reflect on their contemporary times, shape their world image, and receive support for their orientation within an increasingly complex and uncertain reality. In the study circles' social environment adult individuals learn more about themselves and the world they live in through the exchange of experiences and through direct dialogue with others. The habit of meeting and spending time with others in study circles is subconsciously founded through socialisation. The study circle, which is fundamentally a dialogical institution, contributes to the transferral of internalised interaction-codes rooted in common historical experiences. The socially and culturally formed codes being discussed are thankfully not an immovable structure with fixed contents and meaning (comp. Ajagán-Lester et al., 2003). They constitute the intersection of the rules of conduct from different eras, which however is constantly interpreted and reinterpreted in a game of negotiation which always occurs when people are in dialogue with each other. The codes are thus more or less open, more or less integrative, and are always socially and culturally regulated.

The explanation of the popularity of study circles is primarily found in the great freedom adult participants enjoy in designing the study process in accordance with their own needs and prerequisites in a collective atmosphere of mutual co-operation and the open exchange of ideas. The study circle developed as a democratic project and, as such, should reflect the values of democracy in both form and content.

But how and by whom is the decision made as to whether a study circle becomes a study circle in the normative sense indicated above? The assumption is made that a study circle is fundamentally a self-governing study form. Thus, it is the participants themselves who determine the form of the study circle. The question becomes more difficult and more complicated if one considers that society/the state shoulder the greatest part of the responsibility for financing study circle activities. As a financing authority, the state determines the framework which directly steers the activities. Therefore, there sometimes appears to be an inherent conflict between the study circle's pedagogical autonomy on one hand, and the state in its role as the 'guardian' of that autonomy on the other.

Mentalities are understood to be mental and emotional structures affected by ideas, habits and practices from past generations (that hardly have any connection to their original functions), of latent unarticulated collective moods (feelings and intuitions) and of cognitive schemes which fabricate intentions and stage actions. On both individual and collective levels, the working forces of mentalities is 'crystallising' in the same way Bourdieu described with the term *habitus* [8] (Bourdieu, 1977; Berner et al., 1977) as:

> 'a system of lasting and transferable attitudes (dispositions), which, at the same time as it integrates an individual's previous experiences, functions in every given moment as a matrix for the way the individual understands, values, and acts' (Berner et al., 1977: 53).

[8] Habitus denotes here an individual's attitude (pattern of behaviour). Mentality refers to collective psychosocial structures of imaginations, attitudes and experiences which may explain (and motivate) the disposition of groups of people to act and behave in specific ways.

Bourdieu and Passeron localise this 'system of attitudes' in the individual's primary socialisation without excluding the roll of future experiences for the formation of the *habitus*.

'The relation has to be understood in such way that these future experiences constantly are experienced, interpreted, and incorporated in the individual's way of looking at things according to certain principles that have been assimilated in early childhood' (ibid. s. 54)

Mentalities are culturally shaped and, at the same time, they shape the culture. They operate in communication, are refined in communication, and manifest in both individual as well as collective behavioural patterns, in actions, in decisions, and in ways of thinking. The essence of communication is to achieve an influence. When the influence is articulated it is visible and occurs openly. You can always relate to such an influence. But there is also another influence which is hidden and of which those who are exposed to it are unaware. Ödman (1995) coined the notion *immanent pedagogy* to describe all the forms of creeping influence impregnating our lives. This pedagogy is inherent to every life situation. The creeping influence of pedagogical acts is rarely or never perceived consciously but is presumed to form mentalities: 'Pedagogy and mentality belong in my way of seeing, close to each other. It is through pedagogical acts that mentalities are shaped, and pedagogy is shaped in turn by those mentalities which 'pedagogues' are carriers of, in a dialectic interplay' (ibid. s. x.)

Participation in study circles is tantamount to gaining access to a community or to a social network nexus. Every individual participant brings to the community their own human capital, which consists of knowledge, abilities, feelings and beliefs, experiences and capacities. When human capital sets in motion 'by means of communication of habits of doing, thinking, and feeling' from one to the other a new sort of capital – social in nature – is generated. Social capital has a relational character as it is created when relations between people are changed in communication in order to promote some activities. Simultaneously, this is an act of learning since all communication is educative.

Human capital is an individually bound resource in human nodes, while social capital is to be found in the links (relations) between individuals. Coleman (1990) further stressed the difference between social capital and private resources by claiming the character of social capital is something connected with a public-good aspect, i.e. 'social capital is not the private property of any of the persons who benefit from it' (ibid.: 315)

Research and evaluation studies focused on the learning process from the participants' point of view indicate that study circles function as social venues characterised by reciprocity and trustful social relations, both formal and informal, entailing learning of some kind. We tend to put an 'equals' sign between the notions social capital and learning. As social capital 'refers to features of social organisations, such as trust, norms and networks that can improve the efficiency of society by facilitating co-ordinated actions' (Putnam et al., 1993: 167), and directs attention to sociability (Koniordos, 2005), so too is the case with the learning process taking place in study circles.

Flexibility seems to be the study circle's most distinct characteristic. Four components combine to make up the concept of the study circle which can in many ways be said to be ingenious, namely, the loose framework, the informal character of the study situation, the collective learning environment, and the participants' genuine interest in knowledge. The interaction in study circles is influenced by certain conditions which appear to be decisive for the educational climate and, of course, the quality of the learning outcome. These are the lack of a curriculum and grading and thereby the absence of explicit demands on the participants' performance, as well as the fact that it is voluntary, which contributes to a more relaxed climate. Such an environment is a combination of two kinds of community claimed to be inherent to modern societies, i.e. a casual community and a stable community (Lundberg, 2005).

The expectations of the circle leaders and participants are often guided by their previous experience of education with traditional work methods, which mostly govern how the teaching is organised. In addition, there are traditions and institutions. However, it is part of the study circles pedagogical heritage of a weak framework of outside regulations to break with the traditional (school-like) working methods. However, there is a built-in paradox in the pedagogy implemented in study circles owing to the fact that students' influence over the work forms is normally large. In accordance with the democratic state of order in study circles the participants are free to choose either a self-directed learning method or an old-fashioned teacher-oriented one.

Study circles contribute to opinion-building among participants and their individual ability to take action, but there is doubt as to whether they can be considered a body for collective and co-ordinated action for the purpose of social change. On the basis of studies that have been conducted (SUFO 96; Borgström et al., 1997; Larsson, 1999; Gougoulakis, 2001; Byström and Säfström, 2005; SUFO 2) we suggest that the study circle has a multitude of different meanings for the participants. Among other things, they offer knowledge for business and pleasure, the enrichment of leisure time, social resources, an increase in one's self esteem and courage and personal development. At the individual level, the effects that can be shown are in the form of increased self-confidence and a stronger ability to take action. Larsson (1999) indicates, however, that the lack of collective action has less to do with the circle having failed as a work form. Rather, it has more to do with a weakening of the power base of civil society in canalising the citizens' political commitment, which may have a negative effect on the state of social capital for society's future development.

Participation in study circles was once a matter of a collective project, which in turn gave rise to the collective processes of learning and action. This type of co-operative study tradition has been increasingly replaced by more individual-oriented interests. However, this does not prevent study circles from playing an important role in that participants develop a common understanding and share interests that concern their own communities. SUFO 2 emphasises a number of examples of efforts where adult education's collaboration with the local community has been developed and augmented.

Study associations are ascribed a mediating role in public life because of their ability to establish linkages between diverse segments of society contributing to the mitigating of incompatible interests and fostering a culture of negotiation and compromise. In this sense, study circles appear to function as local public arenas for reflective and deliberative exchange on questions of importance for the participants' living conditions, at the same time stimulating participation in public debate. Metaphorically, study circles are the generator of social capital through a refining process of mainly two very scabrous raw materials: the public good on one side, and the private good on the other. Social capital becomes acquired at the very moment the participants are in a communicative relation with each other, and it is composed of knowledge, abilities and competences for a meaningful life, as well as in public and private life.

Some conclusions on the contextualisation of study circles and their relation to social capital

The overall context of the present study is the rapid development of our society and the new demands this places on citizens' ability to retrain, learn new things and learn continuously in a lifelong perspective. One of our key concluding remarks is that the small but conceptually essential contribution of adult education/study circles to social capital is theoretically grounded in Granovetter (1985), Putnam (1993; 1995; 2001) and Rothstein (2001; 2002).

The second conclusion is that the same characteristics and roles of study circles were found in the contexts of both states under comparison, however, they depend on the state tradition and direct financial and research support.

A brand of learning that gives citizens an overall picture and understanding of the changes taking place is assumed to generate security. It is also assumed to enhance people's employability in a working ethos that seeks colleagues able to assume responsibility, work independently and, not least, co-operate. The challenges of our time stem from three circumstances symptomatic of social change. These are changes in the social structure, in how we communicate and how we use our time. There has always been change. What is new is the rapid pace at which the changes are taking place, supported by increasingly sophisticated electronic information technology. Changes that used to take a lifetime may now happen within a generation or even faster.

One conclusion from the above is that when planning operations vis-à-vis adults/the elderly, both in working life and in society in general, one needs to take account of each individual's possibilities and abilities. This is because these vary widely – not least because of the differing social conditions. Changes in the economy and in the community may be handled more smoothly the better the preparedness and the resources of the citizen and the more they are involved in this process (see Granovetter, 1985).

Popular education in Sweden has so far exhibited a fantastic ability to adapt to social change, thanks to harmonious collaboration with and active support from the state and the community. It has been an open and flexible arranger of educational activities for individuals and different associations. De facto, popular education and the study circle offer a public meeting place where people may gather to discuss the questions that social change generates, to get support to create opinion and belief in their own ability to think for themselves and, together with others, work out forms for common solutions to problems. Faced with an uncertain future, popular education must once again choose a vision and an instrument for learning and teaching. Or not choose. Whatever the choice, it will demand an analysis of the consequences for those directly involved and for the community in general.

The three perspectives presented in this article are not mutually exclusive; rather they are seen as convergent. They relate to one another dialectically and are each other's preconditions. Popular education as an institutionalised practice has emerged from civil society but has also, for its consolidation, depended on the active support of the national parliamentary power. How relations between society, the state and the participants have been formed and how the interplay between the actors in popular education has developed are questions which, it is hoped, become clear through an investigation of the main agents of the popular education field. The specific relation between the Swedish state and the popular education organisations follows for the most part the same neo-corporatist pattern (Rothstein, 2001)[9], which characterises the relations between the government and major interest organisations. This is justified through the specific way in which social programmes have been institutionalised and can serve as an explanation of the maintenance and generation of high degree of trust and social capital in Sweden. In Slovenia, the relations between the government and major interest organisations are under the developmental impact of socio-economic circumstances (state independence in 1991, joining the EU in 2004, the political turn in 2005). The role and state of adult education which in turn defines the role, state and results of study circles are therefore not yet in the final phase of establishment. Despite the documented growing trends there are at the moment heavy pressures to bring about the direct economic contribution of study circles to society.

The main points regarding study circles in the two countries for the social capital concept may be summarised as follows:

1. Participation affords the possibility of extending one's social contacts and hence increasing one's social capital. It also involves an opportunity for personal development, new knowledge (experience and skills) and new interests.
2. The study circle is a social context for civic communication through democratic forms of social intercourse.
3. The study circle is an invaluable arena for moulding and developing civil society.
4. Popular education and adult education as institutions offer a social opportunity structure for the education of all. Their forms depend partly on the self-selected need to learn and partly on what society intends. Swedish popular education may offer a model for the vision of a different educational system better adapted to meeting the challenges and demands of the new era – the information age – for lifelong learning.
5. The study circle is an intermediary body. At its best it affords its members security, meaningfulness and self-confidence. It provides the community with responsible citizens.

[9] Moreover, Rothstein has in his writings convincingly stressed the role of the state in making social capital in Sweden and in Nordic countries. He also makes a connection between the occurrence of a high level of trust and social capital, on one hand, and a low level of corruption, on the other.

6. Establishment of the 'common' arena (e.g. action goal) is of particular importance in post-modern society. Participation in a study circle represents, in the first instance, an environment for collaborative learning. This can cause people to grow, extend their knowledge and develop various capabilities on the basis of their own experience and questioning. This is a quality of learning that, by extension, increases the individual's prospects of personal well-being and more active involvement in the life of the community.
7. Study circle teaching theory assumes its specific character as lying at the intersection of two apparently irreconcilable functions: to learn for adaptation and to encourage for change. What is ultimately decisive is the quality of the open discourse and the composition of the autonomous circle group. Group/common learning is an alternative to the prevailing individual learning environments.
8. The unique ramifications of the study circle stemming from its nonformal, free and voluntary character contribute to the even distribution of pedagogical power among the circle members. No one is better than anyone else. The relationships of authority are not given but are negotiable and are legitimated in the interplay of equality, which is of crucial importance in societies where this was sanctioned for decades.
9. Study circle leadership is fundamentally an idealistic assignment. It is associated with virtues such as true commitment to the subject, social competence, knowledge of people, sensitivity, flexibility and organisational ability. Idealistic assignment is probably a prerequisite for engagement/ activation for change including change associated with creation and maintenance of social capital.
10. In the study circle the participant is made visible. What could contribute better to social capital's creation and maintenance?! He/she takes part in a process of learning which they are invited to actively influence. The participant can successfully influence their own learning since they have control over the time for thinking, problematising and exchanging ideas with others.

If meetings in study circles reflect a genuine Swedish 'model' of social community in which adult citizens use it as a public arena for communication, this might become the same in Slovenia but only if state support will allow the continuation of the trends (e.g. of the growing motivation for participation, growing number of organisations which offer study circles, the growing diversity of results – including social capital). To achieve this aim and to use the abovementioned advantages of study circles, a recognition of the arguments emerging out of the pure field of (adult) education is needed. Theorists have proven that study circle communities appeal to the need for strong personal integrity with social engagement – solidarity and individualism/privacy at the same time (comp. Rothstein, 2002) – and 'half anonymity' (comp. Florida, 2001). It is just about right given the way people seem to be, behave and communicate as a society in an effort to find out solutions for the public good in a spirit of consensus. In a macro perspective it might be claimed that the 'free and voluntary' study circle communities foster a specific political culture which is in harmony with the prevailing state ideology. Certainly, the state support for popular education is also grounded on such pragmatic considerations. State and society (*folket*/the people) constitute a harmonious unity emphasising collective co-existence and solidarity, security and effectivity, a community of values and trust.

As Swedish society has never been neither pure communitarian or entirely liberal, although it is composed of a liberal 'union of unions' (comp. Waltzer, 1992), this model might be – at least from the educational point of view – still relevant to Slovenian society. Popular education as an essential part of the societal pedagogical apparatus, including co-operation with the major civil society organisations, is in favour of that national target by using means like discussions in more or less organised forms e.g. study circles), mutual understanding and shared values (Rothstein, 2002). Social movements have played an important role in Sweden's social, economic and political life because of their 'protest' character, their widespread organisational network with local associations/units all over the country, their relative autonomy towards the state and their responsibility whenever the state has delegated public duties to civil society's organisations. (ibid.) In this framework study circles might therefore further contribute to social relations and networks through promoting learning, in the first place, which can be beneficial for social life, spare time and the economy. This is at the same time an expected trend and issues a proposal for politics and professionals – to support self-governing active citizenship through non-individual learning settings.

An ultimate remark

In the present article, we made a first attempt to outline the main characteristics of popular education in Sweden and Slovenia, with a focus on possible effects and consequences participation and learning may have for the creation and maintenance of social capital in the two countries. We are fully aware of the tentative nature of the results and conclusions discussed in this article.

We are convinced that the kind of civil learning which takes place in the non-formal settings of popular education in the examined countries is an authentic way of civilised communication enabling individual growth and collective/social progress in both the short and long term.

However, from a societal point of view, not all learning is always good or beneficial. '*Folkbildning*' and the learning it promotes is an essential matter for society provided that some fundamental conditions are at hand, that is facilitating participatory (self-directed) learning which is free and voluntary, especially democratic, by being open to all citizens and economically supported by the common (community, society).

The idea of popular education is emancipating, critical, reflective and progressive. It rests on democracy's morals regarding human rights, equality and justice, respect for everyone's preferences and life choices, by guaranteeing everybody's active participation in society's life.

The pedagogical-philosophical thinking of popular education as outlined in this article, together with a willingness to learn more from non-formal educational traditions in different countries, could as a suggestion form the basis of comprehensive wide-ranging studies on the European Union level.

Apparently, we are in need of more and profound knowledge of other countries' *folkbildnings* – traditions in search of common grounds for designing and building up a new European (our new?) adult education policy: a policy of a new European '*bildung*' serving the creation of a new identity which ought to be inclusive and thus democratic, pluralistic and thus multicultural and cosmopolitan whereby every citizen is respected, needed and active.

Literature

Adam, Frane, Makarovič, Matej, Rončević, Borut and Tomšič, Matevž (2005) *The challenges of sustained development: the role of socio-cultural factors in East-Central Europe*. New York: Budapest Central European, University Press.

Ajagán-Lester, Luis, Ledin, Per and Rahm, Henrik (2003) 'Intertextualiteter' (Intertextualities), in: Englund, Boel& Ledin, Per (eds) *Teoretiska perspektiv p} sakprosa* (Theoretical Perspectives on Factual Prose). Lund : Studentlitteratur, pp. 205-240.

Andersson, Bo (1980) *Folkbildning i perspektiv. - Studieförbunden 1870-2000. Organisering, etablering och profilering.* (People's Education in Perspective 1870-2000. Focus on Adult Education Organisations). Stockholm: LTs förlag.

Arvidson, Lars (1985) Folkbildning i rörelse. Pedagogisk syn i folkbildning inom svensk arbetarrörelse och frikyrkorörelse under 1900-talet - en jämförelse (Popular Education in Movement. Pedagogical View in Sweden's Labour Movement and Free Churcianism Movement during the 20th Century – A Comparison). Högskolan för Lärarutbildning i Stockholm. Institutionen för pedagogik: CWK Greerup.

Bahovec, Igor (2005) *Skupnosti: teorije, oblike, pomeni* (Communities: theories, forms and meanings). Ljubljana: Sophia.

Beck, Ulrich (1998) *Vad innebär globaliseringen? Missuppfattningar och möjliga politiska svar.* (Was ist Globalisierung? Irrtümer des Globalismus – Antworten auf Globalisierung). Göteborg: Daidalos.

Bergstedt, Bosse and Larsson, Staffan (eds) (1995) *Om folkbildningens innebörder* (On the Meanings of Popular Education). Linköpings universitet: Mimer.

Berner, Boel, Callewaert, Staf and Silberbrandt, Henning (1977) Skola, ideologi och samhälle. Ett kommenterat urval franska utbildningssociologiska texter av Bourdieu/ Passeron, Baudelot/Establet, Poulantzas. (*School, Ideology and Society. Commentaries on Selected French Texts in the Sociology of Education by Bourdieu/Passeron/ Baudelot/Establet, Poulantzas*). Stockholm: Wahlström&Widstrand.

Bogataj, Nevenka (2005) Slovenskim študijskim krožkom v novo desetletje (To the forthcoming decade of Slovenian study circles). In: študije in raziskave; 12, *študijski krožki - od zamisli do sadov v prvem desetletju Andragoški center Slovenije*, pp. 83-97.

Bogataj, Nevenka (2006) *Razumevanje pomena gozda za trajnostni razvoj študijskih krožkov* (Understanding of the Role of Forests for Rural Sustainable Development in Study Circles), PhD. thesis, unpubl.

Borgström, Lena; Gougoulakis, Petros and Höghielm, Robert (1997) *Lärande i studiecirkel – En studie av en pedagogisk miljö* (Learning in Study Circle. A Study of a Pedagogical Milieu). Stockholm: Lärarhögskolan.

Bourdieu, Pierre (1977) *Outline of a theory of practice.* Cambridge: Cambridge Univ. Press.

Bourdieu, Pierre (1985) The Forms of Capital. In: *Handbook of Theory and Research for the Sociology of Education.* (ed. by J. G. Richardson.) New York, Westport, Connecticut, London: Greenwood Press, pp. 241-58.

Bron, Michal. Jr. (2004) 'From Parallel Society to Civil Society: Surfacing from Authoritarianism. *Journal of Adult and Continuing Education.* Special Issue: Adult Education and Democratic Civil Society in Post-Communist Countries. pp. 5-20.

Byström, Jan and Säfström, Fredrika (2005) Studiecirkledeltagare 2004 – Tv} rapporter om deltagare i studieförbundens cirkelverksamhet. (Participants in Study Circles 2004 – Two Reports Regarding Participants in Study Circles Organized by Popular Educational Associations). Folkbildningsr}det utvärderar No 1 2005.

Castells, Manuel (1999) *The information age: economy, society and culture.* Malden, Mass.: Blackwell.

Coleman, James S. (1990) *Foundations of Social Theory.* Cambridge Mass: Harvard University Press

Černoša, Slavica, Malečkar, Vilma (1997) Analiza delovanja študijskih krožkov v šolskem letu 1995/96 (Analysis of study circles in the 1995/96 school year). Ljubljana: Andragoški center Republike Slovenije.

Elands Birgit H.M., Wiersum K. Frierk (2003) Forestry and rural development in Europe: research results and policy implications of a comparative European study: forest and nature conservation policy group. Wageningen, Wageningen University.

Eyerman, Ron and Jamison, Andrew (1991) *Social movements. A cognitive approach.*. Cambridge: Polity Press in association with Basil Blackwell.

Florida, Richard (2001) *The Rise of the Creative Class. And How It's Transforming Work, Leisure, Community and Everyday Life.* New York: Sane Agency & Susan Schulman.

Friedrich, Carl J. (ed.) (1993) *The Philosophy of Kant.* New York: The Modern Library.

Future objectives 2010: Education and training in Europe: diverse systems, shared goals for 2010; Strategic objective 2: Facilitating the access of all to education and training system.

Fuwa, Kazuhiko (2004) Introduction. *Journal of Adult and Continuing Education.* Special Issue: *Adult Education and Democratic Civil Society in Post-Communist Countries*, p. 2.

Giddens, Antony (1994) *Beyond Left and Right: The Future of Radical Politics.* Cambridge: Polity Press.

Gougoulakis, Petros (2001) *Studiecirkeln. Livsl}ngt lärande...* (Study Circle. Lifelong Learning ...). Stockholm: HSL Förlag. PhD thesis.

Gougoulakis, Petros (2006) *Bildning och lärande. Om folkbildningens pedagogic.* (Bildung and Learning. On the Pedagogy of Popular Education). Stockholm: ABF& Bilda.

Government Bill 1997/98:115.

Government Bill 1997/98:115. Lära, växa, förändra [Learn, Grow, Change].

Granovetter, Mark (1985) 'Economic Action and Social Structures: The Problem of Embeddedness'. *American Journal of Sociology*, No. 91.

Hake, Barry (2000) 'The Rise and Fall of Adult Education Institutions and Social Movements'. In: Cooke, MacSween (eds) *The Proceedings of the Seventh International Conference on the History of AE.* Peter Lang.

Hardin, Russel (2005) 'Is Social Capital Declining?' *AXESS Magazine*. (Theme: Social capital). Issue 5, 2005 (www.axess.se).
http://www.surrey.ac.uk/politics/ETGACE/Final-Report-Screen-version.pdf
http://evropa.gov.si/evropomocnik/question/43-9/
http://www.folkbildning.se/download/271/x/FBR_fickfakta2003_engelsk.pdf

Johansson, Inge (1985) *För folket och genom folket. Om idéer och utvecklingslinjer i studieförbundens verksamhet.* (For People and by the People. On ideas and trends in the work of study circle associations). Stockholm: LiberUtbildningsförlaget

Klemenčič, Sonja (1995) *Učimo se v študijskih krožkih* (We are learning in study circles). Ljubljana: Andragoški center Slovenije.

Kondylis, Panajotis (1981) *Die aufklärung im Rahmen des neuzeitlichen Rationalismus.* Stutgart: Klett-Cotta-Verlag.

Koniordos, Sokratis M. (2005) *Networks, Trust and Social Capital. Theoretical and Empirical Investigations from Europe.* England/USA: Ashgate Publishing Company.

Krajnc, Ana (2005) Kaj je odločalo o nastajanju študijskih krožkov? (What was it that initiated study circles?) Študije in raziskave 12. *Študijski krožki – od zamisli do sadov v prvem desetletju* Nevenka Bogataj (eds) - Ljubljana : Andragoški center Slovenije, pp. 33-45.

Larsson, Staffan (1999) 'Studiecirkeldemokratin' (Study Circle Democracy). *Civilsamhället* (Civil Society). SOU 1999:84, pp. 243-280.

Larsson, Staffan (2001) Study circles as democratic utopia. A Swedish perspective. In: Bron, A. Schemmann, M. (eds) *Civil society, citizenship and learning*, Hamburg Münster, pp. 137-167.

Liedman, Sven-Eric (1997) *I skuggan av framtiden. Modernitetens idéhistoria.* ŠUnder the shadow of the future. Modernity's history of ideasĆ. Stockholm: Bonnier Alba

Lindén, Carina and Kvarnström, Christina (1999) Baskompetens. Grunden för kompetenshöjning. [Basic Competence. A ground for competence raising]. Svenska EU-programkontoret, Nutek, Rådet för arbetslivsforskning. Rapport nr 3.

Lundberg, Anders P. (2005) 'Om gemenskap. En sociologisk betraktelse'. (Regarding Community. A Sociological Reflection). Lund: Lund Dissertations in Sociology, Nr 65.

Lundkvist, Sven (1979) *Folkrörelserna i det svenska samhället 1850-1920.* (Popular Movements in Sweden 1850-1920) Stockholm: Almqvist & Wiksell International.

Micheletti, Michele (1994) *Det civila samhället och staten – Medborgarsammanslutningarnas roll i svensk politik.* (Civil Society and the State – The Role of Citizens' Organisations in Swedish Politics). Göteborg: Fritzes AB.

Mohorčič-Špolar, Vida (2005) 'Participation of adults in education-2004'. *Novičke*; summer 2005.

Možina, Ester (2000) 'Pismenost odraslih v Sloveniji - pozabljeni kapital'; (Adult Literacy in Slovenia). In: *Pismenost, participacija in družba znanja.* 4. andragoški kolokvij z mednarodno udeležbo. - Ljubljana : Andragoški center Republike Slovenije, pp. 9-11.

Odredba o standardih in normativih v izobraževanju odraslih, (2000) Ur.l. RS, št. 43/2000.

Ödman, Per-Johan (1995) *Kontrasternas spel. En svensk mentalitets- och pedagogikhistoria.* (The Game of Contradictions. A Swedish History of Mentality and Education). Stockholm: Norstedts Förlag AB.

Preston, John (2004) A continuous effort of sociability: learning and social capital in adult life. In: Schuller, T. et al. *The Benefits of Learning, The impact of education on health, family life and social capital*, pp.119-136.

Putnam, Robert D. (with Robert Leonardi and Raffaella Y. Nanetti) (1993) *Making democracy work. Civic traditions in modern Italy*. Princeton, N.J.: Princeton University Press.

Putnam, Robert D. (1995) 'Bowling Alone: Americas Declining Social Capital'. *Journal of Democracy*, 1: 65-78.

Putnam, Robert D. (2001) *Bowling alone: the collapse and revival of American community*. London: Simon & Schuster.

Report (2003) Študijski krožki: letno poročilo: 2002-2003 (Study circles: yearly report 2002-2003) Nevenka Bogataj, Ana Jasmina Oseban. Ljubljana: Andragoški center Republike Slovenije.

Rothstein, Bo (2001) 'Social Capital in the Social Democratic Welfare State'. *Politics and Society*, Vol. 29 No. 2, June 2001: 207-241.

Rothstein, Bo (2002) 'Sweden: Social Capital in the Social Democratic State'. In: Robert D. Putnam (ed.) *Democracies in Flux. The Evolution of Social capital in Contemporary Society*. Oxford: Oxford University press.

ReNPIO (2004) Resolucija o nacionalnem programu izobraževanja odraslih v RS do leta 2010 (Resolution on national programme of adult education in republic of Slovenia), Official paper RS 70/2004, http://www.uradni-list.si/1/ulonline.jsp?urlid=200470&dhid=70475

Slee, Bill (2003) Understanding Forestry in Rural Development, Volume I – Main Report, 119 p.

SUFO 96. (1996) Cirkelsamhället. Studiecirklars betydelse för individ och lokal samhälle. (Circle Society. The Meaning of Study Circles for Individuals and Local Community). The final report SOU 1996:47.

SUFO 2. (2004) Folkbildning i brytningstid – En utvärdering av folkhögskolor och studieförbund. (Popular Adult Education in Times of Transition. An Evaluation Report on Folkhigh Schools and Circle Study Organisation). The final report SOU 2004:30.

The Swedish National Council of Adult Education, 2003: http://www.folkbildning.se/download/271/x/FBR_fickfakta2003_engelsk.pdf (June, 2006)

Vestlund, Gösta (1996) *Folkuppfostran, folkupplysning, folkbildning: det svenska folkets bildningshistoria - en översikt.* (People's Education, People's Enlightenment, People's Bildung: An Outline of Sweden's History of Popular Education) Stockholm: Brevskolan;

Waltzer, Michael (1990) 'The Communitarian Critique of Liberalism'. *Political Theory*, Vol. 18 No1. Sage Publications, Inc, pp. 6-22.

Wuthnow, Robert (1996 [1994]) *Sharing the Journey. Support Groups and America's New Quest for Community*. New York/ London: Free Press.

8. Polish Traditions of Self-Organisation, Social Capital and the Challenge of Europeanisation

Anna Gąsior-Niemiec and Piotr Gliński

Introduction

International and national surveys yield data revealing the weakness of civic engagement and corresponding low level of social capital in Poland that is measured, in particular, in terms of membership in voluntary organisations and the level of generalised trust. A variety of valid explanations has been offered to account for this state of affairs (cf. for instance Sztompka, 1993; Eyal, Szelenyi, Townsley, 1998; Smolar, 1999). Rarely, however, has one been invited to reflect on the methodological premises of such survey research (cf. Adam's chapter in this volume), to look behind and beyond the indicators (cf. Howard, 2003) and to contrast the survey data with evidence of other patterns and features of societal self-organisation and collective action which are not as frequently and readily measured.

As a consequence, the international rankings of countries focused on social capital and discussions concerning important theoretical and empirical issues related to civic engagement seem skewed, at least in the case of post-Communist countries like Poland. They appear both biased in favour of the quantitative type of research, predisposed towards an 'ideologically correct' – defined as 'modern' – formalised type of civic engagement and not sensitive enough to contextual factors such as economic development and the quality of formal institutions (cf. Jasińska-Kania, Marody, 2004; Fidrmuc, Gerxhani, 2006).

The apparent lag behind Westernised modes and dynamics of the creation of social capital is, as a result, mainly attributed to the legacy of Communism and/or conceptualised in terms of backwardness. Existing informal, traditional, weakly formalised and spontaneous patterns of citizens' involvement in the creation of a common good remain thus, to a significant degree, analytically marginalised. At the same time, factors accounting for their (uneasy) co-existence with the modern, formal membership-based model of societal self-organisation are largely unrecognised as are the diverging internal logics which animate the different modes of participation in collective action. Further, the variegated impact of Europeanisation on the different patterns of self-organisation is often neglected.

In particular, there has been little research into the compatibility of the different modes of civic engagement with the institutional framework of modern governance that is being implemented in countries such as Poland with encouragement coming from the process of European integration (cf. Boerzel, Guttenbrunner, Seper, 2005; Gąsior-Niemiec, Gliński, 2006). The quite intricate relationships between the institutional settings, civic engagement and the different modes it takes as well their influence on the capacity for collective action (premised on social capital) are too often taken for granted without, for instance, recognising the fact that membership in formal – 'modern' – civil society organisations accommodated within the new modes of government may not *per se* necessarily contribute to the civicness and 'good' social capital or, *vice versa,* that informal networks based on strong, for instance territorial, ties could actually be essential for the creation of the common good in an environment perceived as institutionally unstable/unfavourable and plagued by economic underdevelopment.

The key aim of the chapter is therefore to provide a certain corrective to the aforementioned, predominant tendencies and conclusions in academic papers dedicated to civic engagement and social capital by looking at the Polish case from the point of view of several co-existent, both complementary and competing, modes of societal self-organisation and patterns of collective action premised on social capital. Apart from mapping out the phenomena and processes and tracing any signs of their Europeanisation, an attempt is also made at their analytical systematisation. While, for technical reasons, no extensive analysis of internal, contextual factors such as economic development and the quality of institutions is included, the chapter refers to and builds upon recent related findings by Fidrmuc and Gerxhani (2006). The findings convincingly show that the often stated gap in social capital between the West and the East of united Europe needs to be related to both past and current economic and institutional factors.

Introducing the Polish case

Three different modes of civic engagement might be identified within contemporary Polish society. They could be labelled 'modern associationism', '*ad hoc* actionism' and 'traditional self-organisation'.[1] Notably, only the

[1] The three modes constitute broad analytical categories. Empirical cases of civic engagement

first mode – implicating formal membership in registered associations and foundations – is as a rule captured, measured and analysed by means of the survey research on social capital mentioned above. The other two modes appear frequently to be 'excluded' from quantitative, comparative research projects (cf. Gliński, 2004). They are predefined as non-civic or rejected as a topic of research because of methodological difficulties related to their operationalisation and measurement. Thus, they basically constitute an 'arena of forgotten sociology' or popular culture documented by selective and idiographic qualitative research and mass media coverage. The three modes appear to be rooted in different historical and current experiences of the Polish state, nation and society. Consequently, they seem governed by quite diverging logics which involve different approaches to both citizens' participation and production of the common good. Moreover, their relations with the formal institutional arrangement vary.

The three modes of civic engagement are faced with the challenge of Europeanisation, which is defined in the paper as the (perceived and experienced) normative and institutional pressure to introduce and satisfy standards of modern democratic governance experienced by Polish elites within the framework of European integration (cf. Ladrech, 1994; Radaelli and Featherstone, 2002). Given the focus of the paper, pressure leading to the greater involvement of 'social partners' in governance settings and processes is our predominant interest (cf. Boerzel, Guttenbrunner, Seper, 2005). Based on the principles of partnership, subsidiarity and complementarity in the public sphere, state actors, market actors and civil society actors are all to become integrated in a variety of policy and territorial networks with the public administration usually taking the lead and shouldering tasks such as co-opting, co-ordinating, (co)funding and (co)monitoring. [2]

---

may of course and do exhibit mixed features thereof. Recent in-depth qualitative research conducted by Gliński et al. (2006, forthcoming) focuses on the *activity styles* of modern NGOs and distinguishes, for instance, *10 different styles* whose characteristics overlap, intersect and cross-cut with the more general typology offered in the paper. Earlier attempts at categorisation involved for example a publication by Gliński and Palska (1997) who distinguished four categories of civic engagement in Poland: verbal, declarative, enclave and empirical civic engagement. Later, Gliński (2004) divided civic engagement into collective and individual. Within the category of collective civic engagement, he listed a sector of non-governmental organisations, civic local communities and informal groups, movements and initiatives.

[2] While the process brings a much desired improvement to the balancing of state-society relations, its actual mechanisms and consequences might give rise to some misgivings and doubts. *Inter alia,* the status of social partners appears to draw civil society organisations into an ever tighter institutional coupling with public administration actors. The supposed gains measured mainly in terms of infusing public decision-making, public goods and services provision with social awareness,

While it is by no means the only factor of normative, institutional and behavioural pressure affecting the three types of actors, the impact of new modes of governance clearly matters, for instance in terms of creating new opportunity structures. Taking advantage of the opportunity options is premised on both compliance with dominant discourses and on fulfilling relatively rigid institutional and organisational criteria. Thus, only actors who are able to fulfil the conditions become in turn reinforced by the new modes of governance. Actors lacking in such ability are defined as incompetent and/or illegitimate and, as such, barred from participation in new governance arrangements or marginalised. In this way, certain types of civil society actors and modes of self-organisation may be appreciated or devalued even regardless of their actual capacity for enhancing collective action and creating the common good. Another important aspect of the Europeanised modes of governance of civil society actors and patterns of civic engagement is constituted by the ambivalent impact of the ever closer coupling of the actors (as social partners) with the public administration given the sustained and overwhelming public opinion revealing a distrust of the latter (cf. Wciórka, 2004; CBOS, 2006b; cf. also Fidrmuc and Gerxhani, 2006).

Structure of the paper

We start with a brief discussion of the picture of 'Poles among Europeans' as it emerges from typical comparative, quantitative research on social capital and civic engagement, such as the European Value Study (EVS) and European Social Survey (ESS). In the section that follows we move beyond the survey approach and present insights regarding other modes of civic engagement that complement the relatively one-sided picture emerging from the survey data. We point to variegated characteristics and functions of the different modes and identify their strengths and weaknesses from the point of view of social capital and the capacity for collective action. Next, concentrating on the modern vs. traditional divide – which to a certain extent corresponds to the analytical distinction between Putnamesque and Olsonian modes of self-organisation (cf. Knack and Keefer, 1997 as quoted in Fidrmuc and Gerxhani, 2006), we analyse major symptoms of institutional change

accountability and transparency might, however, be dimmed by – the real or perceived – co-optation of social partners into largely discredited, formal institutional structures as well as their complicity – real or perceived – in corrupt dealings thereof (cf. CBOS, Wciórka, 2004:38, 42; Zybertowicz, 2005; Żukowski, 2005).

that affects the respective modes of collective action within the framework of Europeanisation. Finally, in concluding, we briefly discuss the prospects as well as the existing and potential threats to enhanced civic engagement related to its coupling with the deficient formal institutional arrangement of the Polish state.

'Poles among Europeans'[3]: social capital and active citizenship

The European Value Study (1990, 1999) reveals that in terms of civic-ness and social capital measured by proxies such as generalised trust and membership in voluntary organisations an apparent divide between Western Europe and post-Communist Europe emerges. The level of active citizenship measured by the percentage of respondents stating that most people can be trusted, membership in voluntary organisations, the level of activity in such organisations as well as the involvement of citizens in politics all show an overall downward trend eastwards. According to several such indicators, Poland is rated low or very low in the ranking of European countries (ibid.: 68 ff).

Data on generalised trust in Poland obtained through the EVS and the Polish CBOS (Public Opinion Research Centre) surveys[4] are almost identical. According to the 1999 EVS, for instance, only 18.4% of Polish respondents declared that one can in general trust most people, whereas 81.6% said that one ought to be cautious. To compare, in the top-ranking countries like the Scandinavian countries or the Netherlands, 60% to 80% of respondents thought they can trust people in general (cf. Trutkowski, Mandes, 2005; Wciórka, 2004).

The low rating is confirmed by data produced by the European Social Study (ESS 2002). According to results obtained through the ESS, Poles declare the lowest level of trust in others among all studied nations (23 European countries and Israel). There are no significant differences in generalised trust between the inhabitants of rural areas and cities. At the same time, the

[3] Since a recent publication with the same title extensively presents and discusses data from the European Value Study 1990, 1999 (Jasińska-Kania, Marody, 2004), we decided not to repeat the analyses but simply to refer to them. Apart from this, our chapter also partly utilises findings of a 2005 CIVICUS research project (which include data from the 2002 European Social Survey, available from both the Klon/Jawor Association and IFiS PAN), alongside numerous CBOS (cf. Wciórka, 2004; CBOS, 2006) and IFiS PAN surveys (1993, 1997, 2000 referred to in Gliński 2000).

[4] The CBOS data are reported in the paper following the CBOS summary report for the 1998-2004 period by Wciórka, 2004 and selected 2006 CBOS research communiqués.

overwhelming majority of Poles place a high level of trust in their immediate family (86% definitely, 12% somewhat), their more distant family (47% definitely, 40% somewhat), their co-workers (26% definitely, 53% somewhat) and neighbours (26% definitely, 48% somewhat)[5]. A plausible interpretation of these figures would stipulate that personal relations, sharing everyday experience and prolonged relationships form the basis of trust in the country. The 1998 – 2006 CBOS survey data show that the level, grounding and direction of trust in Polish society have remained stable (cf. Wciórka, 2004; CBOS 2006a).

In terms of formal membership in voluntary organisations and active participation in organisations, the EVS data again place Poland at the bottom of the international ranking, with indicators equal or slightly higher than in Romania, Bulgaria, Russia and Lithuania. The ESS, CBOS and IFiS PAN surveys of civic engagement, measured in terms of the Polish population's membership as well as declared participation in formally registered NGOs bring similar results. In 1990 only about 5% of the Polish population declared they were involved in such organisations. By 1995, the proportion of active participants had risen to 13%. Hence, we may say that in the first half of the 1990s there was a clear increase in thus measured civic engagement in Poland. By 1999, however, the level of participation had dropped to 9% (Gliński, 2000) while a survey conducted in 2002 puts the participation of Poles in non-governmental organisations (NGOs) at 12.4%[6].

Nevertheless, conclusions pointing to a persistent gap in stocks of social capital in Poland based on survey data appear in need of further elaboration. Both methodological weaknesses of the survey research and insufficiently recognised contextual factors could shed new light on the discussed phenomena. The following reservations are thus raised in the chapter with a view to complementing the survey-based conclusions with new insights.

- First, it should be mentioned that the category of civic engagement measured in terms of declared formal membership in voluntary organisations does not seem to encompass all patterns of collective action in which Poles are involved. For instance, depending on the

[5] Data provided by the Klon/Jawor Association (cf. the 2005 CIVICUS Civil Society Index report from Poland, draft of January 2005, subsequently quoted as '2005 CIVICUS').

[6] This data is not fully comparable because of the slightly different methods used in the EVS, ESS, CBOS and IFiS surveys; for example, the 2002 ESS was conducted on a slightly younger respondent population (15 plus) and, as it turned out, 15-17-year-olds were the largest 'active' group in Poland.

premises adopted by particular analysts some types of formal associations are at the start ruled out from statistics.[7]

- Second, because of the relative terminological novelty many respondents – especially less educated ones – who are habitually engaged in local societies, clubs, support groups etc. – might during a survey not perceive or declare this type of civic participation as 'membership in voluntary organisations, associations and foundations', seeing it instead as an integral part of everyday life and/or tradition.[8]
- Third, participation in collective action may not necessarily be framed in Poland by formal organisational membership but could be triggered by other stimuli such as, for instance, mass media or locally embedded leaders ('patrons').
- Fourth, some forms of civic collective action – such as *ad hoc*, cross-sectional, protest, co-ordinative and/or redistributive networks might show a tendency to arise at both the grassroots and national levels quite spontaneously whenever formal institutions appear to fail to cope with problems perceived by public opinion as a threat to the common good in a manner typical of new social movements (cf. Kubik and Ekiert, 2001).
- Fifth, as Fidrmuc and Gerxhani (2006) argue generalised trust is not the most adequate measure of social capital. Moreover, both trust and formal membership indicators do not correlate convincingly with other indicators of social capital, such as e.g. social altruism (ibid.; cf. also Wciórka, 2004; CBOS, 2006b; Żukowski, 2006).

Modes of civic engagement

Therefore, we propose that the category of civic engagement as indicative of social capital should in the Polish case accommodate three analytically distinguished modes of citizens' self-organisation or participation in collective action with a view to the common good. The three modes encompass:

(1) '**Modern associationism**' represented by civil society organisations[9] that after the systemic breakthrough of 1989 coalesced into the so-called non-governmental *Third Sector*. Through constant emphasis on

[7] These may not only be trade unions and political parties but also e.g. local fire brigades for some reasons judged as not being civic enough.

[8] It is to be remembered that only as late as the 1990s terms such as 'non-governmental organisation', 'foundation' and 'voluntary associations' actually entered public discourse in the country.

[9] Subsequently in the paper they are referred to as NGOs.

'networking', this type of civic engagement is supposed to foster 'modern' (i.e. bridging and linking) types of social capital (cf. Rose, 2000). It is favoured as a basis for social partnership in new governance settings. It could be first of all characterised by formal, business-like organisational and financial operational rules, monetarisation of membership and services, as well as its increasingly sectoral and urban anchorage etc. '**Professionalisation**' might be identified as a dominant feature of participatory logic inscribed in this mode of self-organisation.[10]

(2) '***Ad hoc* actionism**' evidenced by one-off or intermittent contributions of various kinds made by individual Poles to support actions that they consider being 'for a good cause'. These may range from spontaneous, mass financial, material and human assistance to victims of various disasters, participation in manifestations of solidarity with victims of political repressions and/or protests against economic exploitation to grassroots, informal networks to manage social crisis situations such as those resulting from natural catastrophes (cf. Sitek, 1997; Ekiert, Kubik, 2001; Fidrmuc and Gerxhani, 2006). Both spontaneity and mass media stimulation are their operational characteristics, whereas '**solidarity**' might be identified as a dominant feature of the logic inscribed in this mode of civic engagement.[11]

(3) '**Traditional self-organisation**' exemplified best by a parish or local community initiative is typical of rural and small town Poland. Many such initiatives are based on religious, territorial and neighbourhood ties and/or created under the patronage of old type local intelligentsia – countryside teachers, doctors, parish priests etc. (cf. Kurczewska, 1998, 2000). A considerable role is also played by organisational ties and resources related to the local survivors of popular organisations

[10] Apart from the preliminary insights offered in the chapter, further research should investigate in-depth causes of the apparently modest anchorage of this mode of civic participation in the social fabric as well as the reasons for its weak membership base as demonstrated, among others, by the aforementioned international surveys (cf. Gliński, 2004). Moreover, more research is needed to investigate the causes of the very low level of trust that Poles place in actors identified with this mode of collective action (cf. Żukowski, 2006).

[11] Apart from the preliminary insights offered in the chapter, future research interest called for by this type of civic engagement should be related to its – puzzling in the light of both the scale and frequency with which its instances occur – apparently little bearing on the level of generalised trust as reported by the aforementioned survey research reports. At the same time, it would be worthwhile to enquire more about the reasons for the constant unwillingness of the average Pole to become involved in such activities on the basis of formal, organisational membership. Another question which begs an answer in this context is whether/why this mode of collective action is indeed not illustrative of/conducive to social capital.

supported under the previous political regime (popular sports clubs and societies of rural housewives are good examples thereof). A significant proportion of these traditional civic initiatives are never formally registered despite the fact that they frequently play a role of vital public good providers.[12] In academic, state bureaucratic as well as the urban *Third Sector* discourses, 'traditional self-organisation' is often taken to constitute a 'worse', 'pre-modern' or 'anti-modern' mode of civic engagement, relying strongly on bonding social capital. It is occasionally accused of blocking the process of social change by preventing local communities or certain social enclaves from 're-structuring' and 'modernisation' (cf. Rose, 2000; Marody, Wilkin, 2002; Bartkowski, 2006). '**Reciprocity**' might be identified as a dominant feature of the logic inscribed in this mode of civic engagement.[13]

Strengths and weaknesses of 'modern associationism' in Poland

The modern non-governmental sector has exhibited a relatively strong dynamic over the last 15 years in the country. Over 90% of formally registered Polish NGOs were created after 1989 and the major change factors were mechanisms of self-education and self-development typical of civic movements as well as foreign aid. This aid was monetary, organisational and relating to cultural and political expertise.

In 2004, there were about 53,000 NGOs registered in Poland (45,891 associations and 7,210 foundations), excluding e.g., trade unions, political

[12] As in the case of the other two modes, the civic-ness of such grassroots organisations may not be taken for granted. It should be kept in mind that under Communist rule many of them became schools of clientelism, corruption, claimant attitudes and learned helplessness.

[13] Increased research interest aroused by this type of civic engagement should be related to investigating its 'pre-modern' or 'anti-modern' character manifested in the seeming prevalence of bonding social capital and strong reliance on the reciprocity norm. On one hand, these features could indeed block modernisation processes in rural areas by mobilising endogenous social resources for the sake of 'survival' in the circumstances of permanent underdevelopment and lacking competitiveness (cf. also Inglehart, 1997; Firdmuc and Gerxhani, 2006). Admittedly, this mode of collective action rarely intentionally aims at promoting the public interest that exceeds the boundaries of a given local community. On the other hand, however, it must be perceived as in many cases a rational and, indeed successful, mode of coping with marginalisation, deprivation and of maintaining social cohesion in an economic and institutional milieu which is still far away from the threshold of the turn towards post-materialist values. Further, the fact that even most resourceless members of such 'disfavoured' communities tend to be attributed the status of in-kind 'participants' and 'contributors' rather than just 'clients', 'recipients' or 'addressees' of public goods and services – as is usually the case with modern NGOs – is worth stressing.

parties, voluntary fire brigades, parents' committees, churches and religious denominations.[14] According to the estimates of the KLON/JAWOR Association only about two-thirds of the 53,000 registered NGOs are active, about 90% of these organisations were established after 1989, 25-30% are less than three years old and of those that no longer exist 70% 'dropped out' within the first three years of their existence. We may therefore assume that more than 1/4 of the NGOs registered in Poland are not functioning or even non-existent while only 30% of the NGOs' members are active (Dąbrowska et al., 2002; Gumkowska, Herbst, 2005).

Depending on the definition adopted, the non-governmental sector employs 64,000 to over 100,000 people, i.e., from 0.58% (Dąbrowska et al., 2002; Gumkowska, Herbst, 2005) to 1.2% (Leś, Nałęcz, 2001) of those employed outside of agriculture. However, about 65% of NGOs do not employ any regular paid staff. Membership in NGOs is correlated with urban-rural opposition (modern NGOs are an urban, especially metropolis type of phenomenon) and education (it is a social phenomenon dominated by well-educated people). As of 2002, 15.7% of big city dwellers declared membership in NGOs, in cities of up to 100,000 of residents the figure was 12.6%, while in the countryside it was 9.7% (ESS 2002).

The non-governmental sector is funded to a large extent by public money. Public funds comprise 29.6% of the sector's income (16.5% comes from local governments and 13.1% from the central government).[15] However, the greatest growth dynamic is displayed by income from economic activity: in 2003 this reached 20.7%, having doubled since 2001. Donations from private individuals contribute 4.7% of the sector's income, although most probably this is a large underestimation given that as much as one-quarter of the organisations declaring an income from this source do not reveal the amount of the donations; donations from firms and institutions contribute another 7.0%. Income from abroad has been decreasing rapidly

---

[14] It is worth noting that the inclusion of other organisations, many of which belong to the 'traditional' (Putnamesque) ones, would increase the number of registered NGOs to about 100,000. Even so, the number obviously does not capture all of the 'traditional' civic initiatives as many of them function in an unregistered way as informal groupings and networks. The adopted definition thus 'excludes' a considerable share of civic initiatives in the country, not mentioning the fact that 'ad hoc actionism' also remains outside of its scope. Nevertheless, the available research is mostly focused on the *Third Sector*.

[15] Still, the involvement of public resources in the financing of the non-governmental sector is claimed to be two or even three times as small as that in Western European countries. This argument is frequently used by NGO representatives who lobby for an increase in public funding for the sector and – notably – by Third Sector researchers as well. The issues of bureaucratisation and governmentalisation of the Third Sector are, however, rarely discussed in this context.

since 1997 and amounted to 7.6% of the income of the NGO sector in 2003 (Gumkowska, Herbst, 2005).

One of the most serious barriers to the sector's development is the poor financial state of most NGOs. Seventy-eighty percent of all NGOs in Poland have no assets worth mentioning and only about 20% have financial reserves. The enormous material differences within the sector aggravate this problem even further. There are a few rich organisations while the vast majority are small and economically fragile. The growth of income differences within the non-governmental sector is a cause of unease. In the 2001-2003 period the percentage of the poorest organisations grew from 15% to 21% and at the same time – as we have already noted – there was as much as a doubling of organisations' income from economic activity and most probably there was also growth of the so-called grey zone in the area of individual donations (ibid.).

As mentioned, the size of the town in which they operate is a very important factor that adds to the variety of organisations. There is a clear correlation between the location of associations and foundations and the type of their resources and activities as well as the range of their activities. The difference not only involves the fact that there are more organisations in the cities, but also that the organisations which operate in cities are bigger, richer, more professional and work on a larger scale.

The correlation between five types of locations, divided according to the number of inhabitants, their administrative role and the distribution of NGOs, is as follows: small towns and rural areas (27% of the organisations), towns with up to 50,000 inhabitants (14%), cities with more than 50,000 inhabitants (19%), voivodeship capitals (28%) and Warsaw (12%). In terms of density, Warsaw and the voivodeship capitals take the lead. It should be noted that in the case of other types of organisations such as associations of an economic nature, traditional voluntary fire brigades or social committees, the relationship between the level of urbanisation and the density of organisations is the reverse (cf. Bartkowski, 2002).

Institutional change

Over the past few years we have witnessed a prolonged institutional change in Poland with respect to the place and role of the non-governmental sector in the state and in society. The process began with reforms of the territorial self-government in 1990 and 1999, continued with the introduction of institutions of social dialogue in the administration in 2000, laws concerning social work and the social economy, and culminating in adoption of the

Law on Activity for the Public Benefit and on Volunteering in 2003 and the establishment of a governmental *Civic Initiative Fund* in 2004/2005.[16]

The 2003 law has as its premise the introduction of a new model of co-operation of the state in partnership with non-governmental organisations and to a significant degree facilitates the activity of Polish NGOs. This is because the law introduces, among other things, special tax relief for certain categories of non-governmental organisations and enables their easier access as service providers to commissioned public services. The law also obliges local government units to work in partnership with non-governmental organisations. The obligation involves the negotiating and passing by local government units of so-called 'annual programmes of co-operation with non-governmental organisations'.[17]

In addition, the law allows citizens to designate 1% of their taxes in support of NGOs. Finally, it regulates the legal status of volunteering. *Inter alia,* it makes it possible for volunteers to be covered by insurance, be reimbursed for costs incurred whilst undertaking volunteer work etc. These regulations are said to go along with the constitutional principle of subsidiarity. They are also intended to increase the transparency and accountability of the public administration, local government and non-governmental sectors working in co-operation.

The law has, however, been criticised for its overcomplicated and imprecise language – a vague definition of paid activity for the public benefit can serve as an example. Also, objections are raised against the scope it leaves for arbitrary decisions on the part of both the state administration and mixed or 'partner' bodies such as the Council for Public Benefit. Ambivalent feelings are also stirred by the fact that the law provides opportunities which may be seized by and enjoyed primarily by powerful and professionalised organisations. Moreover, it does not take account of nor adequately regulate many pathological phenomena which occur in the non-governmental environment such as clientelism at the point of contact between non-governmental organisations, local governmental units and central administration.

[16] The Civic Initiative Fund programme was the first general programme in Poland to finance non-governmental organisations from the budget on a competitive basis. 30 million zlotys (about EUR 9 million) annually was earmarked for this purpose. The establishment of the Fund was spurred by a failure to safeguard funding for NGOs by means of the 1% tax deduction to which every Polish taxpayer is entitled by the 2003 law. As of 2004 only 80,000 taxpayers, i.e. about 0.25% of adult Poles, which means 0.35% of taxpayers, used the 1% allocation option.

[17] As of 2004, motions concerning programmes of co-operation with non-governmental organisations were passed by slightly more than 50% of local governments in Poland. In many cases, this was done for the sake of appearance only.

The institutional change has been radically enhanced and shaped by normative and institutional pressure related to the process of European integration. In particular, the implementation of the first round of EU structural funds (2004-2006) opened new and great opportunities for Polish NGOs. They have been admitted to the competition for grants in many 'soft' (i.e. labour market, human resources, R&D, science and culture-oriented) components of programmes (co)financed by the EU structural funds. Further, they have been co-opted as social partners to manage and monitor programmes (cf. Gąsior-Niemiec, Gliński, 2006). In addition, further enormous opportunities are likely to arise with implementation of the National Development Plan for the 2007-13 period.

Internal barriers to the Third Sector's development

Apart from the slowly changing and unstable external, institutional arrangements, not the least important source of difficulty in the Polish NGO sector's development is its own weakness. Some internal flaws stem from structural – still unchanged – conditions inherited from the previous regime. The excessively privileged position of some post-Communist organisations such as sports clubs and associations is a case in point. Other weaknesses include the already mentioned phenomenon of clientelism, which takes place alongside the sector's activity. Yet others are manifested by a decline in significance attached to the monitoring function of social organisations and the practice thereof.

One of the most serious weaknesses relates to difficulties in building a modern membership base of non-governmental organisations. Very few organisations carry out a dedicated programme of membership-building involving an active search for support within society – a fact which, in a significant measure, is caused by a particular mental resistance to persuading anonymous fellow citizens to actively participate in some pro-social activity. The barrier is also connected, without doubt, to the low level of generalised trust and social capital in Polish society. However, it may also be linked to the tendency to form 'close-knit' and 'closed' – guaranteeing loyalty, efficiency and success – organisational forms in the face of the fierce competition for resources and a trend to professionalise, none of which prioritises membership-building.

Another visible weakness of the sector is its difficulty to create a common representation. Despite several attempts – since 1996 there have been proposed all-Poland and regional forums for non-governmental initiatives, networks and thematic coalitions etc. as well as an attempt undertaken in

2002 to federate the Polish non-governmental sector – the building of forms of common representation of non-governmental organisations meets with continual resistance and criticism within the milieu.

Differences of interest between particular organisations, regions and areas of activity, the competition for resources and 'influences' and, finally, the stances of leaders often effectively block the concluding of an agreement. Apart from those differences of a more or less objective nature, sometimes various animosities and personal ambitions are negatively decisive in the matter. As a result – in spite of a few moderately well-functioning coalitions and agreements in some areas of activity – no coherent, generally accepted mode of representation for the sector or building thematic platforms has been created, although these are commonly supposed to be a standard in the EU. In addition, to a significant degree such co-operative frameworks are stipulated as conditions to be entitled to receive assistance from European funds.

Quite a different problem is constituted by the frequent breaches of the sector's self-regulatory and ethical standards. Seven years ago the Polish non-governmental sector elaborated a Charter of Principles. Several regulations for thematic areas were also formulated. Unfortunately many organisations still do not comply[18] with these ethical principles. A lack of transparency, unhealthy competition, 'going through the motions' instead of real activity, a lack of branch and sector solidarity and clientelism are not infrequent. By the same token, it is not uncommon to exploit one's non-governmental status for ethically dubious economic or political purposes.[19] These pathologies cause unease among NGO members at large – as many as 60% of respondents in the 2004 representative survey of the *Third Sector* stated that corruption *within* the Sector is a serious problem (cf. Klon/Jawor 2004 report cited in 2005 CIVICUS).

Finally, the phenomenon of the sector's 'oligarchisation' is another cause for concern. There is a danger that the 'partnership arena' emerging after the institutional change analysed above might become significantly 'colonised' by a particular kind of 'soft oligarchy' which mainly involves non-govern-

[18] Research shows that approximately 70% of NGOs are not even aware such standards apply (cf. Dąbrowska et al., 2002; 2005 CIVICUS).

[19] One of the most notorious examples of the phenomenon is so-called eco-extortion – effective bribes taken by pseudo-ecological organisations in exchange for the withdrawal of legal objections to investments endangering the environment. Other examples concern cases of NGOs incurring exorbitant administrative costs, providing staff with disproportionately high salaries, scam cost reimbursements etc. Manifest pathologies, involving criminal activities and involvement in the grey economy are quite another problem (cf. also Frączak, 2004 as well as numerous press reports).

mental activists representing the biggest and strongest organisations. There is a tendency on their part to enter into oligarchic and corporative relationships with representatives of local government, central and regional administrations and even with representatives of the media or the intellectual elite (cf. Palska, Lewenstein, 2004; Lewenstein, Palska, 2004; Dudkiewicz, 2004). It needs to be added, however, that according to survey research as many as 60% of non-governmental organisations in Poland seek contacts with politicians in order to improve their situation (Dąbrowska et al., 2002). This indicates clearly that the vices of the 'oligarchs' do not make them unique – for pragmatic reasons all types of NGOs often seek patronage in the world of politics and public administration.

Strengths and weaknesses of *ad hoc actionism*

On one hand, all kinds of surveys consistently confirm that approximately 80% of Poles do not belong to any NGOs. On the other hand, according to the ESS data 46.6% of Poles think that to be a good citizen one should be active in organisations or associations, although only 17.9% feel that organisations and associations are important for society. The data seem to suggest there is a deficiency of socially responsive and/or trustworthy NGOs in Poland (ESS 2002) as the majority of Poles declare that no existing organisations serve their interests (cf. CBOS). Bad memories of forced membership in façade, mass organisations during the previous regime might be adduced as a factor discouraging this type of civic engagement (cf. Howard, 2003; Firdmuc and Gerxhani, 2006 and Bezovan in this volume). However, of more recent origin is distrust of such organisations as inculcated, for instance, by cases of criminal, corrupt and unethical activities undertaken by some NGOs (cf. for example *Rzeczpospolita*, 2006).

On the other hand, a more general hypothesis concerning the unwillingness of Poles to join organisations and formal associations could, however, be put forward which is related to the prolonged and repetitive collective experience of a society functioning in unstable/unfavourable institutional conditions.[20] A long history of training in resistance against formal institutions and practising of violent protests and/or informal, parallel self-organisation *outside* and *against* the framework of the state and formal

[20] The claim is particularly pertinent to the category of *inclusive* organisations as opposed to those that are formed on the basis of 'strong ties' such as 'dobre towarzystwo' [high life] (cf. 'Dyskusja redakcyjna ..., 2005) or family (cf. Tarkowska, Tarkowski, 1990).

institutions seems at least as much a valid factor. The 'anti-organisational' hypothesis seems, on one side, corroborated by persistent distrust in formal institutions recorded by surveys in the transition period. On the other side, it appears reinforced by several CBOS survey data that relate to – something consistently expressed by the majority of Poles – a belief in the need for solidarity and mutual assistance in society. As of 2004, more than half of the respondents acknowledged such a need (56%). This is however, as we are already aware, not translated into a tendency to join formally registered NGOs. These findings then suggest that there is a big civic potential in Polish society that has not been tapped by formally institutionalised civic society organisations. The *ad hoc actionism* in which Poles engage may derive from this untapped potential. It could also be said to be reinforced by a church-stimulated custom of intermittent support for a variety of 'good' causes and charity.[21]

In 2004, 39.2% of adult Poles claimed they had given money or material gifts to non-governmental organisations, social or religious movements in the preceding year. This is 6% more than in 2003 when 33.4% of Poles declared their financial or material support for organisations and social movements.[22] When respondents were asked if they had given any money to the Church/religious associations or if they had dedicated unpaid time or work to them during the last year, 66% of respondents declared they had provided such support (the 2004 SMG/KRC and the Klon/Jawor Association survey).[23] Further, data from the Institute of Catholic Church Statistics reveal that 77% of Poles claim they donate money during offertory, while 70% donate money to the construction or renovation of churches.[24] The fact that while the number of donors has actually increased the amount of money donated to non-governmental organisations has not appears congruent with the previously reported, declared belief in solidarity and mutual assistance in need (2005 CIVICUS).

[21] According to a CBOS report (2006b), the level of trust placed in non-governmental organisations in Poland oscillates around 7% (the net difference between the percentage of respondents who declare trust and those who declare distrust). The data ranks the country at the very bottom of the list of several surveyed countries, followed only by Brazil and China. To compare amongst the top ranking countries, the net level of trust is estimated at nearly 60% - 40% (Kenya, Mexico, Canada, France, Great Britain, the USA).

[22] The data do not include the most common form of charity in Poland – the offertory.

[23] Moreover, in both the 2002 and 2004 CBOS nationwide surveys about 60% of the respondents declared that they did something for the sake of their local community or the needy (Wciórka, 2004: 24; CBOS 2006a).

[24] The research question did not use the phrase 'during the last year', which may account for the higher percentage of 'yes' answers.

In terms of non-church fundraising, 'Finał Wielkiej Orkiestry Świątecznej Pomocy' – an annual, one-day, mass fundraising event by Wielka Orkiestra Świątecznej Pomocy [Great Christmas Charity Orchestra] of Jurek Owsiak has managed in each of the past 14 years to raise several tens of millions of Polish zlotys which the chief organiser has subsequently in the limelight (for both PR and transparency reasons) turned into e.g. life-saving medical equipment donated to public health care institutions (cf. *Metro*, 6-8 stycznia 2006). Auctions carried out intermittently by radio stations (such as *Trójka*) to support, for instance, a particular category of disadvantaged children raise tens of thousands of zlotys at a time.

Many other, TV-staged fundraising events raise hundreds of thousands of zlotys both by means of 'audiotele' techniques and traditional transfer modes (bank accounts and the National Post Office). Appeals for financial assistance to create lifetime funds for the victims of accidents, fire, domestic violence etc. who are 'heroes' of TV documentaries are reported by TV broadcasters as meeting with surprisingly quick and generous responses from television viewers (cf. *Metro*, 17-19 lutego 2006). Appeals by a few established, both church-related and lay, charity organisations such as *Caritas*, Polski Czerwony Krzyż [*Polish Red Cross*] and Polska Akcja Humanitarna [*Polish Humanitarian Action*] – as a rule also supported by the mass media – raise millions of zlotys of individual donations in response to individual appeals.[25]

In terms of voluntary participation in collective action 'for a good cause', the number of Poles contributing intermittently to all kinds of formalised civic initiatives in 2004 was estimated at more than 3 million people (2005 CIVICUS). The research of SMG/KRC, the Klon/Jawor Association and the Volunteering Centre Association conducted in 2004 on a representative sample of adult Poles showed that almost 30% of all volunteers had dedicated more than 50 hours to volunteer work in the last year. On average, these volunteers had worked 6 hours a month in 2004 (ibid.).

On the other hand, Jurek Owsiak's 'Finał Wielkiej Orkiestry Świątecznej Pomocy' mobilises more than 120,000 young people each year during the January street collection day. As mentioned, only part of the potential is actually utilised, managed, registered and reimbursed by modern NGOs. Mostly unregistered volunteers support the Church and church-affiliated organisations and events staged by them, local interest and local community initiatives,

[25] For instance, the 1997 flood-related appeals also supported by the Polish Post and many public and private banks (which lifted fees on cash flows in response to the appeals) produced exceptional results. Individual support for victims of tragic events following the collapse of a commercial hall in Katowice in 2006 is another more recent example (cf. Swoboda, 2006).

mass media interventions. Unregistered volunteers work for local cultural societies, form *ad hoc* defence, self-defence or mutual aid committees etc.

Traditional patterns of self-organisation[26]

The use of the word 'traditional' calls for some more explanation in light of the oft repeated opinion that civil society was really only created in Poland after the systemic breakthrough.[27] While we agree that the modern NGOs that constitute today's *Third Sector* could only fully develop after 1989, 'Polish society after 1989 did not start from zero, neither with respect to non-governmental sector development nor to civil society in general'. Their history encompasses both pre-Communist and Communist Poland. It is worth noting that history reveals a dominance of a relatively specific-local, patron-bound formula of the type of societal self-organisation in the country (Marody, Wilkin, 2002: 79-80; Kurczewska, 1998, 2000; Żukowski, 2006).

Even selective overviews of the history of charity, voluntary social assistance, mutual aid and religious societies and foundations, vocational societies, territorial self-governments, local cultural associations, folk music and dance societies, self-education networks as well as neighbourhood safety and labour groups etc. provide a factual background for the thesis that today's traditional forms of self organisation enjoy a long lineage, dating from well before the advent of Communism. Their modes not only became part of the collective memory and social tradition in Poland but also constituted a vital social resource activated in periods when formal institutions were perceived as hostile and/or as having failed to satisfy the needs of society (cf. for instance Kukliński, Swianiewicz, 1990; Leś, 2000; Wieruszewska, 2002; Kurczewski, 2003; Gąsior-Niemiec, 2003, 2005; Kurczewska, 2000; Juros *et al.* 2004). During the state socialist era, these modes were to a significant degree intercepted by the state apparatus, licensed and taken advantage of. Nevertheless, they were not completely deprived of their civic potential.

---

[26] Traditional self-organisation is still most typical of considerable shares of rural and small town Poland. As mentioned, the surveys focused on formal membership in registered organisations and analyses of the modern *Third Sector* do not seem to be the best possible approaches to analyse this particular aspect of civic engagement. For dubious reasons, some 'traditional' formal organisations such as the approximately 18,000 local voluntary fire brigades – which in reality perform many more public functions than simply providing fire safety (cf. also Kurczewski, 2003) – are usually *excluded* from indices of civil society in the country. The fact that research on civil society and social capital is in Poland to a great extent 'colonised' by city-based members/staff of the big, elite NGOs located in metropolises might have a bearing on this tendency to exclude 'traditional' forms of rural self-organisation from the picture of Polish civil society.

[27] The Solidarity movement constitutes a separate case which is not discussed in the paper.

Formally registered traditional associations

As noted, the People's Republic of Poland[28] preserved and even promoted some of the earlier forms of traditional self-organisation (e.g. popular sports clubs, cultural associations, folk music and dance societies) while striving to control their functioning in terms of political correctness. Otherwise, registered as associations, they continued to perform their public and social functions, intermittently supported financially from the state budget. Even mass organisations favoured by the state under the Communist regime, like *Koła Gospodyń Wiejskich* (Societies of Rural Housewives), despite their centralised structure and programmes, allowed for a degree of grassroots initiative, encouraged resourcefulness, a reliance on local, endogenous resources, and taught co-operative behaviour. Thus, they significantly contributed to the maintenance or even corroboration of local social ties and cohesion. On the other hand, they helped 'freeze' social hierarchies and power relations in the local communities.

Still other associations inculcated an ideology of 'local patriotism' epitomised in the ideals of a 'private' or 'small' homeland that commands both attachment and care (cf. Bednarek, 1996; Gąsior-Niemiec, 2003, 2004). Preaching virtues related to human dignity, patriotism and some sort of public spiritedness, numerous Church-affiliated organisations[29], scouts units and rural clubs also carried out teaching and instruction in practical skills of co-operation for survival in the circumstances of a scarcity of resources. They indeed acted as schools for collective action with a view to the common good.

Notwithstanding their provenience and mission, all of them have been the main source of basic organisational skills for unprivileged rural area and small town residents and – often – a source of 'bridging' and/or 'linking' social capital as well.[30] At the same time, quite frequently they have also been 'schools' of patron-client relations where members of local intelligentsia as well as local Communist party secretaries and officials from local administrative units played the role of patrons vis-à-vis the local com-

---

[28] This part is by no means to serve as a full description of or an apology for the (overall underdeveloped and largely colonised by the state) civil society during the Communist period.

[29] Of note here is that some church-affiliated organisations such as the Oaza movement, which sprung up during the 1980s, may instead be counted as the harbingers of 'modern' and not 'traditional' modes of civic engagement.

[30] Many of them functioned within nationwide federations, which could either be imposed by the state (e.g. *koła gospodyń wiejskich*) or created by associations themselves (e.g. regional cultural associations). Moreover, owing to the 'holistic' and not strictly 'sectoral' scope of their activities, they often managed to mount the support and participation of quite socially distant members of local communities.

munities and associations active within them (Kurczewska, 2000; Gliński, 2004). The majority of such associations and organisations continue to function in rural and small town areas even today (cf. Gąsior-Niemiec, 2003). The 'tradition' of clientelism has not been eradicated either (cf. Kurczewski, 2003). However, as noted in the part dedicated to modern NGOs this particular feature seems to be underlying many other types of societal and institutional arrangements in the country (cf. Tarkowska, Tarkowski, 1990; Zybertowicz, 2005).

Unregistered traditional civic initiatives[31]

Rural communities (*gromady*) and a variety of local informal committees (*komitety wiejskie*) constitute quite another form of civic engagement that was functioning well both before and during the Communist period. The Communist state willingly resorted to the mobilising potential of such traditional forms of self-organisation in rural areas to economise on expenses related to modernisation of the country.[32] Embodying in practice the then discursively 'unrecognised' principles of subsidiarity, complementarity and partnership, *gromady* and *komitety wiejskie* were treated as a prototype 'social partner' in building and/or modernising hard and soft infrastructure: schools, health care centres, children playgrounds and day care centres, local culture houses etc. Yet such an experience was largely missing in urban areas.

The production and provision of such public goods was frequently achieved by means of the joint action by the state (financial support) and local social actors (labour, in-kind contributions, partial financial contributions). Numerous roads, footbridges, water mains, gas and telephone net-

[31] As noted earlier, owing to the corrupt impact of state-society relations during the Communist rule such initiatives could perhaps in many cases be better labelled *quasi*-civic as they were often deficient in terms of the autonomy and freedom of choice available to grassroots members and participants.

[32] Analyses carried out under the Institutional Development Programme revealed rural communities are much more public-spirited than municipal ones. Traditional public meetings are still held and attended in rural areas. 'Village councils, which influence the manner in which some of the money earmarked for infrastructure is spent, are unusually active. (…) The character of social relationships, the strong component of personal relationships, as well as neighbourhood ties, are all factors conducive to increased involvement in achieving the common good. *This explains the relatively high level of civic involvement among the rural population, despite the less varied range, or often absence, of NGOs*' (Marody, Wilkin, 2002: 82; emphasis added). The findings are corroborated by 'Diagnoza społeczna' 2005 (Sułek, 2005; cf. also CIVICUS 2005).

works, bus stops, football stadiums, schools, fire stations and other public goods have been created in the rural areas of Poland due to such civic initiatives (cf. also Marody, Wilkin, 2002: 82). In the circumstances of an economic crisis that has especially affected rural areas following the systemic change of 1989, the return to such modes of self-organisation with a view to the production of public goods and the provision of substitute social services has again become initially common.[33] The role of the Communist state as a provider of the financial share of investments in a public good has nowadays been partly taken over by a local government unit or the European Union (structural funds), while the role of local patrons is played more frequently by locally embedded MPs than impoverished school teachers or medical doctors. The change of the financial 'co-provider' has, however, also been accompanied by changed rules of 'social partnership'.

Institutional change

The process of European integration has *inter alia* spelt the transformation of formal arrangements to provide for vital public goods and services in Poland. From the point of view of traditional civic initiatives typical of rural and small town areas, the transformation means both a desired increase in funding opportunities and an undesired 'technicisation' and bureaucratisation of their own activities. In a nutshell, as 'social partners' they must nowadays first of all fulfil the condition of being registered as a legal entity, employ professional administrative and expert staff, and contribute not only with labour and in-kind support but also with significant financial capital.[34]

Second, they do not just form a *wiejski komitet* and strike a partnership deal with or *via* a local patron. They have to seek out opportunities for financial provision much more actively, prepare complex, formal applications and compete for grants or otherwise take part in public tenders. For the local communities and local initiatives characterised above, the changed rules covering the provision of public goods not only spell a drastic institutional change but also the breaking down of the cultural code that governed the tradi-

[33] This stands in sharp contrast to the almost total socio-economic collapse and disintegration that affected northern and to some extent western regions of Poland, where traditions of such self-organisation were largely absent (cf. Tarkowska, 2000, 2002).

[34] It is to be noted that the present PiS/Samoobrona/LPR government has announced a plan to impose an additional tax on financial resources collected by *komitety wiejskie* with a view to applying for institutional grants, conditioned on the applicant's financial co-contribution. If implemented, it is very likely to undercut the traditional grassroots initiatives even further.

tional pattern of civic engagement before. Namely, the logic of reciprocity has to be more and more substituted by the logic of professionalisation.

Parents' committees, parish councils, church-renovation groups, pilgrimage societies, school clubs, cyclists' groups, local football team fans, neighbourhood networks, societies of 'small homeland' friends as well as many other forms of traditional civic engagement typical of Polish rural and small town areas are then increasingly faced with a dilemma: to modernise, meaning legal registering and fulfilling the (costly) administrative criteria which circumscribe the activity of a formal association or foundation (NGO), or not to register, meaning being excluded from public assistance and the status of a social partner.

The dilemma, as mentioned, is first and foremost related to the emergence of new opportunities associated with the impact of European integration (cf. Gąsior-Niemiec, Gliński, 2006). These opportunities imply *inter alia* fulfilling formal, legally binding and testified criteria of an organisational stability, administrative efficiency, financial accountability and a promise of the professional management of grants. The fulfilment of these conditions is hardly possible on a traditional, informal, spontaneous and voluntary basis without employing permanent staff and engaging in prolonged professional training.[35]

Yet, many of the traditional initiatives remain unregistered mainly because of the discouraging and costly procedures of registration, daily administration and book-keeping. They continue to rely on resources that can be provided by members and the local community at large. In a sense, this mode of functioning seems both simpler, cheaper, more autonomous and more *authentic* – devoid of bureaucratic red tape. On the other hand, clearly the scope of such initiatives is becoming ever more limited. Their membership basis is also shrinking as young people are – for a variety of reasons[36] – more attracted to modern NGOs.

Nevertheless, faced with the new opportunities some traditional initiatives are expanding and/or modifying the scope of their interests, registering and slowly transforming into modern NGOs, at least in a legal and bureaucratic sense. Moreover, quite new initiatives are emerging and taking root, in which the traditional and modern codes that govern patterns of civic engagement are combined. A good example is provided by a quite

[36] Educational and organisational deficiencies typical of rural and small town areas also need to be mentioned as a valid blocking factor in this context (cf. Sztompka, 1993).

[37] In the circumstances of very high unemployment, membership/volunteering in a modern NGO is for instance perceived as a substitute for a job which is then utilised in one's CV.

successful *small school* initiative within which local communities may save a small local school from closure by the authorities if they manage to register a 'small school' association and agree to shoulder some of the expenses incurred in the functioning of the school and to partake in its management. Another, not so successful, example of the institutional hybrid is provided by the institutionally stimulated substitution of the traditional type of co-operatives and/or informal, neighbourhood 'mutual aid' farmer networks with modern associations of farm producers, agricultural service providers etc. (cf. Gąsior-Niemiec, 2003; Wąż, 2003).

Despite the persistence of some traditional forms of self-organisation in certain areas of Poland, selective qualitative research shows that the process of erosion – or 'modernisation' – has actually progressed well. Apart from the ambivalent impact of the generational change with young people being more inclined to join the modern type of NGOs than traditional ones,[37] under the pressure of the socio-economic transformation, the aforementioned institutional and cultural change related to it, the strong ties that are laying the foundations for the emergence of these forms are weakened (cf. Wąż 2003; Marody, Wilkin, 2002; Wieruszewska, 2002). The traditional social basis for such initiatives, like traditional local intelligentsia, is also disappearing or losing its importance due to macro-changes in the social structure (cf. Domański, 2000; Gąsior-Niemiec, 2003; Żukowski, 2006; cf. also Firdmuc and Gerxhani, 2006).

On the other hand, it needs to be stressed that the 'seeds of change' have been planted in some rural and small town areas from the very beginning of the systemic change providing, however, a relatively ambivalent experience. Several innovative, modern NGOs were created there in the early 1990s from scratch by prosperous and knowledgeable city dwellers who decided to settle down in a village, by big urban foreign-donor driven foundations targeting social revitalisation, by local residents who during their university studies and/or stays abroad learnt about new opportunities to pursue personal and community interests etc. or artists taking advantage of the comparatively cheaper rural area living costs (cf. Gliński et al. 2002; 2004; Juros et al. 2004; Burszta and Kuligowski, 2005; Gliński 2006).

Other such modern NGOs were established as not very transparent off-spring of local government units when their executives learnt, for instance

[37] The differential benefits seem obvious in this case: modern NGOs offer a much larger scope of activity as well as being capable of playing a much desired role of substitute employees or at least reimbursing costs incurred by volunteering as well as providing crucial, state-of-the-art training in organisational, financial and lobbying skills.

during study visits abroad or training provided through the EU pre-accession programmes, about new opportunities to receive additional funding for public tasks earmarked for NGO-status actors. Others emerged when local politicians – temporarily unsuccessful at elections – resorted to the practical knowledge gained in parliament and decided to establish NGOs as a framework within which they could continue to function as public figures and garner public financial assistance.[38] Not rarely, NGOs have sprung up as spin-offs of MPs' local offices and/or top administration offices to tap the resources quasi-arbitrarily distributed by multiple semi-public agencies in Poland.

All of these modes, types and forms of self-organisation coexist, compete with one another and exert a mutual influence.[39] The competition for public and private donors' resources is resulting not only in the expected improvement of the quality and efficiency of the organisations' activity in the public sphere but also in mutual hostility and a tendency to resort to clientelist relations. The institutionalisation of mutual co-operation between all public actors at local and regional level required by the 2003 law has so far not improved the situation (cf. Gliński, 2002; Gliński, 2006). Moreover, the change in the dominant logics governing engagement in such initiatives seems ambivalent, to say the least.

In this context, Polish researchers often speak then of the 'delayed modernisation' of civil society (cf. Gliński, 2004) or its growing hybridisation (cf. Trutkowski, Mandes, 2005) in rural and small town Poland. Intermittent qualitative research clearly shows that while traditional associations might become either extinct or fully/partly 'modernised/professionalised', on the other hand the modern forms of civil society organisation may also 'inherit' or 'discover' personal ties and patron-client relations as factors crucial for their financial survival, especially that they cannot rely too much on the 'traditional', endogenous resources of a given local community (cf.

[38] There is little research into the problem of un-civic NGOs in Poland that is signalled by acronyms such as QUANGOS, MONGOS, DONGOS, FANGOS. The problem seems to be related to 'the missing relationship between organisational membership and civic morality' (Bartkowski, Jasińska-Kania, 2004:86). It is possibly also linked to the issue of the 'betrayal of elites' (cf. Gliński, 2004: 239-242).

[39] Some research shows in addition that a cleavage is rapidly developing between small, poor, local community-based NGOs and the powerful, rich city civil society organisations. Expressed by means of the 'we/them' opposition, in the Polish periphery the cleavage takes the form of the opposition between 'we' constituted by local organisations, local government units and local communities and 'them' constituted by the state and the big, urban NGOs (cf. Dudkiewicz, 2004). Gliński, 2006 does not, however, confirm Dudkiewicz's findings.

Skrzypiec, 2002). In such cases the principle of 'professionalism' enters into a very ambiguous relationship with the principle of 'reciprocity'. On the other hand, however, ever more frequently newly founded NGOs invoke local patriotism and regional cultural traditions as their assets (cf. Gliński, 2004). This turn – labelled as new localism – is to a significant extent propelled by EU-related opportunities and a discourse dominated by unity in diversity, cultural heritage, cultural factors of local development etc. (Gąsior-Niemiec, 2003, 2005; Jawłowska, 2003).

Conclusions

The aim of this paper was to look behind and beyond survey data that consistently evidence low levels of civic engagement and social capital in Poland, as measured by membership in voluntary organisations and generalised trust. Resorting to multiple quantitative and qualitative research, we have tried to show that the survey data conceal a much more complex picture of phenomena related to the development of civil society, social capital and their linkages with the modern, Europeanised system of governance in Poland.

Apart from 'modern associationism', typified by formally registered associations and foundations that mostly aspire to become 'professional' and 'competitive' providers of public goods and services, we identified two other modes which are not usually fully 'captured' by survey research on social capital – '*ad hoc* actionism' and 'traditional self-organisation'. These may be claimed to be driven by different participatory logics (solidarity and reciprocity, respectively) and thus to function as elements of a complementary, (pre-modern or anti-modern) 'shadow' or 'parallel' informal institutional system that enables (marginalised) individuals and communities they belong to to 'survive' and even 'develop' despite deficient economic resources and/or unstable/ineffective formal institutions.

Reflecting the different historical experiences of the Polish state, nation and society, all three modes of civic engagement that we have distinguished and characterised also appear then to be very sensitive to current contextual factors such as economic development and institutional arrangements. Informal self-organisation seems in the circumstances to act as a substitute for formal institutional arrangements which are frequently perceived/experienced as deficient/corrupt (cf. also Firdmuc and Gerxhani, 2006). By contrast, formalised, modern self-organisation is developing, or at least is aiming to develop, largely alongside – and not so much parallel to – the formal institutional arrangements of the state.

It might indeed be expected that with higher economic growth – translated into the affordability of civic engagement, accompanied by the enhanced quality of formal institutions – translated into institutional trust – the indicators of participation in modern, both post-materialist and Olsonian civic organisations in Poland are likely to improve (cf. Firdmuc and Gerxhani, 2006). However, one needs to be aware that the process of 'catching up' with the West and closing the gap vis-à-vis the type and stocks of social capital is not to be seen as automatic and inevitable.

Also, while new opportunities are emerging for civil society actors *via* the Europeanisation of governance structures, the high costs incurred by participating in them might in fact instead lead to further professionalisation, bureaucratisation and oligarchisation of the civic sphere instead of enhancing the wider active participation of citizens in it. This seems all the more probable when bearing in mind that the 'monetarisation' and 'commercialisation' of participation in collective action that are the result of the aforementioned processes (and the continuing transformation of the Third Sector) are not fully congruent with traditional Polish conceptions of self-organisation and social work underpinned by the logics of solidarity and reciprocity.

Moreover, while on one hand modern NGOs are ever better prepared for and intent on providing public goods and services as well as representing the interests and values of certain segments of Polish society, their ever closer coupling as 'social partners' with actors representing formal institutions might also act as an inhibiting factor for their enhanced anchoring in the social fabric and/or for increasing their membership base in a situation of the persistent distrust exhibited by public opinion of almost all types of formal institutions and organisations associated with the Polish state. On the other hand, the fact that European institutions are endowed by Poles with much more trust may act as a neutralising/advantageous factor in public perceptions of social partnership, which is predominantly executed due to the availability of the EU's structural funds.

References

Bartkowski, J. (2006) '*Więź społeczna i aktywność stowarzyszeniowa*', in: A. Gawkowska, P. Gliński, A. Kościański (eds) *Teorie wspólnotowe a praktyka społeczna: obywatelskość, polityka, lokalność.* Wydawnictwo IFiS PAN, Warszawa.

Bartkowski, J., A. Jasińska-Kania (2004) 'Voluntary organisations and the development of civil society', in: Jasińska-Kania A., M. Marody (eds) *Poles among Europeans*. Wydawnictwo Naukowe Scholar, Warszawa.

Bartkowski, J. (2002) 'Społeczne determinanty geograficznego rozmieszczenia organizacji pozarządowych w Polsce', in: Gliński P., B. Lewenstein B., A. Siciński (eds) op.cit.

Bednarek, S. (1996) *W kręgu małych ojczyzn. Szkice regionalistyczne*. Wrocław-Ciechanów.

Boerzel, T. A., S. Guttenbrunner, S. Seper (2005) 'Conceptualizing New Modes of Governance in EU Enlargement', NewGov Papers at www.iue.it.

Bourdieu, P. (2001) *Zaproszenie do socjologii refleksyjnej*. Oficyna Naukowa, Warszawa.

CBOS (2006a) 'Stan społeczeństwa obywatelskiego w latach 1998 –2006'. Komunikat z badań (BS/19/2006), Warszawa.

CBOS (2006b) 'Zaufanie do rządu, przedsiębiorstw, ONZ i organizacji pozarządowych w 20 krajach świata'. Komunikat z badań (BS/19/2006), Warszawa.

CIVICUS Civil Society Index report, Poland 2005.

Czapiński, J., T. Panek (2005) *Diagnoza społeczna 2005. Warunki życia Polaków,* available at: http://www.diagnoza.com/files/diagnoza2005/raport_diagnoza2005_110106.pdf.

Dąbrowska, J., M. Gumkowska, J.J. Wygnański. (2002) Podstawowe fakty o organizacjach pozarządowych – raport z badania 2002. Stowarzyszenie KLON/JAWOR, Warszawa.

Domański, H., A. Rychard (eds) (1997) *Elementy nowego ładu*. IFIS PAN, Warszawa.

Domański, H., A. Ostrowska, A. Rychard (eds) (2000) *Jak żyją Polacy*. IFIS PAN, Warszawa.

Dudkiewicz, M. (2004) 'Dwie wizje społeczeństwa obywatelskiego w świadomości ludzi trzeciego sektora', in: P Gliński P. B. Lewenstein, A. Siciński (eds) op.cit.

'Dyskusja redakcyjna – Polak – przyszły obywatel?' (an interview with Piotr Gliński and Tadeusz Szawiel) (2005) *Sprawy Nauki. Biuletyn Ministra Edukacji i Nauki*, nr 12 (115) Grudzień 2005, pp. I-IV.

Ekiert, J., J. Kubik (2001) Rebellious Civil Society: Populra Protest and Democratic Consolidation in Poland 1989 –1993. University of Michigan Press, Ann Arbor.

ESS (2002) Europejski Sondaż Społeczny, wyniki badań. [The European Social Survey, research findings], IFiS PAN, Warszawa.

Eyal, G., I. Szelenyi, E. Townsley (eds) (1998) *Making Capitalism Without Capitalists: Class Formation and Elite Struggles in Post-Communist Europe*, Verso, London.

Fidrmuc, J., K. Gerxhani (2006) 'Mind the Gap! Has Communism Destroyed Social Capital?', CEU Budapest economics seminar series (June 13, 2006).

Frączak, P. (2004) 'Lokalne partnerstwo – siła nieporozumień', in: P. Gliński , B. Lewenstein, A. Siciński (eds) op.cit.

Gąsior-Niemiec, A. (2003) *Europeanisation and Myth-making: (New)Regionalism in Poland.* PhD dissertation (unpublished).

Gąsior-Niemiec, A. (2003) 'Traces of Europeanisation: Poland', *Polish Sociological Review,* 1 (141) (2003).

Gąsior-Niemiec, A. (2004) 'Dziedzictwo kulturowe w edukacji regionalnej na Jasielszczyźnie', in: J. Kurczewska (ed.) *Kultura Współczesna*, Narodowe Centrum Kultury, Warszawa.

Gąsior-Niemiec, A. (2005) 'Nowa lokalność na pograniczu' (unpublished IFiS manuscript).

Gąsior-Niemiec, A., P. Gliński (2006) 'Europeanisation of Polish civil society' (forthcoming).

Gawin, D., Gliński P. (eds.) (2006) *Civil Society in the Making*. IFiS Publishers, Warsaw.

Gliński, P., H. Palska (1997) 'Cztery wymiary społecznej aktywności obywatelskiej', in: Domański, H., A. Ostrowska, A. Rychard (eds) (2000) *Jak żyją Polacy*. IFIS PAN, Warszawa.

Gliński, P. (2000) 'O pewnych aspektach obywatelskości. Aktywność społeczna a integracja wspólnot obywatelskich' in: Domański, H., A. Ostrowska, A. Rychard (eds) (2000) *Jak żyją Polacy*. IFIS PAN, Warszawa.

Gliński, P. (2004) 'How Active are the Social Actors? Deficient Citizenship Versus Day-To-Day Resourcefulness in Poland', *Polish Sociological Review, no 4, 2004.*

Gliński, P. (2006) Style działania organizacji pozarządowych w Polsce. Grupy interesu czy pożytku publicznego? (Raport z wykonania projektu KBN). IFiS PAN, Warszawa.

Gliński, P. B. Lewenstein, A. Siciński (eds) (2002) *Samoorganizacja społeczeństwa polskiego: Trzeci sektor*. IFIS PAN, Warszawa.

Gliński, P. B. Lewenstein, A. Siciński (eds) (2004) *Samoorganizacja społeczeństwa polskiego: III sektor i wspólnoty lokalne w jednoczącej się Europie*. IFIS PAN, Warszawa.

Gumkowska, M., Herbst, J. (2005) Podstawowe fakty o organizacjach pozarządowych – raport z badania 2004. Stowarzyszenie KLON/JAWOR, Warszawa.

Howard, M.M. (2003) *The Weakness of Civil Society in Post-Communist Poland*. Cambridge University Press, Cambridge.

Inglehart, R. (1997) *Modernisation and Postmodernisation*, Princeton University Press, Princeton.

Jawłowska, A. (2003) 'Nowe regionalizmy w Polsce', in: Kempny M., Woroniecka G. (eds) *Wymiary globalizacji kulturowej. Wyzwania badawcze*. Wydawnictwo WSIiE TWP, Olsztyn.

Juros, A., E. Leś, S. Nałęcz, I. Rybka, M. Rymsza, J.J. Wygnański (2004) 'From *Solidarity* to Subsidiarity: The Non-Profit Sector in Poland' in: Zimmer A., E. Priller (eds) *Future of Civil Society. Making Central European Nonprofit-Organisations Work*, VS Verlag für Sozialwissenschaften, Wiesbaden.

Ladrech, R. (1994) 'Europeanisation of Domestic Policies and Institutions: The Case of France.' *Journal of Common Market Studies* 32 pp.69-88.

Leś, E., S. Nałęcz (2001) Sektor non-profit. Nowe dane i nowe spojrzenie na społeczeństwo obywatelskie w Polsce. Instytut Studiów Politycznych PAN, Warszawa.

Leś, E. (2000) Od filantropii do pomocniczości. Studium porównawcze rozwoju i działalności organizacji społecznych. Dom Wydawniczy Elipsa, Warszawa.

Lewenstein, B., H. Palska (2004) 'Organizacje pozarządowe na scenie publicznej Polski okresu transformacji: dynamika rozwojowa i relacje z władzą – analiza badań jakościowych', in: Gliński, P., Lewenstein, A. Siciński (eds) op.cit.

Kukliński, A., P. Swianiewicz (eds) (1990) *Polskie województwo: doświadczenia i perspektywy*. Uniwersytet Warszawski, Warszawa.

Kurczewski, J. (ed.) (2003) *Lokalne społeczności obywatelskie*. ISNS UW, Warszawa.

Kurczewska, J., M. Kempny, H. Bojar (1998) 'Społeczności lokalne jako wspólnoty tradycji - w poszukiwaniu korzeni demokracji'. *Studia Socjologiczna* nr 2.

Kurczewska, J. (2000) 'Społeczności lokalne i inteligenci: <<patroni>> i <<partnerzy>>', in: Domański H., A. Ostrowska, A.Rychard (eds) *Jak żyją Polacy*. IFIS PAN.

Marody, M., Wilkin J. (eds) 2002) *The Vagaries of Institution Building: Poland's Adjustment to the European Union*. EU-monitoring VI, Friedrich Ebert Stiftung, MSAP AE, Kraków.

Metro, 6-8 stycznia (2006) 'Grajcie do końca świata'; 'Pójdą z puszką i termosem'.

Palska, H., B. Lewenstein (2004) 'Biografia społecznikowska', in: Gliński P., B., A. Siciński (eds) op.cit.

Putnam, R.D. (1995) *Demokracja w działaniu: tradycje obywatelskie we współczesnych Włoszech*. Instytut Wydawniczy Znak, Fundacja im. S. Batorego, Kraków-Warszawa.

Putnam, R.D. (1996) 'Bowling alone: malejący kapitał społeczny Ameryki', *Res Publica Nova* nr 6.

Radaelli, C., K. Featherstone, (2002) *The Politics of Europeanisation*. Oxford: Oxford University Press.

Rose, R. (2000) 'Uses of Social Capital in Russia: Modern, Pre-modern and Anti-modern', *Post-Soviet Affairs*, v.16, no.1, pp. 33-57.

Rueschemeyer, D, M. Rueschemeyer, B. Wittrock (eds) (1998) *Participation and Democracy East and West: Comparisons and Interpretations*. Armonk, NY M.E. Sharpe.

Rzeczpospolita, 23.03.2006. 'Pieniądze na pomoc dzieciom wypłacił sobie sam'.

Sitek, W. (1997) *Wspólnota i zagrożenie. Wrocławianie wobec wielkiej powodzi*. Wydawnictwo Uniwersytetu Wrocławskiego, Wrocław.

Skrzypiec, R. (2004) 'Mapy lokalnego uczestnictwa obywatelskiego w Polsce', in: Gliński, P. B. Lewenstein, A. Siciński (eds) op.cit.

Smolar, A. (1999) 'Przygoda społeczeństwa obywatelskiego', in: Nowicka E., Chałubiński M. (eds) *Idee a urządzenie świata społecznego*. Wydawnictwo Naukowe PWN, Warszawa.

Świątkiewicz, W. (2004) 'Więzi sąsiedzkie i życie publiczne', in: M. S. Szczepański, A. Śliz (eds) *Obywatel w lokalnej społeczności. Studia i szkice socjologiczne*, Wydawnictwo Uniwersytetu Opolskiego, Śląskie Wydawnictwo Naukowe, Tychy-Opole.

Swoboda, A. (2006) 'Wielka fala pomocy', Metro, 17-19 lutego 2006.

Sztompka, P. (1993) 'Civilisational incompetence: the trap of post-Communist societies', *Zietschrift fuer Soziologie*, 22 (2).

Tarkowska, E., J. Tarkowski (1990) '<<Amoralny familizm>> czyli o dezintegracji społecznej w polsce lat 80', in: E. Wnuk-Lipiński (ed.) *Grupy i wiezi społeczne w systemie monocentrycznym*. IFiS PAN: Warszawa.

Tarkowska, E. (ed.) (2002) *Lata tłuste, lata chude*. Wydawnictwo Instytutu Filozofii i Socjologii PAN, Warszawa.

Tarkowska, E. (ed.) (2000) Zrozumieć biednego. O dawnej i obecnej biedzie w Polsce. Typografika, Warszawa.

Trutkowski, C., S. Mandes (2005) Kapitał społeczny w małych miastach. Wydawnictwo Naukowe Scholar, Warszawa.

Wąż, K. (2003) Wiejska społeczność lokalna wobec instytucji samorządu terytorialnego na przykładzie gminy Brańsk. (Praca magisterska), IS Uniwersytetu w Białymstoku, Białystok.

Wciórka, B. (2004) Społeczeństwo obywatelskie w Polsce 1998-2004. CBOS, Warszawa.

Wieruszewska, M. (ed.) (2002) Samoorganizacja w społecznościach wiejskich. Przejawy-struktury-zróżnicowania. IRWiR PAN, Warszawa.

Zybertowicz, A. (2005) 'Antyrozwojowe grupy interesów: zarys analizy', in: Wesołowski W., J. Włodarek (eds) *Kręgi integracji i rodzaje tożsamości*, Wydawnictwo Naukowe Scholar, Warszawa.

Żukowski, T. (2006) 'Orkiestry wielkie i małe'. *Ozon*, 18 stycznia 2006.

9. The Path Dependency of Civil Society and Social Capital – the case of Croatia

Gojko Bežovan

Introduction

Civil society is seen here as a concept of transitional societies' ongoing modernisation (Arts, Halman, 2004). There is no reliable empirical evidence to assess the ways civil society has been developing in such a relatively short and turbulent period.

The development of civil society is in different aspects very much path dependent and has deep historical roots. For the purpose of a path dependency explanation analyses of three dimensions of civil society's development will be undertaken.

In the first dimension local, endogenous civil initiatives with real interests and needs of local citizens will be analysed using the results of empirical research. There are indications that civil society rooted in local communities has made achievements and it is very clear it can have some impact on the better developed regions of the country. Croatia shares some important facts regarding social capital formation with other Central European transitional countries.

Governmental funding programmes and the 'government' strategy of civil society development are providing a new space for civil society's 'statehood' development. Civil society organisations 'trust' the government for the reason of acquiring funding and gaining some recognition as a client. Civil society's cliental and politically dependent development is fostering the disintegration of society and strengthening the logic of a 'political society' created by political parties. For this part of the analysis the nature of the empirical evidence is more qualitative than quantitative.

Civil society's development as part of the massive offer of international and foreign organisations creates a specific type of virtual, donor-driven civil society. Civil society in this concept is partly generally imported from the developed world. The clash of this concept with local needs and priorities produces a specific type of global civil society. Empirical evidence for this part of analysis is quite limited and very qualitative in nature.

In the concluding part there will be some speculation on how to 'overcome' the facts related to path dependency and how to analyse the formation of social capital and civil society's development in the future.

Background to the development of civil society

Civil society's development in transitional countries has meant the democratisation of societal associations which indirectly influence the state and economy and promote the idea of pluralism in the public sphere (Cohen, Arato, 1992). The introduction of multi-party systems and parliamentary democracies have been on top of civil society's agenda. A big share of civil society actors from the 1980s became an important part of the political landscape in the emerging democracies of the beginning of the 1990s.

Civil society initiatives in the 1980s came as a radical opposition to the communist party system. With the disappearance of the communist system civil society had a survival problem. For civil society actors, the transition from the outside to the inside of society was more difficult than originally thought. At the start of the 1990s the heroes of the opposition and founders of democratic reforms became incompetent political leaders (Smolar, 1996).

The importance and new roles for civil society organisations for these countries came again in the 1990s from the West as part of technical assistance from developmental agencies or developmental programmes financed by EU funds. These programmes, very often involving experience with developing countries, did not respect local traditions and cultures. The impact of the Anglo-Saxon tradition, as being inappropriate given the local traditions, has been recognised in these programmes (Szabo, 2004).

Citizens who were politically engaged in the communist period or even some political leaders who lost their privileged positions became some of the staff of civic organisations with respective funders supporting them (Siegel, Yancey, 1992) and with their own ideological position protecting their own position and past (Tanjić, 2005). With such a development ordinary citizens lost trust in the politically transformed civil society.

Civic culture and civic initiatives are very limited by the given society's structure, culture, tradition, religion etc. The level of civic engagement is relatively low and not a virtue of ordinary citizens. It is a regional phenomenon that civil society is still weak in its ability to engage the citizens (Celichowski, 2004). Citizens associate with the people they know or form part of a related family. Bonding social capital predominates in these types of citizens' associations. The consequences of such an unfavourable cultural matrix are chronic economic, political and social backwardness (Rimac, Štulhofer, 2004).

On the basis of empirical evidence, Howard (2003) stated that civil society within the region of transitional countries has remained relatively flat and in its infancy for three reasons. These reasons can be understood through the path dependency approach. They are:

- the legacy of mistrust of communist organisations;
- the persistence of informal friendship networks; and
- the post-communist disappointment.

This legacy of mistrust makes citizens hesitant to join any grouping as it brings too many bad experiences of mandatory participation during the communist period. According to Howard (105), '...the more people mistrusted communist organisations, and the more they avoided them during the communist period, the less likely they will be to participate in voluntary organisations today.'

The second reason that civil socicty has remained flat in Eastern and Central Europe is the persistence of informal friendship networks. Howard notes that during the days of communism a vibrant private network developed allowing people to express their true feelings and frustrations outside the public sphere with a small, trusted circle of friends. In an economy of shortage, the informal network of friendship played a crucial role in acquiring everything from consumption goods to services. The need for such networks was reinforced in the 1990s. With governments implementing an economic 'shock therapy' and huge public service reforms, along with consumer goods and services being just as difficult to come by as in the communist period, the informal network and family support once again asserted their importance.

Howard (109) noted '... it does appear that to the extent that they have not changed, the vibrant private networks that developed under communism remain an impediment or an alternative to organisational membership today.'

The final reason is very close to the last statement. The 1989-1991 period represented an enchanted time for most citizens of the former communist bloc. Their world was changing daily – sometimes even hourly – and the illusion of wealth, success, economic security and social welfare still made the concept of democracy and capitalism a noble ideal. Many citizens felt slighted, even cheated, by the new system and found it difficult to break with the idea of a paternalistic state. This frustration '...has only increased the demobilization and withdrawal from public activities in the years since the collapse of communism' (ibid, 29.)

For Howard, the 'common theoretical element of these three causal factors is that, in seeking to survive in a complex and fast-changing world, people use their prior experiences as a reference point for their current choices and actions' (ibid, 113).

Howard makes some suggestions for improving the quality of civil society within the region. He is openly sceptical about success in the foreseeable future. The prospects for change that he presents are generational in nature.

Path dependency

The above analysis by Howard can be interpreted as a path dependency concept applicable to the majority of post-communist countries. The legacy of past experience can be seen as a reason for the slowdown in the modernisation of these societies.

Path dependency (Putnam, 1993) is a concept widely that is accepted in the explanation of current social efforts related to the implementation of a modernised developmental process. 'Path dependency can produce durable differences in performance between two societies...' (193) and the implications for economic and political development are profound. The roots of current obstacles to the modernisation of societies are found almost centuries earlier.

Putnam is even more explicit about former communist societies: 'Many of formerly Communist societies had weak civic traditions before the advent of Communism, and totalitarian rule abused even that limited stock of social capital. Without norms of reciprocity and networks of civic engagement, the Hobbesian outcome of the Mezzogiorno – amoral familism, clientelism, lawlessness, ineffective government, and economic stagnation – seems likelier then successful democratization and economic development' (183). With this tradition in mind, Putnam is not very optimistic about the future of former communist countries.

Some recently rediscovered anthropological and historical analysis provides evidence that different aspects of civil society's development in Croatia are very path dependent. The understanding of Croatian society's modernisation in the last part of the 19th and start of the 20th centuries can give additional support for the importance of the path dependency concept.

The processes of modernisation were being introduced from the outside and above. The economy, industrialisation and urbanisation were spreading more slowly than in other parts of the Austro-Hungarian monarchy (Gross, Szabo, 1992.) Associational life was very modest and under permanent state control.

D. Tomašić (1997) in the 1930s argued about the strong tradition of co-operative and tribal culture in different Croatian regions. This co-operative tradition was founded on the basis of collaboration to protect their members, give them security, build up a sense of justice and collaboration for the public good. This system produces responsible and active citizens. The tribal system was egocentric, for the majority members there was no security and there was the dominance of vertical differentiation. The system produced hard and aggressive, self-centred people with a leading position in society which made collaborative work in the interest of the whole community difficult.

It is very evident that a civic tradition is present in some regions that are better developed economically speaking. The score in the human development index is a function of civil society's development (Bartkowski, Jasińska-Kania, 2004). Regions with a more tribal culture are less developed and with a clientelistic syndrome which influences the style of governance[1].

The concept of amoral familism (Banfield, 1958), the inability to concert activity beyond the family, can help in understanding the potential and limitations of self-organisation, the quality of associational life, civil engagement in the production of social capital. The ethos of amoral familism is 'maximize the material, short-run advantage of the nuclear family; assume that all others will do likewise' (83). Societies dominated by this ethos have a very limited civic life, a very weak organisational infrastructure and a developed culture of mistrust.

Amoral familism has been recognised as part of political culture that influences social capital's formation (Bartkowski, Jasińska-Kania, 2004). A dependence on family ties reduces trust in others and leads to a weaker feeling of control over one's life.

For Arnes and Bein (2004) the civil society concept falls on fertile grounds in the Central European cultural area. The influence of the Latin Catholic Church, with its significant differences compared to the Byzantine-Eastern Church had long-lasting impacts on the shape of societies and states. This explanation can be used to further distinguish the intermediate cluster of countries (Central European with Baltic) and post-totalitarian (Belarus, Bulgaria, Rumania, Russia and Ukraine) related to the norms and beliefs in the European Values Study (Arts, Gelissen, Luijkx, 2003).

The variety of value orientations in contemporary and future Europe can, according to Arts, Hagenaars and Halman (2003), be explained by the

[1] The analysis and conclusion of D. Tomašić are quite comparable with the Putnam (1993) research for Southern Italy.

path dependency approach, nation-specific values and institutions which are rooted in different historical traditions and socio-economic circumstances.

To illustrate the different levels of social capital here, we refer to the findings from the European Values Studies measuring the level of networks through the free time which citizens spent on activities of civil society organisations. Differences are clear for all three groups of countries with the density of activities being highest in the EU countries and the lowest in non-EU countries. The different levels of potential for the modernisation of new EU members and non-EU members are very path dependent. This corresponds to the connection of trust and networks, which offers part of the explanation of the difficulties of civil society's development in countries with a trust deficit (Rimac, Štulhofer, 2004).

Graph 9.1 Free time spent in civil organisations in different countries

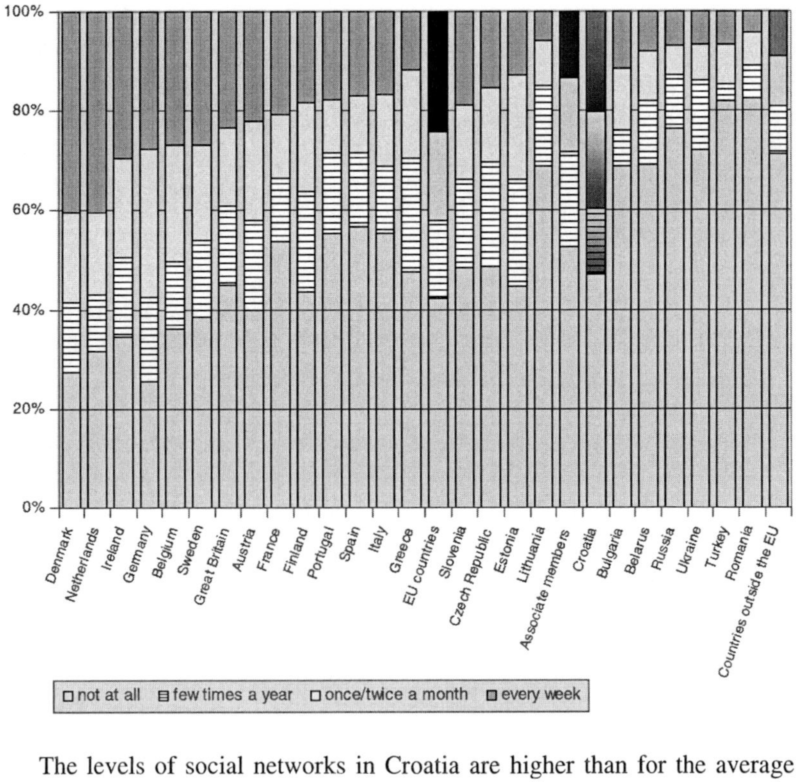

The levels of social networks in Croatia are higher than for the average of the new EU members. Further, among the transitional countries both Croatia and Slovenia have more post-materialistic values (Arts, Halman,

2004). During the communist period, the development path in Croatia and Slovenia was more open and liberal than in other transitional countries. This produced more fertile grounds for civil initiatives.

The embeddedness of civil society organisations

The embeddedness of civil society organisations will be analysed using an empirical indicator of recent research on civil society's development in Croatia[2]. Embeddedness means the interconnection of organisations and their environment (Granovetterm,1985). An analysis of civil society indicators will provide evidence of how civil society organisations are embedded or rooted in their environment in Croatian society.

Non-partisan political action

The mentioned survey indicates that since 1990 only 5.3% of Croatian citizens have written at least one letter to a newspaper, 61.8% have signed a petition and 14.6% have participated in demonstrations. For Croatian citizens this whole area comprises a new type of political action related to the development of civil culture. The signing of petitions, unlike the other two non-partisan activities, has become part of the Croatian civil culture.

Graph 9.2 *Frequency of non-partisan political activities*

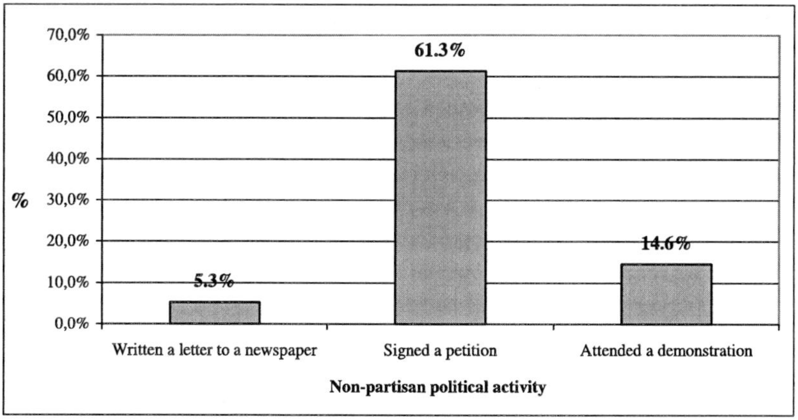

[2] Research evidence of civil society indicators are from the study Bežovan, G., Zrinščak, S., Vugec., M. 'Civil Society in Croatia: Gaining Trust and Establishing Partnerships with the State and other Stakeholders', CERANEO 2005.

Giving to charity

The survey results indicate that 66.8% of citizens have donated cash or other goods such as garments and food for humanitarian purposes in the last year. Giving to charity in Croatia has increased in the last few years thanks to the introduction of new technologies allowing donations by phone or recurring payments.

A slightly higher number of women than men give for charitable purposes, while individuals with higher education levels are more inclined to donate. In some more developed areas cases were recorded of young entrepreneurs approaching civil society organisations to offer support for their programmes. The results indicate that, in general, the public is in favour of a culture of giving. Still there is a lack of trust in giving to charity due to the lack of transparency of charitable organisations (Bežovan, 1995). However, trust in giving to charity is being restored and could potentially be a basis for establishing new types of solidarity among citizens and a stronger orientation of citizens towards the public good.

Membership in civil society organisations

The survey data indicate that 35.2% of Croatian citizens are members of at least one civil society organisation. This indicator speaks in favour of lower participation compared to the data gathered in the 1999 European Values Survey (EVS) when 40% of the citizens declared they were members of a civil society organisation. However, the breakdown of the EVS data reveals that most of them belong to faith-based organisations (12.9%), sports-recreation organisations (11.9%) and trade unions (10.6%), while an insignificant number belongs to social, ecological, women's or some other organisation.[3] A similar membership breakdown was also found in our current research. In general, the membership capacities of civil organisations are relatively weak and, as result of the qualitative analysis, frequently 'big' organisations have members drawn from very narrow circles.

[3] The source of the EVS comparisons used are the original data readouts and, in particular, the paper: Črpić, G., Zrinščak, S. (2005) An Emerging Civil Society. Leisure Time and Volunteering Organisations in Croatia, in: Baloban, J. (ed.) In Search of Identity. *Comparative Study of Values: Croatia and Europe*. Zagreb: Golden Marketing.

Graph 9.3 *CSO membership in different CSO types*

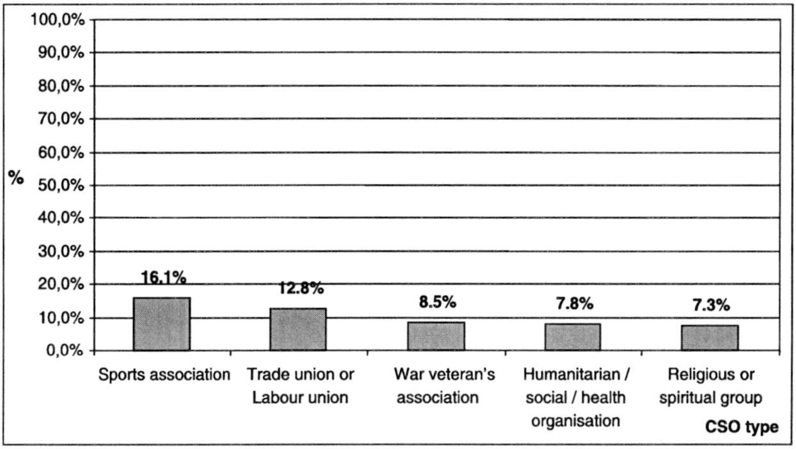

Volunteer work

The survey shows that 38.4% of the citizens were engaged in voluntary work in the last year, defined as providing some support outside the wider family circle to members of their wider community and outside civil society organisations. Citizens typically do not volunteer due to a lack of appropriate values and a lack of information (Ledić, 2001). Volunteering included cases of individual initiatives such as buying things for neighbours and assisting with learning without any compensation. Not surprisingly, respondents with higher levels of education and a higher financial status are more inclined to volunteer. The overall level of volunteering, which involves more than one-third of the population, is an improvement over the EVS 1999 data where the respective figure was only 21.3%, but is focused on formal volunteering for organisations.

Community actions

Activities in the local community are a significant indicator of civil society's development. The survey shows that 21.3% of our sample participated in at least one civil activity during the last year. In addition, 27.1% of the respondents remembered that a meeting addressing community issues was held in their local community in the last 12 months, but only 15.9% of them had participated in at least one such meeting. The voluntary gathering of citizens in the last year for the purpose of public improvement of the community was noted by 38.4% of the respondents. Evidence of community activities can be used in the assessment of the level of social capital.

Civil community actions at the local level are threatened by local political elites and they still struggle with legitimacy issues.

Building the capacity for collective action and resolving of joint problems

The results of the survey indicate that only 7.8% of the respondents perceived the civil society organisations as being active in building community with respect to resolving specific issues, while only 4.5% had actually participated in such activities. Consequently, the role of civil society organisations as a convener that helps in the resolution of local issues is very modest.

Recently, local development has been recognised as the focus of activities for some associations which are building people's capacities for self-organising, mobilising resources and joint activities in order to address the problems of local communities. Within these projects, partnerships with local authorities have been established and a considerable level of trust has been built at the local level. This area of development, although limited in volume, is becoming one of the most recognised areas of civil society organisations' activities: building the local communities and civil society from the bottom up.

The survey indicates that, as far as local community capacity-building is concerned, civil society organisations are perceived to be active to some extent (59.0%) or, less frequently, inactive (18.0%). The success in local capacity-building is mainly assessed as successful to some extent while 22.8% of respondents saw it as unsuccessful.

The research results stress the contribution of civil society to the strengthening of the local community in a mostly affirmative way. This is seen as a new trend of activities of civil society organisations which are engaged in development and that produce some real outputs.

The qualitative findings, as an illustration, describe a certain level of activism at the local level. The citizens are more willing to participate and engage in solving problems where they recognise these issues relate to their personal interest.

With these facts in mind it is evident that civil society has limited roots in local communities and that civil society organisations are not embedded enough in the local environment. The production of social capital through the activities of civil society organisations is in the early stages of its development.

Existence of umbrella bodies

The gathering of civil organisations within networks and umbrella organisations can be seen as usable facts for the analysis of social capital. Based on an earlier analysis (Bežovan, 2004), it is clear that civil organisations are unwilling to join such a network. 39.4% of interviewed regional stakeholders' representatives expressed the view that 40% to 100% of civil organisations are probably members of some umbrella bodies. Some better known umbrella bodies are active at the national level in the areas of sports, recreation, culture, social welfare and health. In some sectors, umbrella bodies are present at the regional level. In cases where the umbrella bodies appear at the county level, their strength appears to be fragmented due to the large number of countries involved.

Distribution of civil society organisations within the country

From previous research we know that civil society in Croatia is an urban phenomenon (Bežovan, 2004). The highest concentration of civil organisations is found in large cities (49.4%) and their spread is mostly limited to urban areas (42.0%). In cities with less than 5,000 inhabitants active associations can hardly be found.

There is one civil organisation for every 160 Croatian citizens. The number of associations per region varies considerably – from 8.3 to 4.9 per 10,000 people. In regions with a higher share of people with a university education more civil organisations are registered. More than one-quarter of all associations are registered within the wider Zagreb area – a percentage similar to Zagreb's share of the total population in Croatia. Of the registered associations, 50.4% are located in or within the immediate vicinity of the four largest cities.

Building social capital

To assess civil society's contribution to building social capital, the research examined differences in the level of social capital indicators among civil society organisations' members versus other citizens. There is no difference when comparing the level of trust regarding members of civil society organisations and non-members, nor do they differ with respect to their levels of social tolerance of the most marginalised groups. Further, members and non-members do not differ in the public spiritedness indicators, and the widespread mistrust of Croatian citizens does not stop at the gates of civil society organisations. Using the difference in attitudes, or lack of differences, between civil society organisations' members and non-members as an indicator, it therefore does not seem that civil society organisations contribute to the building of social capital among their members. The EVS for Croatia made very similar findings in respect of these issues.

On the basis of the findings it is clear that membership in civil society organisations is not important for building up social capital in Croatia. In that respect it would be important to discuss the influence of foreign programmes where 'membership' is more related with the professionalisation of those involved in civil society. A society with a huge mistrust of different institutions (Table 9.1) produces a limited amount of social capital.

In terms of the analysed indicators and results of the mentioned study there is empirical evidence that civic culture and the embeddedness of civil society organisations are only partly relevant for the local communities. Citizens faced with their own problems at local levels are prepared to take an active part in informal civil actions or to organise themselves in civil society organisations. Citizens' self-responsibility and voluntary engagement, with certain viability, are spread in narrow circles of the emerging middle class representing a new civic culture.

Table 9.1 Public trust in institutions

	A great deal of trust (in %)	**Quite a lot of trust (in %)**	**Not very much trust (in %)**	**No trust (in %)**	**DK (in %)**
The Church	24.9	29.9	29.4	12.8	3.0
The armed forces	1.3	30.2	39.2	14.8	4.5
The press	0.8	11.6	62.8	22.4	2.5
Television	1.3	15.1	65.3	16.3	2.0
Labour unions	1.3	15.1	45.2	21.4	17.1
The Police	6.3	31.7	40.7	17.8	3.5
Government in Zagreb	1.5	11.3	41.7	41.0	4.5
President of the state	7.3	25.9	42.0	19.6	5.3
Political parties in general	1.5	4.5	39.2	50.3	4.5
Non-governmental organisations	5.0	31.2	36.9	10.3	16.6
Major companies	1.8	10.1	39.7	34.9	13.6
Caritas	17.6	47.5	17.6	6.5	10.8
Croatian Helsinki Committee	3.3	20.6	27.6	18.6	29.9
HVIDRA	5.0	18.6	33.7	17.3	25.4

Civil society's dependence on the government

Civil society is shaped to a large extent by its relationships with the government. The Croatian legacy from the 1990s is the perception of civil society organisations forming part of the opposition. The problems with passing favourable legislation for the establishment and development of civil society organisations will have a long-lasting influence on civil society (Bežovan, 2004).

The legacy of the relationships of civil society organisations and governments in other transitional countries is complex, ranging from confrontation to partnership in recent times (Rymsza, Zimmer, 2004), (Celichowski, 2004).

The mentioned empirical research provides new insights into these complex relationships.

Autonomy of civil society organisations

The autonomy of civil society organisations in new democracies is considered a key indicator of an independent and healthy civil society. In Croatia, the paternalistic attitude of the state as well as its tradition of being in absolute control over society challenges the autonomy of civil society organisations (Bežovan, 2004). Consequently, in the opinion of a majority of stakeholders, the state and in particular local authorities, are sometimes too involved in the activities of civil society organisations. For example, environmental civil organisations are closely monitored by local authorities which are worried about local civic activists raising difficult questions about local government's investment plans. Powerful political actors, mostly from political parties, often undermine civil society initiatives that conflict with or do not fit in with their interests.

According to qualitative findings, financial dependence on the state further challenges the autonomy of civil society organisations. The survey respondents mentioned the recent legal amendments with respect to value-added tax as an example of the state's involvement in civil society activities indicative of a systematic governmental policy aimed at undermining organisations that ask unpleasant questions.

The results of the mentioned research have drawn attention to the widespread practice of connections and acquaintances in civil society through which state and political actors 'have their hand in civil society'. This challenges the public credibility of civil society organisations.

Dialogue between civil society organisations and the state

In the 1990s the relationship between the state and civil society organisations was ridden with conflict. Apart from the humanitarian area, there were only a few areas of co-operation and partnership. After 2000 state-civil society relations changed when appropriate rules of engagement were put in place. Counselling bodies working on children's rights, the rights of disabled persons, gender equality, minorities, environmental protection, the protection of human rights, consumer protection and similar issues have recently been established by the state with representatives of civil society organisations. At the regional level and in larger towns similar bodies involving civil organisations' representatives have been established and the signed agreements on co-operation between local and regional authorities and civil society organisations are likely to improve dialogue. These activities are largely produced through well-funded foreign programmes. However, some experts' qualitative findings show that by establishing such consultative bodies the government avoids having to deal with difficult issues, while simultaneously presenting a democratic face to the international public.

The results of the survey show the relatively limited level of dialogue between the state and civil society (see Table 9.2).

Table 9.2 Description of dialogue between the state and civil society

	Number	**%**
Does not exist	14	5.3
Restricted	125	47.2
Medium	112	42.3
Extensive	4	1.5
DK/Na	10	3.8
Total	265	100.0

Regional stakeholders identified several specific problems such as the slow pace of establishing communication, as well as the poor quality of dialogue between the state and civil society. One respondent said: '[m]y personal opinion is that within the associations the awareness of their role and importance is growing, but also the awareness of the need of their development and growth, as well as transparency in their activities. The state also changes its attitude to associations and can see them, in a segment of their activities, as potential partners and not as competitors or enemies.'

According to attitudes, namely qualitative findings, found among the majority of civil servants as a key informant in the research, 'the associations are still considered as a necessary evil'. This means that for the majority of governmental bodies they are not perceived as a partner but more as a troublemaker.

State support for civil society organisations

Financial support from the state is inconsistent as is the process of allocating state funds, and they are not guided by any clear civil society organisation funding policy. Grants are not awarded in accordance with priority social issues or public policies that are being pursued. One respondent concluded that: '[t]he criteria for allocating funds from the state budget, as well as from the regional and local budgets, are still not clear'. In addition, experts pointed out that no evaluations of state-funded projects have been carried out, making the identification of the lessons learned impossible.

According to a comment from respondents the government started with financial support under the pressure of foreign organisations and an international audience. The financial support of the state is very often perceived as way of neutralising critical positions regarding the government.

The dominant governance style does not influence the role of civil society organisations as a partner to government. The state has a negative impact on social capital when it starts to organise activities which are, by the nature of their competence, part of civil society business. Path dependency is important for explaining these relationships.

Virtual civil society

The issue of the virtual civil society is known from previous research in Croatia (Bežovan, 2004). This phenomena was previously recognised in the region as a complex part of the relationship (Deakin, 2001; Celichowski, 2004). For some analysts it involves a concept of global civil society's development developed by technical assistance from the outside (Anheier, Glasius, Kaldor, 2001).

Howard (2003) is more explicit when stating that the strengthening of civil society in such an arrangement does not work. For him '...both domestic governments and international donors should intensify their efforts to strengthen local groups and organisations, but they need to reinforce their energies in a way that would encourage and reward groups for expanding their activities, membership, and constituencies, rather than simply providing a well-written missions statement and a nicely designed Internet site'[4] (161).

The war conflict in Croatia and in the region meant the presence of international organisations with specific missions related to humanitarian issues has had a specific influence on local organisations and the path of their development. The Anglo-Saxon concept of the role of civil society organisations has shaped the specific image of these organisations in the eyes of the general public[5].

The mentioned survey says that civil society organisations in Croatia are still receiving the biggest amount of funding from foreign donors. Well-developed and very professional civil organisations obtain the majority of funding from foreign donors. These foreign programmes, using a top-down approach, produce specific types of temporary and unstable networks, promote new ideas, make international connections and produce a specific type of influence. Traditional society does not have the capacity to enter into a real partnership with such programmes.

There is some speculation in the media promoted by people with certain reputations that the foreign-funded programmes for civil society's development are following a donor- driven agenda that is highly influenced by the political interest of the country providing the donation.

There is no evidence that such a 'forced' development of civil society produces social capital. It might involve a specific type of social capital relevant to the progress of globalisation and the participation of the civic elite in global civil society programmes.

Recent debates on the role of the state and para-state organisations in partnership with foreign organisations stress the issue of 'meta level civil society' development in Croatia (van Teefelen, 2005). It seems that these organisations do not have problem with 'legitimacy' with being involved in that way in this sensitive and fragile sector.

---

[4] Recent debates in Croatia perceived such an involvement of foreign and semi-state organisations as developing the 'meta level of civil society'.

[5] In a programme of foreign support for civil society's development the dominant term is non-governmental organisations. Several surveys indicated that ordinary citizens have negative views of non-governmental organisations. The wording and contextualisation of the civic idea in the local tradition are very important for the acceptance of civil society by other stakeholders.

Conclusions

Path dependency is a crucial approach to understanding civil society's development and in assessing the production of social capital through the activities of civil society organisations in transitional societies.

The research suggests that social capital is developed more through informal networks at the neighbourhood level than through membership in civil society organisations. Citizens are ever more willing to be involved in activities at that level and they do experience the importance of practicing the norm of reciprocity for the sake of a safe neighbourhood.

Qualitative researches, especially separate case studies of civic actions, are important for making new findings on the nature of this social capital. Family and friendship ties still play dominant roles and it is unclear whether this is also applies to people from younger generations.

The paternalistic position of the state pushing civil society organisations into a marginal position means they are still not fully legitimised actors in public life. The development of social capital in this relationship will depend on civic activism, the citizens' capacity to self-organise and, related to that, democratisation processes and the new governance culture.

The production of social capital in the activities of civil society organisations largely depends on the embeddedness of civil society organisations and the relations with their constituencies. Civil organisations as part of foreign funding programmes can be seen as an important actor producing social capital relevant for globalisation processes. Some of these activities, such as the top-down approach or donor-driven agendas, are very questionable in terms of building trust in civil initiatives.

Do the recent developments provide evidence that civil society in Croatia is paving the way for modernisation with a new style of civic engagement of the emerging new middle class? Empirical evidence says that social capital is being produced on the road of society's transformation from traditional to modern. Here we agree with Howard that any change in the quality of civil society is generational in nature. The research findings point to the new ranks of middle-class people who are well-educated, well-off, who represent the new civic culture that is willing to join civil society organisations and to act as a convener of new initiatives. It is here that the seeds of limited bridging social capital are appearing.

Literature

Arens, M., Bein, D. (2004) 'The Origins of Civil Society Structures in Central and Eastern Europe through the 18th Century', in: Zimmer, A., Priller, E. (eds) *Future of Civil Society- Making Central European Nonprofit-Organisations Work*, Wiesbaden: VS Verlag für Sozialwissenschaften. CD-ROM.

Arts, W., Hagenaars, J., Halman, L. (2003) 'The Cultural Diversity of European Unity: an Introduction', in Arts, W., J. Hagenaars, L. Halman, *The Cultural Diversity of European Unity. Findings, Explanations and Reflections from the European Values Studies*. Leiden-Boston: Brill.

Arts, W., J. Gelissen, R. Luijkx (2003) 'Shall the Twain Ever Meet? Differences and Changes in Socio-Economic Justice Norms and Beliefs in Eastern and Western European at the turn of the Millennium', in: Arts, W., J. Hagenaars, L. Halman *The Cultural Diversity of European Unity. Findings, Explanations and Reflections from the European Values Studies*. Leiden-Boston: Brill.

Banfield, E. C. (1958) *The Moral Basis of a Backward Society*. New York: The Free Press.

Bartkowski, J., Jasińska-Kania, A. (2004) 'Voluntary organisations and the development of civil society', in: Arts, W., Halman, L., *European Values at the Turn of the Millennium*. Brill: Leiden-Boston.

Bežovan, G. (2004) *Civilno društvo*. Zagreb: Nakladni zavod Globus.

Bežovan, G. (1995) 'Neprofitne organizacije i kombinirani model socijalne politike.' *Revija za socijalnu politiku*, 3: 195-214.

Celichowski, J. (2004) 'Civil Society in Eastern Europe – Growth without Engagement', in M. Glasious, D. Lewis, H. Seckinelgin (eds) *Exploring Civil Society- Political and Cultural Contexts*. London/New York: Routledge.

Cohn, J.L., Arato, A. (1992) *Civil Society and Political Theory*. Cambridge, MA: The M.I.T. Press.

Črpić, G., Zrinščak, S. (2005) 'An Emerging Civil Society. Leisure Time and Volunteering Organisations in Croatia', in Baloban, J. (ed.) *In Search of Identity. Comparative Study of Values : Croatia and Europe*. Zagreb: Golden Marketing.

Deakin, N. (2001) *In Search of Civil Society*, New York: Palgrave.

Granovetter, M. (1985) 'Economic Action and Social Structure: The Problem of Embeddedness.' *American Journal of Sociology*, Vol. 91: 481-510.

Gross, M., Szabo, A. (1992) Prema hrvatskome građanskom društvu: društveni razvoj u civilnoj Hrvatskoj i Slavoniji šezdesetih i sedamdesetih godina 19. stoljeća, Zagreb: Globus.

Howard, M. M. (2003) *The Weakness of Civil Society in Post-Communist Europe*. Cambridge: Cambridge University Press.

Ledić, J. (2001) Biti volonter/volonterka? Istraživanje uključenosti građana u civilne inicijative u zajednici kroz volonterski rad, Rijeka: SMART.

Putnam, R. D. (R. Leonardi, R.Y. Nanetti) (1993) *Making Democracy Work*, Princeton: Princeton University Press.

Rimac, I., Štulhofer, A. (2004) 'Sociokulturne vrijednosti, gospodarska razvijenost i politička stabilnost kao čimbenici povjerenja u Europsku uniju', in: Ott, K. (ed.) *Pridruživanje Hrvatske Europskoj uniji – Izazovi institucionalnih prilagodbi*. Zagreb: Institut za javne financije / Zaklada Friedrich Ebert.

Rymsza, M., A. Zimmer (2004) 'Embeddedness of Nonprofit Organisations: Government-Nonprofit Relationships', in: Zimmer, A., Priller, E. (eds) *Future of Civil Society – Making Central European Nonprofit-Organisations Work*, Wiesbaden: VS Verlag für Sozialwissenschaften.

Szabo, M. (2004) 'Civic Engagement in East-Central Europe', in: Zimmer, A., E. Priller (eds) *Future of Civil Society – Making Central European Nonprofit-Organisations Work*, Wiesbaden: VS Verlag für Sozialwissenschaften.

Siegel, D., J. Yancey (1992) *The Rebirth of Civil Society: The Development of the Nonprofit Sector in East Central Europe and the Role of Western Assistance*. New York: Rockefeller Brothers Fund.

Smolar, A. (1996) 'From Opposition to Atomisation.' *Journal of Democracy*, Vol. 7: 24-38.

Tanjić, Ž. (2005) Osoba prije države i kapitala, *Kana*, 4: 4-5.

Tomašić, D. (1997) *Društveni razvitak Hrvata: rasprave i eseji*. Zagreb: Hrvatsko sociološko društvo, Naklada Jesenski i Turk.

Van Teefelen, M. (2005) Croatia, in: Co-opearting Netherlands Foundations for Central and Eastern Europe, *Annual Report* 2005.

Notes on the contributors

Frane Adam is a Professor at the Department of Cultural Studies and the Department for Sociology at the Faculty of Social Sciences, University of Ljubljana, Slovenia. He is the Head of the Centre for Theoretical Sociology, Ljubljana. The main topics of his research are democracy, elite formation, socio-cultural indicators of modernisation and development.

His recent publications include, along with M. Makarovič, B. Rončević and M. Tomšič, *The Challenges of Sustained Development: The Role of Socio-cultural Factors in East-Central Europe* (2005, Budapest & New York: CEU Press) and, with B. Rončević, 'Social Capital: Recent Debates and Research Trends', (2003, in: *Social Science Information*).

Igor Bahovec, Ph.D. in sociology, is a research fellow at the Faculty of Social Sciences, and assistant at the Theological Faculty, University of Ljubljana, Slovenia. The main topics of his research are community, social capital, religion, post-modern culture, and inter-religious dialogue.

His recent publications include *Communities: Theories, Forms, Meanings* (2005, Ljubljana: Sophia, in the Slovenian language).

Gojko Bežovan is a Professor of Social Policy and the Head of the Department of Social Work, Faculty of Law, University of Zagreb, Croatia. He is the Head of the CERANEO (Centre for Development of Non-Profit Organisations) in Zagreb. The main topics of his academic interest are social policy, welfare mix, civil society, and housing policy.

His recent publications include *Civil Society* (2004, Zagreb: Globus, in the Croatian language).

Nevenka Bogataj, M.Sc. in geography and Ph.D. candidate, is a researcher at the Slovenian Institute for Adult Education in Ljubljana, Slovenia. The topics of her research are non-formal learning, study circles, educational needs in the rural environment, and sustainable development.

Her publications include 'Considering the contribution of study circles to civil society in Slovenia' (2004, in: *Journal of Adult and Continuing Education*).

Anna Gąsior-Niemiec is a research associate at the Institute of Philosophy and Sociology, Polish Academy of Sciences in Warsaw, a member of the European Studies Unit, an Assistant Professor at the Department of Political Sciences at the Rzeszow University in Rzeszow, Poland. The main topics of her research are regional governance, regionalism, the social construction of space, territorial marketing, Europeanisation and migration.

Her publications include 'The Management of the Future. Regions and Corporations' (2005, in: A. Kukliński, K. Pawłowski (eds), *Europe – Strategic Choices*, vol. 2, Warszawa-Nowy Sącz).

Piotr Gliński is a senior research associate at the Institute of Philosophy and Sociology, Polish Academy of Sciences in Warsaw, the President of the Polish Sociological Society (PTS), and an Associate Professor at the Department of Humanities at the Białystok University in Białystok, Poland. His research topics are civil society, local communities, and new social movements.

His latest works include, along with D. Gawin (eds), *Civil Society in the Making* (2006, Warsaw: IFiS Publishers).

Petros Gougoulakis is Assistant Professor at the Department of Social and Cultural Studies in Education at the Stockholm Institute of Education,. The main topics of his research are study circles, the pedagogy of education, ethics and democracy.

His recent publications include 'Higher Education in Sweden' (2005, in: *Science and Society Journal of Political and Moral Theory*).

Angelca Ivančič, Ph.D. in sociology, is a senior researcher at the Slovenian Institute for Adult Education in Ljubljana, Slovenia. The topics of her academic research are participation in lifelong learning, lifelong learning and social inclusion, education and active citizenship.

Her publications include 'Active citizenship in the changing society: evidence from six European countries' (2004, in: F. H. Columbus (ed.), *European economic and political issues: vol. 8*, Hauppauge (New York): Nova).

Matej Makarovič is an Assistant Professor of General and Theoretical Sociology at the Faculty of Social Sciences at the University of Ljubljana, Slovenia. His academic interests encompass sociological theory, societal development, and political sociology.

His recent publications include 'Social capital in Slovenian organisations: the missing resource?' (2005, in: I. Svetlik and B. Ilič (eds), *HRM's contri-*

bution to hard work: a comparative analysis of human resource management. Bern: P. Lang).

Margreet Nuus was a research assistant at the Department of Political Science at the Faculty of Social Sciences, Leiden University. She holds a master's degree in political science. The title of her thesis was 'Towards a better understanding of Dutch youth's intentions to vote' (2003). She is currently an auditor at the Netherlands Court of Audit.

Darka Podmenik, M.A. in communication sciences, is an independent researcher living in Ljubljana, Slovenia. The main topics of her research are active citizenship and other forms of direct and non-traditional modes of participation, and qualitative research methodology.

Her publications include, along with co-authors, 'Learning active citizenship and governance in Slovenia' (2001, in: A. Snick et al. (eds), *Learning citizenship and governance in Europe*, Leuven: Catholic University of Leuven).

Vinko Potočnik is a Professor of the Sociology of Religion at the Faculty of Theology, University of Ljubljana, Slovenia. The main topics of his interest are church religiosity, rituals, the family, and values.

His publications include 'Leitung der Kirche und kirchliche Kommunikation in Ost(Mittel)Europa' (2001, in: P. M. Zulener et al. *Kirche im Aufbruch: zur pastoralen Entwicklung in Ost(Mittel)Europa – eine qualitative Studie*, Ostfildern: Schwabenverlag).

Mateja Rek, M.A. in Management of Nonprofit Organisations, is a Ph.D. candidate and research assistant at the Faculty of Social Sciences at the University of Ljubljana, Slovenia. The topics of her research are social capital and European civil society, organisational theory and the knowledge society.

Her publications include 'The Dilemmas of Transnational Civil Society in the EU' (2006, in: *Družboslovne razprave*, in the Slovenian language).

Peggy Schyns is an Assistant Professor of Political Science at Department of Political Science at the Faculty of Social Sciences, Leiden University. The main topics of her research are political cynicism, social cohesion, income and life satisfaction, subjective well-being, social and political participation, and quality of life.

Her publications include *Income and life satisfaction, A cross-national and longitudinal study* (2003, Delft: Eburon Publishers).

Matevž Tomšič, Ph.D. in sociology, is an Assistant Professor at the Department of Cultural Studies at the Faculty of Social Science, University of Ljubljana, Slovenia, and a research fellow at the Faculty of Social Sciences. His research interest includes political sociology, i.e. elites, democracy and development in post-socialist societies, the sociology of intellectuals.

His publications include *Political Stability in the New Democracies* (2002, Ljubljana: Znanstveno in publicistično središče, in the Slovenian language).

Urban Vehovar, Ph.D. in sociology, is an Assistant Professor at the Faculty of Education, Koper, Slovenia and at the Faculty of Education, University of Ljubljana, Slovenia. Topics of his academic interest cover corruption, democracy and economic development.

His publications include *Judicature in Slovenia: a politico-sociological essay on the condition and role of the judicature in Slovenia in the period of transition*, (2001, Ljubljana: FDV, in the Slovenian language).

Siniša Zrinščak, Ph.D. in sociology, is an Associate Professor of Social Policy at the Department of Social Work at the Faculty of Law, University of Zagreb. He is President of the Croatian Sociological Association. His primary scientific interests include the sociology of religion and social policy, and in particular Church-State relations, the social role of the Church, religious and social policy changes in post-communism, and the role of Europeanisation in the social policy development of post-communist countries.

His recent works include 'Generations of Atheism: Patterns of Response to Communist Rule among Different Generations and Countries' (2004, in: *Social Compass*).